The Lost Knowledge

Alain Hubrecht

FOREWORD

I have written this book to let everyone in on something that may well be the best kept secret in the world for thousands of years. In this volume you will find a novel in which you can follow the progress of two people who discover the elements needed to understand the secret.

Considering that the hidden secret is still highly topical today, you should not be surprised if the book gives rise to fierce debates between those who belong to groups that 'knew' about the secret – and therefore denied its existence – and scientists who did not know about it but still denied its possible existence, because it was far removed from the laboratories of their universities.

In any case, you will see that there are some places in the world where scientists work on presenting the secret in line with the fashion of the time and use its power to reconquer the world, as happened several times thousands of years ago when real emperors used the secret over the centuries, from generation to generation.

ACKNOWLEDGMENTS

I would like to personally thank the following people for their contributions to my inspiration and knowledge, and for other kinds of help in creating this book: Chris Dunn, François Favre, Volodymyr Krasnoholovets, Jean-Paul Lemonde, Bertrand Méheust, Jean-Pierre Petit, John Quackenboss, Paul Smith, Henri Stierlin, Russel Targ, Jacques Vallée, and special thanks to David Griffiths for the translation and to Rhys Thomas for the cover picture.

DISCLAIMER

REFERENCES

References in parenthesis are available in the addendum having the same title.

Chapter 1

September 5th 2009, Succuronis, Sardinia

All is quiet. Susan and Rano cower in the depths of the nouraghe (2.2). The morning chill makes them shiver. It is still dark. Fine dew covers their sleeping bags as a cell phone alarm sounds, quickly switched off by Susan, who turns over in her bag.

"Rano, Rano, wake up! It's almost the time."

"Hey… let me sleep! It's cold outside, and I've been freezing all night!"

"No, let's get moving. There are only ten minutes left and I haven't flown 7,500 miles and then driven for ten hours for some lazy asshole to screw up my trip!"

Rano squirms as he gets out of his sleeping bag, stretching and yawning noisily. He gets up and catches up with Susan as she is rolling her sleeping bag up. They are ready in five minutes, crouching on their heels in the alcove in the depths of the cave, just in front of the corridor leading to the entrance to the nuraghe.

They switch off their pocket flashlights and wait in the total darkness. They have difficulty in making out some stars, just visible in the small piece of sky they can see at the entrance to the nuraghe. Then, in just five seconds, there it is… in front of them, brilliant, incredibly bright and almost blinding. It is as if a laser beam has struck them. They are amazed at such power, but it also has such a supernatural aura to it.

Now that their eyes have got used to it, they see that the inside of the nuraghe is bathed in a bluish light, so bright that they can read the labels on their sleeping bags. They sit back, not knowing what to say... the result of their experiment has surpassed all their hopes/beyond their wildest dreams.

Then it goes away, but not without leaving a tenuous glow, soon replaced by the golden glow of the sun coming over the horizon.

Susan and Rano have witnessed the rise of Venus from the depths of a nuraghe, one clearly oriented in such a way that its corridor allows the rays from Venus to penetrate it completely when the planet rises at the moment when its magnitude is strongest.

Until now, archeologists and historians have continued to argue about the use or purpose of these thousand-year-old megaliths that resemble squat towers. Their builders, the Nuraghi, disappeared with their civilization, taking their secret with them. There is no known method for dating these monuments. No burial ground has been discovered, or traces of fire, food or water. So, they were not used for storage or accommodation, and the theory that they were watchtowers does not hold water either because they were located at the bottom of valleys. The Nuraghi built more than 2,000 of them, only in Sardinia, from north to south and from east to west. In some places they combined with other ancient nuraghi, or were adjacent to others still standing, and sometimes they formed a great muddle that looks like a village when seen from a distance, but on closer examination there is no street layout or means of getting around the place.

There are mysterious towers all over the world, the most similar to the nuraghi being the *brochs* (A-2) in Scotland. Thousands of years later more round towers (E-1)were built, this time in Ireland. There were hundreds of them, and replicas all over the world (E-3). Again, nobody knows what they were for, although the most common name given to them is 'Lantern of the Dead' (E-2). However, there is no evidence that the use of nuraghi and brochs is the same as the Lanterns of the Dead.

One possible factor linking them is their location on geo-biological nodes (E-15). It is very difficult to verify this theory, however, because these geo-biological networks are measured by human sensitivity, like water-diviners, and perhaps time has displaced these networks, if in fact they exist at all.

Susan and Rano emerge from the nuraghe and watch the sunrise in silence from the grass bank in front of it. Susan Gomez is a 32-year-old archeologist with long brown hair framing her long face and small brown eyes. Her tanned skin makes it difficult to tell her nationality. She speaks English, French, Spanish and Italian, which does not make it easier to guess where she is from. In fact, she is Hispano-French and her parents met in Los Angeles.

Rano Saret is her Chinese assistant. He recently joined the campus and is not yet twenty-six years old. He is taller than the average Chinese, and quite athletic. He was awarded a grant by his government to participate in Susan's mission within the framework of international archeological cooperation. In return, the United States hopes to send their archeologists to China on some interesting mission. Who knows, there may be hundreds of still-unexplored pyramids (E-4)?

They travelled to Sardinia together and have had time to get to know each other a little better. Rano is a quiet young man who still has a lot to learn about Western society and the world in general, but he speaks perfectly good English, which makes things easier.

Susan did her thesis on archeoastronomy (E-15) at UCLA (E-16) and, realizing that the orientation of the nuraghi could be based on movements of the stars, applied to her university for a grant to study the subject in greater detail. Indeed, a recent study demonstrates a certain link between the orientation of their entrances and sunrise during the solstice, and also between moonrise and its zenith. Most of the nuraghi, however, point towards a star, something that previous studies have not been able to prove.

After in-depth analysis of the data and drawings available, Susan discovered that the planet Venus was a good candidate, but only at certain moments of its journey around the Sun. Early research had confirmed the orientation of the nuraghi towards the Moon and the Sun, but they could also be built to line up with the rising of Venus. Historians have used their knowledge of civilizations to date these monuments, although it is impossible to know the date of construction to an accuracy of 500 or 1,000 years. Susan wanted to check if her hypothesis made sense and decided to observe Venus rising from inside a nuraghe. She chose a compatible date using her astronomy software and was successful in obtaining funding for her trip.

The always breathtaking sight of the sunrise comes to an end, with the Sun shedding its flamboyant red dress to put its more common yellow clothes on.

"Wow, what were these constructions used for?" asks Rano as he plays with some pieces of grass, ripping the tops off and throwing them as far as possible, like rockets.

"That's why we're here, to try and understand," replies Susan, looking out to sea. "What is now sure is that they were built based on the rise of Venus."

"Let's go back inside the nuraghe to think about it now that there's some light," says Rano, who stands up and flicks off some small pebbles stuck on his pants.

"Watch your head! You already hit it yesterday evening. I wonder why they made these entrances so low. Even a dwarf would have trouble standing up!"

Susan follows Rano, crawling behind him to squeeze into the imposing structure. The walls are more than a yard thick, and sometimes a staircase appears to lead up to the next floor; some of the bigger nuraghi even have three levels. Continuing on their way, and after climbing a few feet, they reach a small round room with three niches where they can sit.

The two archeologists sit down facing the corridor.

"Despite looking closely," says Rano, "I can't see any detail or script that could give us a clue. Apparently, they did things here that had something to do with the appearance of Venus".

"What if they just came to pray?" Susan suggests.

"Maybe, but just think of the work needed to build this thing! All that effort just to pray? Also, since it is aligned to a star or planet, Venus perhaps, the prayers wouldn't last very long!"

"Yes, you're right; it had to be something that didn't take too much time, or something that had to happen at an exact moment."

"Why don't these rooms have windows?"

"Imagine that these niches were used to accommodate other people, who surrounded a main person in the center."

"Let's go and check out some other nuraghi, then think about all this calmly before getting into a survey of the bibliography on the basis of our discovery," says Susan.

"Right," says Rano as he closes his laptop. "What's for sure is that they wanted to see Venus rising when the planet was at its brightest. Some archeoastronmers have thought that their orientation had to do with the sunrise, but it's easy to confuse sunrise with Venus rising, since Venus rises – or follows the sun – just a few minutes later. This time lag can even be up to four and a half hours when the elongation (9) of Venus is at its maximum."

The two archeologists then walk back down the valley to their rented Jeep.

Chapter 2

September 11ᵗʰ 2009, Edwards Air Base, Mojave Desert

Alex gets up early so as not to miss the event. He still has some way to go before arriving at the base in California, and the return is announced for the end of the day. Indeed, today is the day the Space Shuttle *Discovery* is scheduled to land at Edwards, putting an end to STS-128, another eventful mission thanks to the debris that can damage the protective layer of the Shuttle's heat shield, so essential during re-entry into the atmosphere. After several checks and attempts at repair, NASA decided to bring the Shuttle back early, although the landing had to be postponed as a result of a rather threatening hurricane. Alex's new job means that he has to be present when the Shuttle returns. His company is in charge of preparing the Shuttle for its ride home to Cape Canaveral on the back of a Boeing 747. It is a brand new job for him and a very enjoyable one too. It gets him away from the click of computer keyboards in the windowless office of his former workplace. The work may have been a little more intellectual, working on programs to configure missions, but he missed the open air and when he had the chance to change jobs he decided that this one was for him, that he was going to travel a bit and fulfill one of this childhood dreams at the same time. So, if all went well, the Shuttle would be landing today and he has exactly three hours to reach the landing site. He had received an e-mail the evening before confirming that the Shuttle would not land at

Kennedy Space Center as planned, so his company's services were required. He had just enough time to pack his suitcase and check that he had everything: camera, laptop, infrared camera and the procedures, which he would have to read over again. It was all quite tricky, in fact. His colleague Mike, who was going to accompany him on this first mission, had hurt his ankle the evening before at the bowling alley and told him he could not make it. Alex decided to go ahead on his own if he wanted to keep this new job. His office charged NASA two million dollars a year to sign off the Shuttle in Florida, and if he got it wrong he would be in big trouble. His job was to check the condition of the Shuttle before signing it off, code some references, and check that all the elements had cooled down correctly before it could be handled with a crane and mounted on the back of the 747. He also had to take photographs to check for any visible defects in case they were accused of damaging the craft during transport. The Shuttle re-enters Earth's atmosphere at almost 1,000 degrees and they could be accused of ruining it with thin ropes that look more like something you could hang your wash on! Everything seemed in order, so he set off in his brand new Chrysler Magnum, the envy of his neighborhood.

Alex Bergen has just turned thirty, and his short blond hair gives him a certain Dutch air. He is proud of his career so far. In reality, he was never really sure what he wanted to do for a living but he had always been attracted by science. After wondering about biotechnology for a long time he decided on photonics, an emerging science with job opportunities in several markets, but also an exciting one as a result of all the new discoveries. It is also a cutting-edge specialty in which there is not too much competition. Basically, it is an interesting thing to study with very specialist skills. He works out every morning – whenever possible – to keep his athletic body trim, and drives to the beach to hit the surf whenever he can. He loves going there at dawn, sometimes coming across a few other courageous souls who brave the cold morning water. The rising sun gives a strange aura to the scene. From the beach it looks as if there are flocks of seagulls out on the surf, but in fact they are surfers, waiting to catch a good wave. Alex is also pleased with his waterfront apartment in Huntington Beach. The town is not too far from Los Angeles, and even though it is full of trendy places the apartments cost less than in downtown L.A. Despite his success, Alex has not found his other half yet, although he did not want to get involved with anyone before he graduated and got a decent job.

Thinking of his situation, Alex observes the monotonous road stretching out in front of him on the way to the air base, where crowds are already gathering along the roadside to witness the return of the Shuttle. His brand new pass does the job and he soon finds himself on the apron near the runway. He checks his map and heads for a gray building near the control tower. He presents his credentials; the personnel are friendly, although a little tense. His is given an office and nobody bothers him for about ten minutes, so he makes use of the time to re-read his notes and check his equipment. There is an incredible coming-and-going of civilians and military personnel wearing passes of all kinds. Finally, at around 8 p.m. the imminent arrival of the Shuttle is announced over the PA system; it will land in around thirty minutes. Only a few people are allowed to be outside, although he is not one of them. He must be content with looking through the windows, although he is pleased to see that they are quite well located. He takes some photos of *Discovery* when it lands at high speed before disappearing off to the left at the end of the runway. Once the all-clear is given he pulls out his pass and, carrying all his gear, rides in a Hummer to the place where the Shuttle has stopped. A cordon has been placed around it and special vehicles are attending to the astronauts. He takes advantage to take a few photos. The Shuttle is really impressive; up close it is much bigger than he expected. The hatch opens and he sees the astronauts emerge, closely escorted to the vehicles by military personnel. Suddenly, while taking a photo with his telephoto lens, vehicles he sees some forms move on top of a hangar on the other side of the runway. He zooms in on the place where he saw the movement but cannot see anything. He wants to focus back on the runway but again sees a shape, and has just the time to take a photo without focusing in too precisely. Turning round to keep the Sun off his face, he looks at what he has just photographed. He enlarges the dark form and makes out the shape of a man lying on the roof. Another zoom, and he makes out a camera – no, a gun! – one of those long rifles with a sight on top like in Iraq. That's it, a sniper's rifle! Good God, he has discovered a hidden marksman, who is surely about to do something that his mother-in-law would not approve of. He elbows his way through a crowd of technicians and approaches a soldier near the vehicles where the astronauts with the astronauts inside. He shows him the photo and explains it as quickly as he can, while trying to appear as discreet as possible. The soldier looks at him, asks him to show his pass, looks at him again, but at no time does he look towards the hangar where the sniper is hiding. For a moment Alex thinks that even he is under suspicion. The soldier grabs his walkie-talkie and murmurs something unintelligible into it. He then tells Alex to stay close to him until a more senior officer comes. Alex is amazed; the solider still does not look in the direction of the sniper. His calmness staggers him even more. He has not got over his surprise when a man in a suit comes up and asks him to follow him through the crowd. He tells him that what he saw is normal, and it would be good if he would let other people do their jobs properly, explaining that what he saw is normal security procedure. He confirms that the perimeter of the base is under high surveillance and it is impossible for an unauthorized person to be there, and even less that an unauthorized weapon could get in. He is allowed to return to the Shuttle, taking care not to look towards the hangar. Even so, he would like to know what a sniper is doing there if everything is supposedly under control! Alex patiently waits for everyone to move away from the spacecraft to start work. He has to show his pass again to pass through the cordon. There are still about fifty people busy around the Shuttle, but according to the procedure he can start work already. Not really knowing what he needs to photograph, given that it is the first time he has seen a Shuttle close up, he takes dozens of shots of the 100-ton beast. A quick look in the direction of the hangar reveals that his 'colleague' is no longer there. Just as well; that makes him feel better. The infrared camera allows him to check that the surface of the spacecraft is cooling off correctly. Alex will have to make another check one hour before the Shuttle is loaded onto the Jumbo, which is already waiting on another taxiway. He has reference images in his laptop that allow him to give the go-ahead to the workers. He approaches the Shuttle again because he has to photograph the joints of all the openings. That is the area in which changes during handling are observed most often. He climbs the ladder that leads to the door of the spacecraft – now closed – and is about to take some photos when he sees that some seals have been put on the door. He is quite used to seeing seals on his electricity meter or at a crime scene on TV, but he does not understand why seals need to be put on a Space Shuttle. There is nothing in his notes about this, and Mike is not there to help him out. Taking care not to disturb the straps, he continues shooting as if nothing was amiss, although he takes the opportunity to take a good photo of the lead used in the seals. His mission finally ends late in the evening and he gives the green light to the workers; his responsibility stops here and a supervisor from his company takes over. He still has at least four hours' work and they have already connected enormous spotlights to light up the extraordinary scene in which the Shuttle will be placed on top of the Boeing 747.

Alex puts his gear in the car and heads for his hotel, where a well-deserved meal awaits him. Already stressed out from carrying out his first 'packaging' of a Shuttle on his own, the episode with the sniper made him nervous and he will be happy to get a good night's sleep. Once in his room, he takes a shower and then starts to transfer the photos to his laptop while watching the news on CNN. Out of curiosity, and without thinking too much about it, he runs through the photos to find the zoom shot of the lead on the seals. A design on the lead, in the shape of a cat's paw, catches his attention. He enlarges it a little and reads the four letters 'CATS,' and on each toe of the paw there is an even smaller logo. He makes out a skull, a bolt of lightning, a drawing that looks like an explosion … but cannot make out the last one. It could be satellite antennae, or perhaps solar panels.

The next evening, after dropping by the office to deliver the photos and sign some papers, he switches his computer on and looks for information on the logo on the seals. He discovers that CATS is a subsidiary activity of SAIC (T-2), a company with strange ramifications, and above all strange responsibilities. He learns that the company prepares nothing less than the budget of the US Congress and the three armed forces, designs lunar exploration vehicles, manages Internet domain names all over the world, carries out counter-terrorism operations and research into nuclear fusion, plasma engines and detonation engines such as those used in the prototype of the ultra-secret Aurora aircraft (T-3). And that is just what he finds in the public domain on the Internet! Strange companies with all kinds of ramifications. Even so, this does not tell him why CATS closes the doors of the Space Shuttle and not NASA.

Chapter 3

September 16th 2009, University of Los Angeles (UCLA), California

Back in California, Susan hurries along to the archeology and history library of her university, one of the best libraries in the United States. Susan is very proud of having been accepted at this university. The Campus is more like a small town than a university. Its buildings reflect a variety of styles; some of them, white and ultra-modern, sparkle in the year-round sunshine. Others, built of brick in a style that recalls Venetian architecture, emerge from the greenery of a park. The students' car park is full of sports convertibles. Susan's parents could not afford to send her to this university, but her excellent grades and her entrance exam score earned her a grant from the government.

Based on the knowledge that there is a relationship between the orientation of the nuraghi and the rise of Venus when the planet is at its brightest, Susan is carrying out research on historical and archeological articles on Venus and a ceremony associated with the phenomenon. She comes across an article that describes sculptures showing women giving birth, with a symbol of a star opposite them. The article refers to a dolmen discovered in Belgium, carved in such a way that a woman could give birth in it; the dolmen faces south-east. Susan then decides to investigate some population statistics. Ancient cemeteries are incredible sources of data on population fluctuations.

Thanks to carbon 14 dating it is possible to carry out censuses retrospectively. Susan obtains access to graphs showing birth peaks in particular years in a search for the quietest periods.

In the meantime, Rano is working with his astronomical software and, based on the information discovered by Susan, is researching possible light fluctuations from Venus. He reaches the conclusion that its light varies for 584 days before returning, for an earthbound observer, to its point of departure. Even if Venus takes 224 days to go round the sun, it needs more than twice the time before its cycle, seen from Earth, intersects. However, he discovers that there are other much longer cycles that make Venus even brighter as a result of other factors. Every eight years, then every forty, and finally every 480 years, Venus reaches its brightest levels (S-1). After researching dates in the past for these brightness cycles, Rano meets with Susan to give her the result of his calculations. Amazed, Susan sees that there were many more births during these brighter phases of Venus.

"So, the nuraghi could have a link to births, but what, and why?" Susan asks.

"Perhaps the nuraghi were built so that women could have their babies there?" Rano replies.

"Imagine," he says to Susan, his eyes shining, "that when Venus appears very brightly on the axis of the entrance, the mother would be crouching at the end of the corridor, in the dark. The people accompanying her have just covered the glowing ash pan that allowed them to take up the right position. They reassure the woman in labor, who asks when her baby will be born. The contractions that started a few hours before do not seem to speed up, and are increasingly painful. She is assisted by three people, each one in a niche: one supports her, while the other two hold her arms. They wait for the magic moment. Suddenly, without warning, the baby starts to push, harder and harder. The mother tries to help the baby along, breathing in and out constantly. The position of her legs, wedged against the two corners of the corridor and the room, means that she could not be in a better position to give birth. The midwives reassure her, support her and mark out the rhythm. At a given moment, the corridor lights up as if someone had flicked a switch. Far off, a brilliant point of light appears, shining strongly. Its rays seem to be reflected in the wide eyes of the mother. A final effort, a contraction of her entire body, and she feels the baby come out. It is taken away by a midwife, who carries it in her outstretched arms towards the bluish light of Venus. A baby's cry breaks the morning silence, and far off, the insects suddenly stop filling the air with their noise."

Rano stops talking and Susan looks at him, stunned and speechless.

"But where did you get this idea from, and since when are you good at telling stories?" Susan asks.

"I don't know; it just came to me like that. I suddenly had this vision before me, and everything seemed to fit perfectly".

"Hm, maybe you're right. So the nuraghi would have been built for childbirth, and at the same time to know if the child was born when Venus rises. But, what interest could they have in doing that?"

"Maybe we need to look for more reliable information on birth statistics and the position of the planets, in particular Venus?"

"Yes, but there we're getting into astrology. First of all, astrology was not around at the time, and then... why just focus on Venus when astrology covers all the planets and the constellations in the zodiac?"

"Sure, but let's see if there are articles about this anyway, without necessarily mentioning astrology, OK?"

Having decided that, they say goodbye and return to their own research, Susan in the library and Rano on the Internet.

After a while Susan discovers the work of Michel Gauquelin (8), a psychologist who dedicated his life to tracing a relationship between peoples' character and the position of a planet close to Earth at their time of birth. He came across the link by chance, while trying to see if a statistical study could validate astrology. The study did not lead to anything, but Gauquelin discovered another phenomenon by chance, not taking astrological methods into account but nevertheless involving certain planets which, based on their position at the moment of birth, would have an influence on the character of a newly born child. To be sure that his results were not too subjective, he used the double blind method used in tests on pharmaceutical drugs, i.e., the doctor is not told which pills are the placebos or the real medication.

His work highlighted the fact that a planet needs to be in a series of particular positions to have a positive influence on a baby. The best position would be when the planet had just risen, and in the following twenty minutes. The effect is also present when the planet is at its highest point in the sky, and in the two opposing positions to these first two. Gauquelin thus associated particular character traits to each planet close to Earth, although he had difficulty in finding traits related to Venus.

Pleased with her discovery, Susan goes to see Rano in his office.

"I've found a researcher from the 20th century who demonstrated that certain planets have an influence on a person's character for life if he or she was born during the rise of that particular planet. There are other valid positions, but they have a lesser effect."

"Well, well," says Rano, getting out of his chair to look at the charts that Susan has spread out on the table. "It's really amazing, it looks like a slightly inclined cross. What kind of phenomenon could have an influence on a baby? Look, it's equally active when the planet is on the other side of Earth, which means that the phenomenon is not stopped by the thickness of Earth!"

"Yes, it really is surprising. But why did the people concentrate on Venus when, according to Gauquelin, it's the planet with the least effect?"

"Maybe the effect is not related to character, and Gauquelin didn't look for it because he used the effects of astrology as his basis?"

"OK, so what are we talking about, then? You know what? We should try to see if there are other monuments in the world that are also oriented towards the rise of Venus, and see if we can find other clues there or from other sources."

ALAIN HUBRECHT

Chapter 4

October 20th 2009, McLean, USA.

Alex has returned to his usual work routine but is still intrigued by what he discovered at Edwards Air Base, and anyway he is becoming increasing bored with his work. After mulling things over, he decides to contact SAIC, the company that put the seals on the Shuttle, and manages to contact their photonics department without too much trouble. America is great for that … you can change jobs on a sudden impulse.

He had to obtain clearance to work on TOP SECRET projects from NSA, at quite a high level, i.e., Cosmic Top Secret in Cryptography, which he later found out was called ECE (Extraterrestrial Communication Exchanges). He did not have much trouble getting the clearance. He is a US citizen with a clean police record, does not gamble, and has no debts or 'questionable' female acquaintances. It is just a case of waiting for the State Security Services to carry out their checks; they will ask his neighbors about him, go through his garbage and do who knows what else.

SAIC has as many as 112 offices in California, with its headquarters located at McLean. The company employs over 40,000 people, and its second-biggest complex is in San Diego, which is where Alex will work. It takes over an hour to get there from his home, but the route is all freeways with very little congestion; it takes him just as long to get to downtown LA. The building where he works is identical to the other company buildings: enormous with reflecting glass windows. The company employees could easily be accused of being too proud of where they work; in fact, they love to call their street 'SAIC Drive'.

Once hired, he joins the research team working on a new technology for fighting cancer. The idea is to use the light at a frequency of several terahertzes to carry out tissue spectrometry from samples taken. He is told that certain potential applications are very sensitive and that is why certain areas of the project need clearance.

The building is crowned by an enormous logo with the company name. As usually happens in secret projects, people only know a bit of it but not the ultimate objective. Alex spends most of his time in a laboratory workshop where they assemble and test pieces of the apparatus. At other times he shares an office with two people who are working on the same project. He soon realizes that he is better qualified than the others, no doubt because photonics is not one of SAIC's most common specialties. Moreover, he is a good speaker and soon becomes the spokesman for his group in presentations, which puts him in contact with higher executives and the project leader.

Chapter 5

November 2ⁿᵈ 2009, Newgrange, Ireland

Susan's research on other monuments that could reveal information about the same ceremony as the one held in the nuraghi shows that there is an enormous megalith in Ireland whose axis faces sunrise at the winter solstice. This 6,500-year-old monument resembles an enormous tumulus with a diameter of over 250 feet (2.1). It is covered with grass, and has an immaculate white façade on the south-east flank made from stones containing quartz crystals. When this side is lit up by the sun it can be seen shining from miles away (a bit like the ancient pyramids in Egypt when they had their original covering).

She applied for – and received – a grant to visit the site and analyze it with a view to corroborating her theory on the nuraghi.

She arrived in Ireland the day before starting work, and after spending a night in her hotel to recover from jet lag she decided to head straight for the megalith. She had plenty of time to read about its history, the civilizations that had inhabited Ireland, and the different theories explaining the use of the megalith.

The site was a twenty-minute drive away, and when she arrived, she was greeted by a very imposing sight.

An analysis of the surroundings on Google Earth showed that there must have been hundreds of identical sites in the past, some built of wood, others of stone, and the rest heaped up in a tumulus. Much of the wood and stone had disappeared, removed by the weather or the local people, but the ditches, embankments and other knolls were still visible. She counted no less than eleven within a radius of just over half a mile. God only knows what these tumuli or archeological digs could reveal. Just a stone's throw away, and as big as the one at Newgrange, stands the megalith of Knowth. It contains a kerbstone – the very complete and extremely complex K15 – that describes all the events of the year, the stars, other heavenly bodies, the phases of the moon, the system of months and weeks … and dating to more than 5,000 years ago.

The Newgrange megalith was only discovered in 1966, by a famer who wanted to remove earth from a hillock located in his fields.

Susan parks her car and walks the hundred yards to the monument. Her archeologist's pass allows her to enter the site, currently closed to tourists. The entrance to the megalith is very strange. Large stones engraved with spiral signs stand in front of the entrance. After walking around the megalith, Susan realizes that the door is crowned by a skylight which, according to previous studies, allows the sunlight to penetrate right into the corridor at sunrise on December 21st.

The internal architecture involves a long tunnel that ends up in a room whose function is unknown. Here too, it is surrounded by three niches where people could stand up – midwives too. She takes out her compass and measures the orientation of the corridor, noting it down at around 135 degrees. She walks back, observing the slanting daylight and how it highlights the designs on the stones. As she is about to go outside she sees a sign engraved above the door on the stone separating the door from the skylight. She had heard about it in 'The Book of Hiram' by the freemason journalists Christopher Knight and Robert Lomas. These journalists claimed to have observed specific engravings on several megaliths, diamond shapes whose angles corresponded to the angle of the sun at sunrise and sunset during the spring and winter solstices. They noted that the angles varied depending on the latitude of the megalith, and also that light from Venus enters the corridor at Newgrange once every eight years. Indeed, Venus has longer cycles than that of its orbit around the sun, which lasts 224 days. It has a cycle of 584 days, which corresponds to its cycle seen from Earth, and another one of eight days during which the key positions of the planet during one orbit are very bright. The Mayans, for example, were fully aware of these cycles and described them in meticulous detail in the Dresden Codex. Therefore, it is possible – by the rule of the least common multiple – to define the longer periods of twenty-nine, 243 and even 5,128 years.

After memorizing these figures, Susan started to wonder if the engravings were linked to old Masonic practices, and if they had some relation to the practices around childbirth, or rather to improve it. As she dreamily passed her fingers over the grooves in the rock she wondered if she was touching a very well-kept ancient secret, or maybe lost knowledge.

Chapter 6

November 15th 2009, SAIC, San Diego

Alex had worked at SAIC for a few months now. His skill at making clear presentations of stages of development had earned him praise from his superiors. He had just finished a meeting where he presented the budget and the development schedule for a spectrograph light emitter. Most of the people had already left the room, but one stayed behind at the back. Alex had not seen this man since he started at SAIC, and he had not uttered a word during the meeting. Alex had learned some time ago that you never ask a person's name in SAIC. This temple of secrets had rules that were more akin to the secret service than an industrial company. As Alex finished putting his papers away in his briefcase and switched off the video projector, the man stood up and closed the door. He turned round to face Alex.

"An excellent presentation, I would like to congratulate you. My name is William Minsmann but please call me Bill. I would like to have a word with you in private for a few minutes."

Alex was not too surprised. People had said that the project had several branches, and some of them needed to be handled with discretion, although until now he had not met anyone working on it. The most he had received were details of the budgets and the code names to be inserted in his presentations. He sat down and waited to hear something new.

"You've been with us a few months now, and your bosses tell me they are pleased with your work. We've checked out certain things about you and we think that you should be transferred to another unit. Today you have shown that you are right on top of your part of the project and I have no doubt that it would be easy for you to hand over your files to someone else. I represent one of the branches of the project that is classified 'Confidential' and I would like you to join my team. I think I could make better use of your skills. You would have less paperwork and a bit more technical stuff to do, which is, after all, what you trained for."

Alex continues listening, but his body language clearly shows that he already agrees with the proposition.

"This spectrograph is officially designed to detect the presence of cancer cells. You know that, but you've probably realized that it contains elements that are not used in cancer screening tests, and that its high-powered stage is also over-dimensioned. Indeed, we are working on a very sensitive project, and what I am going to tell you must never be repeated to anyone except other people working on this aspect of the project. Are you with me?"

Alex nods, but the other man seems to expect something more, so he feels obliged to express his agreement more enthusiastically.

"Agreed, you can count on me," he says with a dry throat.

"Right, here's what it's about: for the last 15 years, SAIC has recovered the Stargate project, initially started by the CIA and the Pentagon in the 1970s during the Cold War (14). At the time, they were frightened out of their wits by undetectable Russian nuclear submarines loaded with ballistic missiles. Our satellites also showed suspicious activities in some secret research centers and we had no way of knowing what the Russians were working on. The Stanford Research Institute performed statistical studies on the psi phenomenon, and were contacted to see how their best subjects could detect the position of Russian submarines or see what was going on inside the secret factories. The tests were set up by the head of the unit, Russel Targ (P-12), but one of the brightest guys there, Ingo Swann, developed a fairly effective method. Using his method, they were able to provide information on targets that was seen to be reliable in 65% of cases, which is not bad at all, but still leaves too much room for error. In the early 1990s the CIA and the Pentagon decided to withdraw their support for the project, which is when we recovered it and classified it 'Secret Defense'. In fact, some of our services do things it's better not to speak of outside these walls. The guys who were working on this one had a very particular reason for being interested in the psi methods developed by the SRI team. Don't hold it against me if I don't give you more information at this point, it's too soon to do that. We still have strong suspicions that psi powers can be improved by the exposure of a person to a certain light, or rather a certain particle, and that the particle needs to be endowed with certain characteristics."

These last few words make Alex sit up straight in his chair.

"Listen, first you say that SAIC believes in psi powers, and then you say that they could be influenced by light?"

Bill sighs but continues with his explanation:

"I can't go into detail on why we think this, but they seem to form a solid basis. That's not the issue. Our problem now is that the team working on this part of the project is behind schedule, but we have an agenda and certain dates cannot be postponed under any circumstances. That's why we want to reinforce the team. Are you on board?"

"Of course I am, as long as the clearance level isn't higher than the one I have now."

"Don't worry about that. As I said, we have already vetted you and your profile is in line with our criteria. We already recommended you for a higher clearance in case you had to change teams. They don't give out a COSMIC ECE level every day, you know."

"By the way," asks Alex, trying to sound offhand, "what do the letters ECE mean? I've never heard that acronym."

"ECE means Extraterrestrial Communication Exchanges also known as Exchanges of Extraterrestrial Communications". Bill looks Alex straight in the eye and waits for his reaction.

"Wow, what are you telling me? Are we going to speak to aliens? Hey, you didn't tell me that before asking if I wanted to join you! That little game could be a bit dangerous. I think I need a little more time to think things over."

"Whoa, take it easy. The term 'extraterrestrial' covers a lot of things, and at least so far there are no little green men in the project. The use of the term means that we are going to work with information exchange equipment orbiting Earth."

"Nothing more than that, are you sure?" says Alex, doubtful but nevertheless very excited. He is not really afraid of flying saucers and the subject has always interested him, but even so he does not want to be used as a dummy in a "beam me up, Scotty" kind of test into an alien spaceship.

"I swear that we are not considering anything that could put your life in danger, although you might be required to participate in flights to the ISS (T-4), where your presence could be needed."

"Wow, the ISS … tell me I'm dreaming!"

"No, you're not dreaming. It is a matter of taking the machine up to the ISS and, based on your profile, you're the best person to go with it. Your physique is another reason we've chosen you to join the team."

"So no little green men, is that a promise?"

"Well, not exactly, I swear to you that we don't expect anything l like that, but there are parts of the project that even I don't know anything about, and to be frank with you, there are some things that nobody here masters. That's why we're asking you to show a little goodwill and trust our good intentions."

"Well, it all seems quite exciting, and a trip to the ISS is well worth a bit of mystery. In any case, from what I know of the machine, I don't think it's a weapon of any sort, especially against aliens. OK, then! Where do I sign?"

"Pass by the clearance office tomorrow. They'll give you a new pass and will take some biometric prints (S-4)."

Bill stands up and takes his leave of Alex, congratulating him on his choice and giving him a few practical tips on his new role.

ALAIN HUBRECHT

Chapter 7

November 17th 2009, Huntington, California

Susan returned from Ireland with thousands of photographs and she has already spent several days examining and classifying them with her usual attention to detail. The day after her return she goes to see the chancellor of her university to bring him up to date on her research and to ask for a meeting with the most senior freemason possible. She tells him that her research compared certain theories linked to the origins of the freemasons and that she would like to check out some hypotheses. The chancellor explains that the masons use rituals for enthroning ceremonies and access to higher levels. He gives her an idea of what he can do for her. Susan is not a member of the confraternity, but she knows from the rumors around UCLA that the chancellor must surely be one. She does not know which lodge, or at what level, but has learnt that there are thirty-three levels and explains that she hopes to find her answers by directly speaking to a member at the highest level. The chancellor stands up and closes his office door, then turns back but does not return to his desk. Curiously, he sits down in the chair next to hers and begins to act much more openly than expected for a college president. His body language has changed in just a few moments. The man in front of Susan is now someone else. Even the tone of his voice has changed, now softer, calmer, and apparently more human, without that authoritarian air that he usually adopts in the presence of students.

"Dear Susan … I take it I can call you Susan?"

"Uh, yes, of course," she replies, caught off guard and wondering what he really wants to say to her.

"It's no secret, and I am not revealing anything out of the ordinary, if I tell you that most of the big secular universities are run by freemasons. Dan Brown's successful novels have disseminated our ideas among the general public, even if they are full of errors, intended or not. Above all, freemasonry is a school. Rather than a political, financial or humanist instrument, it is really a school for life. You learn to respect your peers and also develop the basis for a clear vision for life, of one's own life. Only after this learning process takes place can each person make a choice about what to do with information, and I can't deny that sometimes this choice goes beyond our control, unfortunately. However, every association, brotherhood or even church has members who make mistakes. We're flesh and bone and fallible and will always be so, no matter how united we are. These choices and the importance of the mistakes we might make are not linked to a status or 'level' as you call it. The notion of 'level' is mainly linked to the basic vocation of freemasonry, in other words, humanism, a vocation that is less and less required for posts of responsibility in our society, I must confess. By asking to speak to someone at the top of the ladder you are not necessarily contacting someone powerful or rich, rather someone who likes to dedicate his or her time or life to improving in the areas of discretion, humility and perseverance. His actions will be judged by some as highly inscrutable and irrelevant to our twenty-first century lifestyle, but we believe that this search for something higher should go ahead, and that it is the cornerstone of our brotherhood. It's our soul, our essence.

As for your specific request, I would recommend that you talk to one of our historians. A French historian who is preparing a study on the history of freemasonry comes to mind; it will be the first to be openly published by our order. It is intended to be comprehensive and covers all the continents. You probably know that we are present almost everywhere in the world. To give you an idea, just look at the number of countries' flags that have a triangle on them. The only reason for using a triangle is to refer to the freemasonry convictions of that country's government or royal family. Take the strangest example: Cuba. Its flag has a triangle, and the island also has the highest concentration of Masonic lodges, and everyone knows about the ideological war between Cuba and the United States, a country that is also largely run by Masonic presidents.

Look, here's an inside story ... NASA, our national pride, is simply a branch of the freemasonry movement. The space missions during its glorious years were full of Masonic codes, an enormous 'wink' to our brothers all over the world. The symbols and landing coordinates of the LEM on the Moon often made references to freemasons' values.

As is the custom, I will personally contact our mason sister and give her your details. If she accepts, she will contact you."

ALAIN HUBRECHT

Chapter 8

November 25ᵗʰ 2009, SAIC, San Diego

Alex has joined his new team. He still works in the same building, but on another floor. The access system is stricter and he needs to have an iris print taken in order to enter the area where he works. He is told that their job involves modifying the spectrum of light emitted by the machine, and above all to increase the power emitted to the highest possible factor. That is the function of the big module from which thick cables emerge. The light emitted is also sent to a different stage, giving access to other types of lenses. The spectrum emitted is complex, and Alex is asked to work on the polarization function, which does not operational yet. Apart from being right-hand circularly polarized, it must be negative (10), and nobody on the team has been able to achieve this efficiently. Alex, who still needs to fully understand this notion of negative polarization, is summoned to a highly confidential meeting called only for people with the same ECE clearance. He is not familiar with the meeting room, and makes quite a few phone calls before he learns that it is located underground. Taking the elevator indicated to him, he is surprised by the time it takes to reach what must only be level -1. He steps out of the elevator and two grim-looking guards tell him to walk towards a red door. It is the first time he has seen a red door in SAIC. It is also the first time he is body-searched. In any case, all cell phones have been prohibited in his team for some time, as have cameras, of course. Finally, after the search, which he is used to after so many spot checks by the internal SAIC police, the armored door is opened. In front of him, a winding corridor prevents him from seeing what is in the middle of the room. Strangely, the walls are covered in black carpets and sunlight enters the room in the form of tiny lights that seem to imitate the Milky Way.

The atmosphere is warm yet mysterious. It feels to Alex as though he has entered another world, as if he has gone from a dehumanized world of technology to an oasis of peace. He follows a corridor that curves gently upward, as if lifting his soul. He is now at the end of the corridor, and a space opens up before him – not as big as he expected – with room for around fifty people. The rows of chairs are already half-full. In front of them he makes out an empty space with an object in the middle covered with a black cloth.

None other than Ed Dixon, his department director, starts speaking. This means that the meeting is on the international level if the boss has come to McLean, a quiet town located north of Washington.

He recalls that this meeting is being held under the COSMIC TOPO SECRET ECE level, and that each participant is sworn to secrecy on what he or she will see. He even takes pleasure in remembering that the internal SAIC Police do not need to envy the Military Police. They know no limits, and do not even have to observe the laws of the United States.

The people remain silent, aware of the importance of the event. Everyone knows that the black sheet hides a mysterious object that is subject to extreme secrecy. They wonder how such a relatively small thing could be of interest to SAIC, which is more used to sending vehicles to the Moon or writing the US Navy's budget.

Ed Dixon's presence highlights the importance of the occasion. Alex also notices that some of the people present are not like usual researchers, but more like politicians or military personnel, even though they have to have the same level of clearance as him. Alex recognizes Richard D'Amato, the National Security Council member who often gives conferences on aliens, and the unmistakable Jacques Vallée, omnipresent in any major event on exopolitics, extraterrestrial technologies and telepathy. This is the same man who worked as scientific adviser to Steven Spielberg on 'Encounters of the Third Kind'. This discreet, modest man was linked to the origins of the Internet, now called ARPANET, the domain that made him rich to the point that he could dedicate much of his time to research into aliens. He stands apart from most other ufologists (P-15) for his rather surprising opinions; like the psychologist Carl Gustav Jung (P-5), Jacques believes that the UFO phenomenon has more to do with psychology than flesh-and-blood aliens that are similar to us. Alex is nevertheless surprised to see Jacques Vallée here, considering the level of clearance needed to attend this presentation.

The eagerly-awaited moment arrives, and their boss approaches the imposing bulk still hidden beneath the sheet. Picking up one corner, he yanks it aside and reveals a box with four legs. The unit resembles a stretcher with a metal chest on top. There are two types of satellite dishes on the chest. The people present seem disappointed, but are still bewitched by the strangeness of the object. After a pause, Dixon continues, explaining that it is, in fact, the Ark of the Covenant, or at least what they thought it should have looked like in the past. He explains that, according to their information, this object so often referred to in ancient documents is no more than a container. The usually quoted documents describe all the stages of its manufacture and explain that its mission was to protect the tablets inscribed with the Ten Commandments. There are, however, other versions that claim it is capable of great exploits: light phenomena that give access to a mysterious power, or an opportunity to speak to the gods. This is reason enough for SAIC to undertake a close-up examination of the content of the Ark and its original purpose. It is clear that the tablets of the Ten Commandments cannot be at the source of the phenomena described, although, of course, the concept of 'tablet' is rather more evolved now. Ed Dixon continues by explaining that the

Ark would have initially been conceived for use in King Solomon's temple, and then transported elsewhere for protection from invaders and thieves until its trail was lost.

Surprisingly, they are now shown a photograph of the Great Pyramid of Cheops, directly linking it to the fact that the sarcophagus in the King's Chamber inside the pyramid seems to be the same size as the apparatus inside the Ark. This comparison has not been made by chance. According to studies by Chris Dunn (P-3), the pyramid was have been a wave amplifier, and the supposed sarcophagus was the place where a very specific wave from the sky would be transformed and amplified by the Great Pyramid and then stored in the object hidden inside the Ark of the Covenant. The Great Pyramid would be an immense mechanism powered by hydraulic energy, like the armillary mechanisms of Rome. The galleries and rooms below would be a kind of ram pump, with no need for a motor or any external input of energy. The water from the nearby Nile was supplied by underground galleries that are still in existence. A chemical process was activated in the intermediate chamber – the Queen's – to produce hydrogen. The level of hydrogen production could be controlled through two ducts leading to this chamber. The pumped water compressed the hydrogen, which was sent to the upper chamber (the King's). The heavy granite beams that make up the five-layer ceiling of the chamber, and the granite pseudo-sarcophagi, were carved so that everything vibrated at a very precise frequency. There was a system at the top of the great gallery to filter the amplified wave that penetrated the slabs of granite, which could slide vertically like a portcullis. This is what archeologists refer to as 'extra doors', but an objective analysis of the place clearly shows that these sliding blocks were able to adjust to any position. It was also possible to eliminate frequencies that were too low or too high. The purified wave penetrated the King's Chamber, filled with the hydrogen generated in the Queen's Chamber. .

According to Ed Dixon, the ducts leading to the King's Chamber were not used to channel the light of a star or any other wave but, just like in the Queen's Chamber, to control the process under way in the chamber. Moreover, some ducts discovered at the summit of the pyramid were identical to those found at the end of the ducts in the Queen's Chamber. A small robot sent through these ducts in 2000 showed that they are closed off by two trapdoors that slide inside the clefts in the wall of the duct. The robot also observed the same clefts as in the ducts in the King's Chamber. Therefore, they must have been used for the same purpose, even if it is still not known how people gained access to these trapdoors in the case of the Queen's Chamber.

SAIC explains why they have rejected the idea that the ducts allowed the light from a star to penetrate as far as the King's Chamber, as many researchers have claimed. The ducts are not straight but oddly curved, with strange detours, and the transit time of a star in the axis of a duct would be no longer than a few seconds, insufficient to capture enough rays to influence the process under way in the King's Chamber. It is also highly unlikely that the south and north ducts would have been 'visited' by stars of interest, especially as they are at exactly the same height when they reach the open air. This restriction is clearly linked to how the pressure of the liquid is managed rather than to an attempt to align the stars with certainty. Instead, SAIC believes that some kind of wave entered the King's Chamber, and that it was transformed and stored in the Ark of the Covenant. They believe that the wave penetrated the thick blocks of the pyramid to reach the King's Chamber. What they want to do is to artificially re-create this wave using a spectrograph. Dixon explains that it is absolutely necessary for the light to be subjected to the electromagnetic layers that surround Earth, such as the Van Allen belt, the magnetosphere or the ionosphere. These layers have the ability to modify the particles that cross them and, although it is still an area that is not fully understood, they also think that it would be easier to take the machine to the ISS in the Space Shuttle, or, to be more precise, the new X.37C military shuttle, almost specifically built for this mission. A frequency generator would be placed inside the pyramid to reproduce the amplification and filtering system, now non-existent but easy to understand, since the vibratory frequencies of the granite elements are known. The Ark and what they imagine are its contents will be placed inside the chest, which also seems to have been carved for the original Ark. It would simply be a matter of placing the Shuttle beyond the Van Allen belt and transmitting the specific light required for the experiment. Even so, SAIC does not want to say any more today about the possible results of this experiment. The audience is told that an even higher clearance level would be required to obtain access to the information. Everyone looks at each other, and murmurs of bewilderment can be heard everywhere. Nobody understands why this could be even more sensitive than information related to aliens.

Out of the corner of his eye, Alex watches Jacques Vallée, who seems to be the only one not to bat an eyelid. Alex realizes that this six-foot-two giant must be one of the people in on the secret.

Ed Dixon calms everyone down and reminds them of the highly classified status of the project. He returns his attention to King Solomon's Temple and shows some engravings. He explains that according to ancient scriptures, its architecture had only one function – to allow the light from Venus to penetrate through a spyhole on a very precise date, when it would hit the surface of the altar. SAIC knows that the Temple was built to house the Ark of the Covenant and also make it work on very specific dates, so they plan to carry out some initial tests with light that has the same properties as the rays from Venus.

For the rest of the year the Ark was hidden in a secret place under the temple. After being exposed to the light from Venus it produced a very special reaction, according to ancient documents. This reaction was clearly beneficial to the people present. To this day nobody really knows about the reaction or its effects, no more so than the real origin of the Ark. SAIC thinks it has identified the phenomenon in question and wants to confirm it by reactivating the Ark.

Ed Dixon then asks everyone with a blue disc on their pass to leave the room. The meeting is over for them, but he tells the others to stay.

Alex looks down at his pass and, to his surprise, sees that there is a small disc in the bottom left-hand corner, but it is red! Alex watches almost everybody leave the room. The rest need about ten minutes to get organized, move closer to the screen and be scrutinized again, not by the internal service this time – they also had to leave the room – but by people who were already present among the guests. "Wow!" thought Alex, he had not heard of meetings in which even the SAIC internal police could not take part. He feels exultant. Just a few months ago he was working for a special transport company. His heartbeat increases; he is so excited. He counts the number of people who have stayed behind – seventeen – including Ed, Jacques and Richard d'Amato.

Ed explains that he is going to open the Ark and that they will be able to see what its inner mechanism looks like. Alex cannot contain his excitement, but he takes up a position that does not block the view of some other people who are already standing up. He cannot believe his luck, but notices that Jacques has not stood up. He concludes that Jacques must have already seen the inside of the mysterious box. Alex is taken aback when he finally looks inside the Ark. It is a kind of lens, an enormous lens, which must be at least fifteen inches across. Alex sees a pantograph system on the side, which must be used to take the lens out of the box, but he also notes that the lens seems to hollow in the middle and contains a slightly opaque and bluish gas. On the other two sides, it appears that ducts enter the lens, but he cannot see where they lead to.

After about ten minutes, Ed asks everyone to return to their seats and turns the floor over to Jacques Vallée. Well, well, a 'Frenchie' taking over from the boss! In a French accent that is fortunately easy to understand, Jacques starts to describe the activities of SAIC.

The company was set up in the 1960s as a cooperative, the only legal form that prevents a private lobby from buying it. Its mission was to handle secrets common to all the armed forces and to NASA, the CIA, NSA and the Pentagon. It was officially charged with drawing up the budgets for all these organizations, and also to watch over certain aspects of the security of the United States, for example the Internet. It has a full hold on the World Wide Web, and could cut off access to all the servers in the world at the drop of a hat if it wanted to. It recently set up PSIC, an information center on anti-terrorist techniques that has the cream of the best available technologies, although the real reason for SAIC's existence is anything that has to do with alien technology. Two other agencies that call themselves private also dispute the territory: RAND and EG&G, but neither of them has the power behind the scenes of SAIC. Jacques explains that he participated in defining the role and structure of SAIC right from the start, or at least the services geared to alien technologies. He explains that he was selected on the basis of his work at Stanford Research Institute and his approach to the UFO phenomenon. Jacques' research had been closely followed by the US government, and when experiments with remote viewing in the SRI started to cover flying saucers it became increasingly clear that the UFO phenomenon was something different from simple appearances of spaceships from distant planets. Jacques' theory is that objects have appeared in the sky throughout history, but they were always strange and difficult to explain with the technology of the time. Nowadays we have aircraft, rockets and missiles, so these appearances are increasingly rare and their resemblance to the flying saucers of our teenage years is less and less. Their shape becomes more eccentric, or rather an absence of form. Their materiality fools us, as does their behavior. Sometimes they seem to experience technical problems, emit smoke, shed ash or molten metal, flounder, or lose altitude and then fly off. How is it that these craft crash in front of us after flying millions of miles across space? Analyses of scraps of molten metal have shown an incredible diversity of materials, but which have nothing to do with those in the objects that visit us. No two crafts are completely the same, and there are thousands of cases. On one hand, they might be real alien visitors, but this would have to be explained by the presence of an incalculable number of civilizations and associated technologies on our Earth. There is an amusing analogy here. It is like a big shopping mall in a large city when the sales are on. Each alien craft would be one person walking along the street; each one knows what it is doing, but it does not worry about the others. Each one speaks a different language, but nobody worries about trying to understand the others' language. They come and go in all directions like ants along the store fronts, totally unaware of all the comings and goings.

At the other extreme, Jacques explains his theory: that these phenomena are not linked to visitors from space but to how the world and the universe are managed, and are closely related to our soul and our consciousness. These paradoxical apparitions are there to tell us something, to lead us to reflect on our presence in this lowly world. One clue is the ability of the phenomenon to adapt to our technological capability in each era, and on each occasion push the apparent performance of UFOs beyond what we are capable of perceiving. Other characteristics could also indicate that the phenomenon challenges our certainty about mastering matter through science. This might encourage us to continue technological research, for example, but it seems to be rather Earth-restricted for such a mysterious thing. Jacques quotes Bertrand Méheust (P-7), a French author who has spent half his life researching passages of stories, science fiction magazine covers and scenes from films about aliens in which the fictional visions were later validated by real observation. His searches have led to a number of successes, and he has found dozens of links between the invented illustrations and descriptions of people's experiences, always *after* the author of the fiction described what he had imagined. This corroborates Jacques' theory, and even seems to show that the forms and behaviors observed by witnesses are identical to the stories previously imagined by us earthlings.

It is more a case of some kind of intelligence, but without knowing what to reference it to. Is it only linked to our soul, as Carl Gustav Jung thought, or to a disincarnate and omnipresent super-intelligence?

Jacques explains that most of the constructions from the past lead us to think that some kind of intelligence has helped the human race at a given time, for example, by building structures with great precision or requiring out-of-the-ordinary resources, even by modern standards. He says that the Ark of the Covenant and the Great Pyramid are perhaps the only testimonies to this 'alliance', and he uses the word carefully. SAIC, whose mission is to carry out research on all kinds of alien intelligence, has decided to recreate an Ark of the Covenant because it believes that it is a way of communicating with those who helped us thousands of years ago.

Nothing more is known at present, and there are many gray areas involving concepts far removed from the first pharaohs, flying saucers and our consciousness.

For around ten years SAIC studied a group of human beings that either seemed capable of attracting UFOs at will or of feeling their presence, and of increasing the frequency of these events without being able to control it. Some people are also able, through concentration, to make UFOs appear, but they need several days of very hard concentration to achieve any results. Others say that wherever they go they can see UFOs, just by looking at the sky for a short time. Others say they have seen UFOs almost every week over a period of ten years. They often have testimonies and have filmed or photographed these objects. There are many of them around the world, the best-known being Anthony Woods (T-1), from

Portsmouth in southern England. When he was eight years old he saw an enormous craft at the far end of his garden. The worrying thing here is that there is a secret base beyond his garden fence where advanced radar research is conducted. He fainted but later recalled the experience, and a few years later he started to observe strangely shaped objects in the sky, either one at a time or in groups. Half of these observations took place above the base. The officers were interrogated but were not at all aware of this almost uninterrupted presence. In any case, here is a sign that the phenomenon watches over human activity that is linked to wave propagation. It immediately leads us to think of other observations made at the height of the Cold War when the rival forces deployed their nuclear missile shields. Now that more and more secret documents are being declassified, it seems that UFOs flew over many of these sites at the time, together with severe perturbations to launching mechanisms, most probably caused by these flights. Yet another strange behavior, apparently aimed at stopping us doing something irreparable. So, why does this not help us discover a new source of energy if this intelligence is so evil?

There are so many unanswered questions.

Coming back to the people who seem better at detecting the phenomenon than others, or even at making it happen, the researchers at SAIC still think that they have something special in their brains or in their DNA, or even in the quantum configuration of some of their molecules. An initial decision was made to incorporate what the rest of the Remote Viewing team of the SRI used to call the Stargate Project. This team's work was classified Secret Defense at the end of the 1980s, but the program was then taken over by SAIC. Their idea was to keep the knowledge connected with this reservoir of information under wraps, i.e., the universal consciousness to which the Remote Viewers connected during their missions. The repeated intrusions of UFO-related phenomena underline a disturbing connection between this omniscient consciousness and these strange aerial phenomena. The twenty years spent exploring the past, the present and the future through Remote Viewing allowed them to define the content and the structure of this universal consciousness. It contains a virtual representation of everything that has existed, and of what will more than likely exist in the future. It does contain information on the future; not *the* future but what seems to be the most likely future. Moreover, its content seems to be organized as information from our memory, by association, by affinity, or by attributes. Not all the details are there, but the things that are important for objects or human beings are present. The most surprising thing is that it is possible to talk to people in the past and in the future, and these virtual people behave as they would have done in their era, which seems to indicate that one is really talking to real people. Other experiments have shown that these virtual people have access to dates from the past or the future, when the real person is alive, and the same goes for objects. An object does not really die even though it loses its function, and experiments have demonstrated that if one looks for an object such as a building it is no longer possible to gain access to it if the building loses its function, and it is through its function that one researches each piece of information. Hence the really intriguing characteristics on the way in which the information stored in this universal consciousness is structured or made available, what some people call the Akaschic Records or what the Bible called the Book of Life.

SAIC believes that the Ark of the Covenant is linked to this and that it could increase the ability of a human being to communicate with this universal consciousness and what we consider as alien manifestations. They believe that the Ark could improve a human being's capacity at that level.

Jacques finishes by presenting the hidden agenda of the spectrograph project, the planned date for the transfer to the ISS, and the planned date for the first test inside the Great Pyramid.

He finishes by reminding everyone of the total secrecy around what has been said during the meeting.

Alex walks back to his office after the meeting, still in shock from the presentation. Everyone around him seems to be isolated in a bubble, tired from the energy required to assimilate what they just heard. So much information in such a short time, so many new facts and potential discoveries, but even so, still so mysterious.

So much so that they would find it hard to keep quiet when they joined their partners at bedtime.

ALAIN HUBRECHT

Chapter 9

December 2nd 2009, Sofitel hotel, Philadelphia

Susan arrived the night before, not wanting to be late to meet the lady freemason who had come from Paris specially to see her. She was in Philadelphia, the old capital of the United States. She has reserved a suite in the Sofitel hotel up on the heights of the city, near the restaurant quarter. It is the first time she has stayed in such a luxurious hotel – almost a thousand dollars a night – but her college is paying because the suite is an ideal place to meet Élise Thirionnet, a specialist in the history of freemasonry. Élise called her the same day Susan had her meeting with her college President. Despite the time difference, Élise managed to speak to her before the day was out. Susan told her how her research was going and gave her an idea about her questions, and Élise confirmed that she could contribute new elements but did not want to say any more over the telephone, and certainly not by e-mail. She proposed a half-way rendezvous, so they agreed to meet in Philadelphia.

The day starts perfectly, with a bright sun shining in a pure blue sky. The area is heavily wooded, which helps the air quality enormously. The woods also attract heavy rain, but everything is built for that, like almost everywhere in the United States. Susan is pleased the weather is good, feels proud to be American and wants to give Élise the best possible welcome. For her, the story of civilizations is the foundation of the human race, something that links all peoples. There are no 'goodies' or 'baddies', just civilizations seeking their way forward. Unlike some people, who believe that history should remind us of the errors of the past, Susan thinks that the traces of the past should lead us to be proud of ourselves and make us want to progress even farther. She knows that evolution is cyclical, like most natural phenomena, and finds it normal that certain phases of development of each civilization have dark or regrettable areas. Moreover, she also believes that each civilization does not start from nothing to end up with nothing, passing through a peak of knowledge and technology. It seems common for civilizations to start from everything, and they only decline in their ability to master their technology and their knowledge. The civilization of the pharaohs could be an example. The civilization discovered in Turkey at Gobekli Tepe even 'committed suicide' by voluntarily burying all the traces of its knowledge. More recently still, in Amazonia, a civilization had been discovered in Brazil that lived completely isolated for its entire duration, from 200 BC to 800 AD. Archeological digs reveal that very ancient pottery had extremely elaborate artwork; only later did it become more of a crude art bereft of decoration. It is one of the best examples a continuous decline starting from the first day of the establishment of a civilization, one which nevertheless lasted for over 1,000 years.

Lost in her reveries, Susan does not hear the doorbell at first. She gets up from the extremely comfortable bed, straightens her skirt, checks how she looks in the mirror and goes to the door.

She is met by the sight of a woman who still looks young, although she is well into middle age. Élise speaks English and the two women seem to hit it off right away. Susan invites her guest into the lounge and asks her if she would like a drink. After discussing a range of subjects such as archeological studies in California or Élise's professional background, Susan comes to the point.

"What do you know about a possible relationship between freemasonry and birth rituals in ancient times?"

"I got a good idea of your research when we first spoke on the phone, and even though I could already answer some of your questions, I searched more carefully through my files. I actually did find traces of childbirth rituals in certain ceremonies, but to tell you the truth I haven't seen any explanations of their significance anywhere, which leads me to think the significance has been lost over the years.

"More than 2,000 years ago, the Temples in either Rome or Athens were built in two zones, one for public ceremonies and the other for secret rituals. That's where the Mysteries (4) come from, like the ones from Eleusis or Mithra. At the time the Oracles were fashionable; they were supposed to able to predict the future. In the public area, at certain times of the year they made arrangements so that fertile women could have intercourse with any man, although nobody knows the reason for this practice. Strings were tied between the columns to create recesses that were called, believe it or not, 'fornix', a term that led to the verb 'fornicate'. True, all this could have been at the origins of freemasonry, but I haven't been able to find any more information on it."

Disappointed by Élise's reply, Susan continues:

"But surely there must be masons who still have knowledge about why these rituals were performed in the temples, or ancient documents to describe them?"

"Unfortunately, no. The growing number of masons after the increase in lodges, together with political and religious quarrels, has led to the disappearance of documents containing, for example, the Mysteries of Antiquity, which are also subject to complete secrecy on the part of enthroned persons. Later on, the push towards modernity led the Supreme Masters to modify the Masonic rituals. That was in the 17th century, and it made the real meaning of these rituals more confusing. Nowadays none of us are able to understand the real messages behind all those documents."

"Tell me more about the Mysteries of Antiquity, which you say are at the origins of freemasonry."

"Archeological digs have unearthed crypts that had not been robbed by burglars, and it appears that they contained a representation of the night sky. The metallic remains of armillary mechanisms (5.3) have also been discovered."

"Armi-what mechanisms?"

"Armillary. They're animated mechanisms that can locate the planets of the solar system or the constellations of the zodiac in space, or rather on a celestial vault. Some of these mechanisms were small, even very small, like the Antikythera mechanism (5.2), while others are gigantic, such as the one that operated in the secret room of Nero's palace (5.3)."

"A secret room?"

"Yes, a few years ago one of the digs near Nero's palace in Rome unearthed an enormous underground room. It's round, with a diameter of around fifty feet. Its ceiling is a semi-sphere, and thanks to a hydraulic system called a 'clepsydra', or water clock, the stars and constellations move around automatically. Nero could know where the planets and stars were in the sky at any time of the day."

"But that's crazy, and what use could it have?"

"In principle, for astrology, but we don't know any more about it. Today's astronomers don't like talking about astrology, and when the Antikythera mechanism was discovered – a genuine marvel of precision with dozens of moving parts that take irregular orbits and calendars into account – they stubbornly claimed it was a teaching instrument for universities over 2,000 years ago. However, when a gigantic system like the one in Nero's palace is discovered, and hidden in a secret room reserved for secret rituals, then we are no longer talking about something just used to teach astronomy."

"But what else could they do with these mechanisms on the basis of what they could observe in the night sky?"

"If we take the Antikythera mechanism, discovered at the start of the 20th century by sponge fishers off the Greek island of Antikythera, we can only wonder at the infinite possibilities of the device. First of all, we should thank the scientists who x-rayed the mass of rusty metal in the decades following its discovery to determine its composition. The object, no bigger than a shoebox, has a handle on one side, and when you turn it you can adjust a date with great precision. You just have to move the needles on one of the faces that represent the Egyptian calendar. At the time, the calendar was exact and almost identical to ours. Once you've set the date, you can turn the apparatus around and you see the Greek calendar, riddled with contradictions, but used in Greece in that era. You can see the planets that were known then, orbiting around Earth and the Moon, and an animation of the Moon's phases, and the signs of the zodiac all around."

"But that's crazy! They knew all that all those years ago?"

"Wait … that's not all. The device was covered in inscriptions, probably instructions for use, and deciphering the inscriptions has taught us a lot more about its potential. It could predict eclipses and took into account particular features of the orbits of certain planets – and some of these only returned every 1,000 years. So, they must have believed those cogwheels that had more than 1,000 teeth. Some were off-center, or the teeth weren't evenly distributed. I'm telling you, it was a real marvel. Oh, and there's a detail that might interest you. Strangely enough, the device had a dial indicating the dates of the Olympic Games and other important games organized in Greece at the time."

"But I thought those games took place on very specific dates every year?"

"Well, not exactly, the dates were calculated on the basis of the position of the stars."

"Why is that?"

"Nobody knows, but this is where I have some information that might interest you. The winners of the events did not receive a cup or a laurel wreath; they were invited to the Temple to choose one of the women there, to do what they pleased with them. The pretty hostesses that drape themselves over today's sports champions and cover them with kisses are a relic of that practice, but then again, its real meaning has been completely lost."

"If I understand it right, the Greeks waited for a particular date to allow these couplings between the local women and athletes from all over the country?"

"Exactly!"

"But what for? Why wait for a very precise date?"

"Maybe it all comes down to the stars. They were keen on astrology in those days. Some people even say that the Essenes, a sect often associated with the life of Jesus, only worked by the rules of astrology. Ancient writings explain that, depending on the configuration of the sky at a person's birth, each human being received bad and good parts to make a total of nine parts. For them, the more good parts a baby received, the better-looking he or she would be later on in life. These ancient documents also describe the criteria behind this beauty: the more good parts you had, the sooner the hair disappeared from your body. The Essenes had also predicted the arrival of the Messiah based on a very precise configuration of the stars, forecasting that, exceptionally, he would receive nine good parts and no bad ones."

"Something doesn't make sense here, because astrology always talks of the sky at birth, not of the date of procreation, but the Antikythera mechanism allowed people to predict the date of the Olympic Games and the date on which mating could take place best, if I follow your theory."

"Think about it, what stops you adjusting the device on the basis of a configuration of stars, watching the stars and the constellations move rather than modifying the date? Once you've reached the best configuration of the year, you look at the date and subtract nine months! And there you have it!"

Susan opens her mouth, but no sound comes out. She struggles for breath. She hears her heart beating in her chest and tries to get her breath back, feeling as if something had collapsed inside her head. She feels the knots of the armchair lining under her hands, which have suddenly gone cold. She looks into space and cannot concentrate on anything. She finally comes back to Élise, who does not know which side to tilt her head to get Susan's attention again. She is almost out of breath as a result of what she has just understood and glimpsed.

"Do you realize what you've just said? Well, it certainly seems to confirm my ideas. Oh, I'm so glad I asked you to come. Let's take five and celebrate this discovery with a nice cocktail! I'm going to call the bar and ask them to bring one up, and then I'd like to invite you to dinner. As you'll, there are dozens of delightful little restaurants near the hotel."

"Oh, come on! It's you, through your questions, who led me to this conclusion. Don't forget that we're talking about different eras, and you are focused on a particular celestial body, Venus if I remember rightly. You need to re-examine all these different elements and see if your ideas can still be confirmed. Don't count your chickens too soon!"

"Oh, yes! I feel it, I'm sure of it, a little light in my head tells me that I'm on the right track. Listen, what would you like to drink?"

Later on in the evening Élise explained the ins and outs of the book she was about to publish. Her approach to the history of freemasonry basically breaks some taboos, such as the one that says the main lodges in the world today do not like to trace their origins back beyond the 17th century. She tells her about the two main currents in the movement – 'operational' and 'speculative' freemasonry – but also about the continuous conflicts with religion. Strangely, in order to be a mason you have to say you believe in God, but that god should not be linked to religion, and for some lodges not under any circumstances, ever. She also explains the parallel systems, stuck on to freemasonry to a greater or lesser extent, such as the Templists and the Templars, the Rosicrucians, the Knights of Malta and finally the Illuminati. Certain levels of freemasonry have communication channels with these orders, but the reason for this remains obscure; the same obscurity that covers the existence of the Illuminati. The two women say goodbye to each other late in the evening after long discussions about mythical sects, and return home the following morning.

Chapter 10

December 15th 2009, UCLA, San Francisco

After returning from Philadelphia, Susan rushed to the library, for two reasons, the first being that it is quiet there; she could get away from her colleagues, her e-mails and social networks and could work much more efficiently. Secondly, a library is still a place where you can consult a number of works and documents that are not available on the Internet. Some people still believe that the Internet lets you find and consult absolutely everything, or download it, but they are very wrong indeed. You have to pay for most scientific studies when you want to access them via the Internet, but they are free if you bother to pass by the library. In the last two weeks she has gathered a real set of data that allows her to validate her ideas and put forward a theory that is entirely original and momentous. After agonizing for ages she decides to contact her President again to ask for another interview. Trembling with excitement, she asks him if he can bring together the highest echelons of freemasonry for a presentation – to be given by her – and knowing that what she will say will have enormous importance for freemasons, science and the human race in general. No less!

The President forgets protocol again, as he did in their first interview. This time, after learning of her request, he turns round in his chair and swings on the two feet that remain on the floor, almost falling backwards. Susan gives him an outline of her theory, asks him a few questions, and he seems convinced that what she says has substance. He tells her that there is a conference planned for the following month – January 2010 – in Washington. The conference is up there on a level with Davos or Bilderberg, but it only brings freemasons together and would be the ideal occasion for Susan to fulfill her wish without people having to travel too far. He promises to find out if the idea is feasible, congratulates her on her idea and urges her to be extremely discreet about her conclusions because the subject could not be more delicate. He also reminds her to keep any of her contacts with freemasons secret.

Susan cannot resist a couple of kangaroo jumps in the corridor after leaving the President's office. The world seems a lighter, brighter place. She feels intense pleasure when she thinks of the extent of her discovery, and starts counting the days to the conference.

Chapter 11

January 23rd 2010, a masonic temple in Washington

Susan managed to get her meeting with the highest echelons of international freemasonry. Naturally, she wrote a document outlining the main ideas of her presentation, which was vetted by a committee of experts. They were impressed by her arguments and approved the meeting. It would take place as a prelude to the World Freemasonry Conference, in a discreet temple in Washington. She has been allocated a ninety-minute session on the second day, to be attended by about fifty people. She will not be able to ask people their names, and certainly not film anything or take photos. The follow-up to her presentation will be exclusively up to those present, and she must keep any information considered too sensitive by her interlocutors to herself.

This is the content of her presentation:

"Over millions of years, the knowledge involved in linking in with the cycle of Venus in order to improve the human race is a secret that has been very well kept by senior freemasons. Early rituals describe, in thirty-three stages, the construction of a temple dedicated to Venus, research into its orientation, the location of the opening where the light of Venus would enter, and the position of the altar where the baby would be born, flooded with the bluish light of the planet. Most early megaliths were places to give birth or, by extension, to mate nine months before. Later, the first Greek temples, and even Roman, were erected for this purpose. "Certain times of the year were reserved for well-disposed women to visit the temples and offer themselves to virile men so that the maximum number of children could be born nine months later under the most favorable conditions, i.e., during the rise of Venus. This knowledge was transmitted under great secrecy, and certain circles of influence tried to diversify the teachings under the form of the Mysteries of Antiquity or through advice given by the Oracles.

"Later, the monotheistic religions tried to destroy these practices, which competed with theirs. Historians have even forgotten the real meaning of the temples. As for the churches, they conserve an altar and a specially-oriented window to allow the light from a celestial body to flood the altar at a particular moment, but the original knowledge has been lost and the Church simply copied practices that are pagan or druid-like in order to keep the maximum number of worshippers and offend people as little as possible. Wasn't going to church and giving birth there a tradition in the early churches? From that to imagining the altar as a place to give birth at the same time as receiving light from a star or planet is just one step that I still do not dare to take. However, let me come back to these mysterious structures built over thousands of years. Their objective was to give birth to the elites, future village or tribal chiefs, or leading figures in cities or civilizations. In the same way that Man has been able to cross animals and plants to improve the species or adapt them to his taste after thousands of years, he would have discovered how to improve not only the human race, but also how to produce future kings and emperors. Having understood the influence of celestial bodies on our character and personality, he could improve, generation by generation, the ability of his descendants to reason and improve their intelligence. There are many testimonies of this from Egypt up to Scotland via Sardinia, Rome and Athens, and they span at least 8,000 years. It seems that our ancestors had discovered particularly interesting properties linked to Venus, and this planet received the full attention of those who, I believe, first created freemasonry thousands of years ago.

"They made this knowledge top secret because it was capable of producing the greatest leaders on Earth, people with great vision who would be able to conquer an empire in less than twenty years and make the best choice in every major decision. It is easy to understand why the emperors who were in on this secret took great care to forbid its practice without their consent, and killed anyone who went against their will.

"The best configurations of Venus were eagerly awaited, and that is how the sects waited for a sign for the coming of their Messiah. It is also why Herod killed all the babies who were born during a particularly rare configuration of Venus, precisely at the conjunction of Venus and Mercury when Venus was at its brightest.

"The ancients called this conjunction the Shekhinah. I will just illustrate the importance of this term with three highly significant examples. The Illuminati, of whom everyone talks about but nobody sees, would have used the symbol of the Chi Ro, long used by the Christians, to recognize each other. This symbol represents the word Christ, symbolized by the two Greek letters Chi and Ro, placed on either side of a six-spoke cross. These spokes represented the superimposition of two three-spoke stars, Venus and Mercury, when they came together with such surprising properties. This was surely the star which guided the Three Wise Men. The six-spoke symbol also appeared on the tympanum of the entry to the crypt of the Basilica of the Nativity in Bethlehem (6) and this tympanum is also cited by local members of religious orders as representing the Shekhinah. The Shekhinah would also be associated with the term Holy Spirit, the famous Holy Spirit which, according to the Old Testament, would enter the newborn child and later allow him or her to read the future and know everything."

Susan finishes her presentation by repeating that the freemasons would have patiently collected the different elements of bringing future leaders into the world and hidden them in their secret rituals, gradually teaching them to followers during the enthroning process. The message was lost over the years, but she believes she has found its very essence.

Her last slide thanks people for attending and includes her contact information. The audience seems to shuffle in their chairs without really knowing what to do. The fact that a non-mason has attended one of their sessions is surprising enough, but that this person should come and tell them where they originated from and what their initial purpose was is quite a surprise, to say the least. Faced with this general hesitation, the organizer escorts Susan off the stage and tells her that they will keep her up to date on the follow-up to her presentation, but in the meantime she should not discuss it with anyone else.

She would not receive any news from them for two weeks and would therefore have to live with the anguish of not knowing the effect her discoveries had on the audience, and if they really were discoveries, or if there was a group – an elite – who were already in the picture about this knowledge.

Chapter 12

February 5ᵗʰ 2010, SAIC, McLean, Virginia

Alex's work is going well. He has contacted the best specialists on Venus, found scientific articles about its atmosphere and orbit, the polarization that the sun's light suffers when it is reflected by the double atmosphere of Venus, and the effect produced on this polarization by the backward turn of its atmosphere. Venus is not only the sole planet in our solar system to rotate 'backwards', its atmosphere also turns against its direction of rotation. The effect is like a backhand shot in tennis – a 'slice' – in the sense that the ball starts turning after hitting the racket.

Alex has found some graphs showing that the sunlight reflected by Venus is polarized in a circular way, i.e., only the photons that turn in a very precise direction are returned. For every wavelength sent back there is a very specific polarization, but all the photons turn in an anti-clockwise direction.

Other graphs show another phenomenon, one that is much less well-known. When the planet approaches its maximum elongation, the polarization of the reflected light becomes negative. This elongation is the angle between Venus and the Sun. It is maximal when Venus is (visually) the furthest from the sun, this distance being observed from Earth (9). Despite his research and the resources of SAIC, Alex has not been able to find a laboratory capable of providing him with the negative polarization filters he needs. Some researchers believe that it is possible to create this effect by piercing a reflective surface with several tiny holes that are around the wavelength to the light to be reflected. While thinking about this problem, Alex is called to a meeting at SAIC headquarters in McLean. He is told that new information is available that could help the project, although it would not modify its elements to a great extent.

Alex has no difficulty finding his company's headquarters. It occupies the whole street, which is not surprisingly called 'SAIC Drive'. The town of McLean seems to be nondescript, but it is just a stone's throw from Washington, the Pentagon and NSA.

As usual, Alex goes through the entry procedures to the building, but they seem even stricter than usual. The surprising thing is that they are carried out by civilians, but civilians with crew cuts, long overcoats and sunglasses, not unlike the characters from the film *Men in Black*!

He finally enters the building and goes up to the floor where the meeting is to be held. He finds himself in a large room with about twenty other people. Ed Dixon is there, and so is Jacques Vallée.

However, the first person to speak is a man that Alex does not know. He is over sixty and seems quite at ease, as if he felt at home. Alex thinks that he must be a member of the board, or at least the senior management. Jacques is sitting to his left, while Ed is opposite, like him. This person starts by explaining that everything that will be said comes under Cosmic Top Secret ECE, a level held by everyone present. Once this is understood and accepted by everyone, he presents a summary of a theory presented in a recent conference. The person behind the theory is a certain Susan Gomez and the presentation was related to freemasonry. Alex thinks it is not surprising that SAIC would have been present at that meeting because, like NASA and the large military groups, they have always been run by freemasons. The JPL, the forerunner of NASA, was created by freemasons, i.e., Ron Hubbard, who went on to set up

Scientology, and Werner Von Braun, the Nazi brain behind the infamous V2 rocket.

They are all here today because Ms. Gomez' discovery could mean a great leap forward in the preparation of the spectrograph and the activation of the Ark of the Covenant. It seems clear that the sought-after parameters of its light are those of the rays from Venus or the Shekhinah, which vary depending on the position of Venus and the time of day. Based on historical data, the alignment of the nuraghi and megaliths such as the one at Newgrange could determine the exact position that the ancients had taken so long to identify.

The speaker then hands over to Jacques Vallée. Alex realizes that he is clearly deeply involved in all sorts of things related to basic research, but also to alien and paranormal phenomena. As he already heard his presentation the other day, he wonders what more he can learn today.

Jacques speaks on behalf of SAIC, and explains that they have been following encounters of the third kind for fifty years. They try to understand why certain people have been contacted and what sets them apart. After much trial and error and several failures, they have found a thread that seems to be plausible. They have discovered that the brains of these contacts were different from 'normal' people at the level of centrioles, which appear to be better arranged. Centrioles are the brains of living cells, and they are found in all the cells of live animals. They are authentic decision-making centers, and are made of microtubules (12.1). Microtubules are polymers that look like tubes, with a cross-section of thirteen tubulin molecules, to make up a total of 300 to 1,000 molecules. These tubes are everywhere in cells. They link the centrioles to cell walls and constitute the cytoskeleton of the cell, and are scattered among the neurons in large numbers. As a cytoskeleton, when they contract or dilate they allow a cell to move.

Centrioles (12.2) are made up two perpendicular parts, each one with nine 'flaps' of three microtubules. These flaps shake like the slats on Venetian blinds, in such a way that each axis of the centriole can determine the angle of impact of a particle such as a photon when it strikes it. Having two perpendicular parts, the centriole can determine the exact direction from where the particle comes. Jacques presents a large number of diagrams, photos and drawings to explain his ideas. The audience seems a bit lost, but everyone knows that they are not there to play hopscotch.

Jacques continues by explaining that the microtubules are also present in large numbers and in an isolated state in cells, even more so in brain cells, around 10,000 per neuron.

Tubulin molecules are polymers, molecules able to adopt different spatial configurations. Here we see two main states, called Alpha and Beta. We will use the term 'dimer'. Sometimes these configurations are identical, like reflections in a mirror. Here we speak of chiral molecules, and the two states as 'left' and 'right', like our hands. The term 'chiral' also means 'hand' in Greek. Biologists have observed that the tubulin molecules located in our neurons can pass from an Alpha to a Beta state quickly, and researchers have been unable to find the reason for this change of state. Even more surprising, these molecules can line up in identical states within the same microtubule and create geometrical figures like spirals, parallel lines, or – even better – all the molecules in a microtubule can acquire the same state (Alpha or Beta). Each neuron contains around 10,000 microtubules, and each microtubule up to 1,000 molecules of tubulin. Around ten million tubulin molecules can be evaluated per neuron. Given that the brain has around 100 billion neurons, that gives a total of one million trillion (10 to the power of 18) molecules that seem to be able to change their state without any explanation. This is why our researchers imagine that these molecules are the interface with our consciousness; there is only one step more to take. Some believe that they are our information storage units, but we here in SAIC think that our memory is stored directly in what we call a 'universal consciousness', a kind of common pot in which every organism in the universe stores its past and present, and where its future can also be accessed. There would be a kind of 'implicit code' that gives us inside access to our information, but other people could also gain access with a bit more experience, a bit like people who say they know how to speak to animals. Indeed, they link in to this universal memory and can read the information emitted from one animal or another.

The synchronized modification of the state of these tubulin molecules located in the microtubules seems to give super-conducting powers to these tubes, or even give them the ability to capture different information in the form of light, sound, electricity or gravity waves. Some people now call these 'inertons', a particle recently invented by Volodymyr Krasnoholovets (P-6).

Susan Gomez's discovery points the way forward, as we can express and know what these changes of state are used for. According to her hypothesis, we think we should no longer focus on the life cycle of these strange structures but on their initialization phase, which would occur during the birth of a baby. The position of Venus at the time of a person's birth would have an effect on these microtubules for their entire life. According to the results of recent research by Alex Bergen, head of spectrometry for our machine, the light that reaches Earth from Venus is constantly modified on the basis of its length and its position in relation to the horizon. Although we now seem to have good knowledge of the light that approaches Earth, we do not know what modifications take place to it when it comes close to Earth and enters its atmosphere. This is why we are going to carry out some light emissions from Space, in order to use these natural layers to modify our artificial light.

Recent scientific studies have shown that this light is the only one that creates life on Earth. The amino acids that are the basic 'bricks' of life need to be lit up by such a light to form themselves, and sunlight does not do this. The twenty or so molecules in amino acids are all chiral molecules, but life only wants those that face left and wants absolutely nothing to do with those that face right. Now, if you inject light into a mixture containing all the atoms needed to create these amino acids, the result shows as many left-facing as right-facing ones. This proportion of each orientation – 50% – literally prevents life from being created. Belgian researchers from the ULB (yet another freemasons' university) have shown that the light emitted from the constellation Orion could influence this proportion due to the fact that it has right-hand circular polarization, as does the light from Venus (9). In fact, these amino acids are constructed from sugars, which also have chiral molecules. These same scholars have shown that the light from Orion mainly comes from right-facing sugars called dextrose, and, based on these sugars, the amino acids can only be oriented to the left. Venus probably played a significant role vis-à-vis our planet hundreds of millions of years ago, and these recent discoveries lead SAIC to believe in Susan's findings.

Given the obvious importance of her discoveries, we would like to invite her to join the project team. It seems clear that we cannot make progress without taking history into account, plus the information that archeological and historical research can contribute. If the ancients made such great efforts to keep a power linked to childbirth, the planets and world domination secret, we cannot continue to ignore their teachings, and apparently all their efforts went in the same direction as ours do now. Indeed, what they tried to improve was the ability of a human being to read the future, to find answers to questions; in other words, to be able to connect with this universal consciousness, the same one that we think our machine will help us to connect to through the Ark of the Covenant.

Jacques leaves it there for this meeting. Once again, the amount of information he is able to convey and summarize in his presentations is impressive. Alex wonders what else he knows but does not talk about, but is very happy at having his name mentioned by the expert. Obviously, he already holds an important position, not just in the project team but also in SAIC in general. He recently moved closer to San Diego, his salary has almost doubled and the assurances given to him by the company mean that he looks to the future with optimism. Even better, the project on which he is working is incredibly interesting. He never though he would do something so exciting in his life, and linked to Space at that. He thinks about everything that has happened to him in the last six months. His parents constantly tell him to keep his feet on the ground, saying that it is surely a temporary thing and that nothing is sure at a time of worldwide economic crisis, but Alex feels more confident with every day that passes. The company is like a great ocean liner cruising across the sea; nothing can divert it from its course. Since starting work here he has observed dozens of anomalies, things that would have otherwise created insurmountable problems, but they seem to disappear without any effort. For example, he has found out that there is a service to sort out any problems related to traffic offenses; you just have to send a parking ticket to the service and you never hear any more about it. His pension is carved in stone, and for a figure that he would never dare to tell his friends about. He has also noticed that a large number of people work on ghost projects. In conversations in the canteen or at the coffee machine, when someone asks someone else what they are working on, the reaction is always the same. They change subject immediately, or say it's not worth talking about. Others say they are only in 'ghost' services in the sense that they need to fill in forms for services to dozens of people who, apparently, do not exist. They then have to send invoices for these services, which contain ridiculous sums, to different federal and state services. In any case, Alex gets on with his job and realizes that it is better not to try and understand what goes on elsewhere, so he does not nose around or ask awkward questions of his colleagues. Everything he knows, he has learnt it by keeping his ears trained at the right time and in the right place. Anyway, what has he got to complain about?

He now has a nice house in a good neighborhood in north San Diego, no more long trips to work, sun all year round, a city center on a human scale, the sea just five minutes from his home, and big waves to indulge his passion for surfing.

After organizing his belongings, Alex stands up and leaves for the airport, as happy as a lark.

Chapter 13

March 2nd 2010, SAIC, San Diego

Susan arrived in San Diego the previous week, and SAIC rented an apartment for her and Rano. They are in the southern part of the city, unfortunately just behind the poorer neighborhoods, but they can easily reach SAIC by bicycle, which is OK. Their apartment block is mostly occupied by Afro-Americans who hang out in the entrance hall, which almost seems to be their living room. They had a bad impression at first, but when they discovered their apartment they changed their mind completely. It was luxurious and in good condition, with a view over the naval base where enormous gray warships bristling with guns seemed to be waiting for some unlikely event to happen. They soon realized that they could also reach the city center easily by bike. San Diego is quite small, a bit like the French quarter of New Orleans, but without the strong Cajun connotations of the old colonial French city. Here, it looks more like a replica of the chic neighborhoods around the Stock Exchange in New York. Indeed, all the best restaurants are located on the main drag, which is just around half a mile long. It starts from the port and climbs up the hill. Cycle-taxis have been a feature for a few years, a fashion from Asia that seems to please people who like ancient practices. However, watching the poor students struggle to pull obese tourists around by hauling them up the main avenue, Susan wonders if they would not be better off finding some other way to make a few bucks.

After a few days settling in and doing official paperwork, probably to allow the security personnel to vet them and see what clearance level they could receive, they finally turn up at the offices of SAIC in San Diego.

Despite his Chinese parents Rano has been granted the same level of clearance as Susan, and can therefore follow her wherever she goes. The level is not Top Secret, but it still allows them to enter buildings and common areas without being accompanied or having to ask for a new pass every day.

They are given a small office, which Susan brightens up in the afternoon with a plant she places somewhere where she can always see it from her desk. Rano has brought a little Buddha from Los Angeles and places it on the ledge of the fanlight above their door. Like he did at college, every morning he puts an offering in front of the statue, usually a sweet or an orange. He is never tempted to eat them if he is hungry, a sweet offered to Buddha is a sweet for Buddha and it would be sacrilege to think that he could eat it later. Susan would never see Rano remove these offerings; he always waited for the office to empty to put them away. It makes her think of Santa Claus, like when parents devise a thousand strategies to make their kids believe he is coming, and the tacit agreement they have later when the kids learn who really leaves the presents, carrying on for a few years as if nothing had changed.

The afternoon of their arrival, after watering her plant Susan and Rano go to a meeting room to describe their discovery. She explains that, based on her reading and observations of megaliths, an ancient practice carried out all over Europe tried to get certain babies born at a very precise moment, linked to the cycle of Venus. In certain regions such as Sardinia it seems that the practice was common and in others it was reserved to only a few people, no doubt the elites. The ancient moments she observed are clearly built so that the light from Venus penetrates inside them when the planet rises, flooding the mother giving birth with that light. The idea was to know if Venus was in a very precise place when the baby was born, no doubt in the moments following the cutting of the umbilical cord. She had examined studies carried out in France, where EEG recordings had been made on the heads of babies during and after childbirth. The traces reveal a very clear modification of the EEG signals before and after labor. Before the birth they seem linked to the mother's, and later change frequency and form, and are, of course, linked to the baby itself. Susan believes that this involves a basic modification of the brain's chemistry, as if great changes take place in the newborn child's body, such as the adaptation of red blood corpuscles, the closure of the *foramen ovale* and the lungs starting to work. While she explains this, she attentively observes that the SAIC people are taking notes non-stop and even seem enthusiastic about what she is saying! She imagines that it all happens in a kind of moment of grace during which the baby is highly receptive to 'something', and that something could be the light from Venus. Some midwives even told her that sometimes they see the baby motionless, as if it was waiting for 'something', and suddenly it moves without anything visible having happened.

Alex is present, of course, and has already made the presentations of the two archeologists in his team. He interrupts her and asks her if she had heard of the microtubules.

Susan shakes her head.

Alex tells her, with the air of a college professor, that two weeks earlier he did not know that microtubules were mysterious elements in our brain, and that they could be like 'flashes' at the birth of a baby. Furthermore, the light from Venus is consistent and particular, and the state of the tubulin molecules would be specific. This discovery would have been made by our ancestors, and the secret kept by the freemasons, although without fully understanding the mechanism that really takes place in our cells.

Alex explains that another strange phenomenon takes place inside the brain a few years after birth, surely linked to what happened before.

"This phenomenon is called neuronal death, or apoptosis. In fact, we're born with 300 billion neurons, many more than we have when we're adults. For some unknown reason we lose two-thirds of our brain cells in the first seven years of life. However, let's leave that aside for now, as we already have enough unknown factors to deal with."

"Do you think that nature tries to eliminate what you call a 'microtubule' that wouldn't have been correctly 'flashed' at the time of birth?" asks Susan.

"We have no idea. Nobody has been able to explain the purpose of this 'collective suicide', but we are now swimming in an ocean of information that very few people can decipher. In any case, we'd like to congratulate you for your work and your conclusions. We heard about your conference in Washington and it seems that you made a triumphal entry into the Pantheon of SAIC."

The SAIC employees cannot get over it. Without realizing it, Susan has put her finger on the role of microtubules in human intelligence, or rather precognition, without suspecting that they are all studying the same molecule within the framework of extra-sensorial communication.

Chapter 14

March 28th 2010, the beach, San Diego

Alex and Susan are in the water, astride their surfboards. Alex convinced Susan to come and visit him at the weekend so she could learn how to surf. He has not been able to resist the charms of this young woman for long, and the time he has spent alone over the past few months is starting to bug him. He also thought it would be a good idea for him to get on well with Susan, and maybe, he secretly hoped, ask her out. Indeed, sessions that involve getting undressed and handling wetsuits certainly help you to get to know someone better. Sure, Susan goes and changes behind Alex's big station wagon but she still needs his help to remove her wetsuit, and that allows Alex to appreciate her curves, not just by looking at them but by passing his hands over them, which he does for a little longer than he normally would. She realizes what he is doing, but makes nothing of it. She admires this man who heads such an advanced technology team, but does not know him well enough yet to know if he would be a good lover or companion. For the time being, she focuses on waiting for that big wave, the one that will carry her along for a few yards and seem interminable because it is so hard to stay balanced on the surfboard while checking the behavior of the wave, as Alex has taught her. The time passes quickly, but at least they have time to talk between waves. They paddle with their hands and stay close to each other. Alex starts telling her about his childhood, and Susan talks of her love for Europe and its ancient civilizations. Alex asks her about Rano, but Susan reassures him – without intending to – by saying that most of the time he is deeply into his mystical practices related to Buddha, and is not as interested as her in the project they are working on. Well, he is interested, but he is already thinking of examining other monuments closer to his roots in Asia. She mentions that Rano has told her about the Stupas (E-5). These monuments, found all over Asia, contain relics of Buddha. Initially, they were stones sculpted in the form of a sphere, the sphere symbolizing the universe. Inside, there is a round pillar symbolizing the axis of the universe. Later on, the Stupas adopted different forms, from the most elaborate to the simplest. They were monuments that called people to prayer and to worship Buddha. Buddhism was born 2,500 years ago, but Rano thinks that the monuments are older than that, and that they had a function that is still unknown to this day. He would like to go out there to study the oldest Stupas and carry out his own research. Susan continues by saying that she prefers to finish her thesis based on her discoveries first. Alex, his throat a little tight, asks her what she is planning on doing afterwards, but to his relief she says that she does not know yet. He looks out to sea and tries to imagine what life would be like with this beautiful and intelligent woman with beautifully bronzed skin. He has never been very good at chatting women up, but the circumstances are on his side here. Inviting her to learn to surf was a great idea, he thinks to himself. He has not taken the step of inviting her back to his place yet and continues to pick her up and drop her off at her apartment. This is the third weekend she has come down to the beach with him. In his usual style, he has not plucked up courage to raise the subject head on and starts beating about the bush. He usually hopes that the woman will take the first step, so he generally ends up empty-handed, with the woman no doubt thinking he is gay. For heaven's sake, wake up, he tells himself as they paddle back to the beach, with the sun starting to set on the horizon. Just go for it, man! He swears he will try something before dropping her off at her apartment, and as it turns out luck is on his side this evening. Susan has difficulty getting out of her wetsuit and calls Alex to help her unzip it. Alex sees her standing next to his big Chrysler Magnum. The tailgate is wide open, which protects them a little from prying eyes. He realizes that she is talking of the zipper under her chin. He pulls it down as far as it will go, suddenly revealing the curve of her breasts. Susan does not do anything to zip up her wetsuit, and seeks out Alex's eyes, although he is distracted by the two areolas he can see on the edges of her neckline. Susan impatiently waits for him to lift his gaze to meet hers. Confused and hesitant, Alex's eyes finally meet Susan's and a smile breaks out on his lips. Susan's body language lets him know she's ready for a bit of fun. The beach is now deserted, as very few serious surfers come to the beaches south of San Diego, and Alex had found a place that was quite difficult to get to, one that few surfers seemed to know. He's glad he did that now. This moment is his, and he seems to be holding all the cards. He places his hands on Susan's thighs without taking his gaze off hers, and delicately kisses her on the lips. Susan shuts her eyes and lets herself go, quite happy to trust her feelings to this man she has only known for a few weeks, but who – so far – ticks all the right boxes for her. The couple finishing changing, and Susan returns to the platform of the station wagon to finish off. Alex's shyness stops him from invading her privacy, but he knows he is on to a good thing.

On the way back they hold hands spontaneously despite the movements demanded by the manual transmission of the Chrysler. Neither of them speak, preferring to let the rosy mist they have just discovered on a Californian beach descend on them slowly.

Alex only breaks the silence as they approach Susan's apartment by asking her if he can come and pick her up later that evening and take her to dinner at the Gaslamp Strip Club, a chic restaurant in the heart of the gaslight district where stunning girls dressed in black help you to choose the meat that you then grill yourself on one of the braziers.

The atmosphere is great, just like the meat, and he already sees himself next to Susan in front of the fire, explaining that meat has to be enjoyed with one's soul and not with a stopwatch. Susan happily accepts, and after dropping her off at her apartment Alex goes home to tidy the place up a bit, hoping that after the meal he will bring her back for a drink, and then see what happens. He feels really happy to be where he is right now.

Chapter 15

April 15ᵗʰ 2010, Rano's apartment, San Diego

It is raining, and Rano has just come home from work. Things are going well for him and Susan, very well even. SAIC has really opened its doors to them, and it is also clear that their university has a higher opinion of them now. The President called them personally to check everything was going OK. Rano is aware that freemasonry is involved because of the easy arrangements that have been made for them, plus Susan's meeting in Washington, their detachment to SAIC, their paid apartments, and access to SAIC resources, which are much more extensive than they ever imagined. Initially, they wondered how this technology company could help them to make progress in their research. They soon realized that the question should be asked the other way round: how their research could make an important contribution to SAIC.

The learned at an early stage that the company was a member of the university library network, so they had as easy access to documents that were difficult to find in the Internet, as they had at UCLA. Above all, however, they were surprised to discover that SAIC had an incredibly rich library of books that were difficult to find, on any subject. These works were precisely the ones they needed to consult to take their research forward. They were about ancient civilizations, spiritual practices, and paranormal studies. They did not find medical books, but they could easily be accessed through the university network. True, the originals were kept in the headquarters at McLean, but they had all been scanned and could be consulted on the company's internal broadband network.

Rano, always interested in ancient technological discoveries, had already researched everything he could find about the Antikythera mechanism that Alex had told them about.

He then did some research on other giant mechanisms of which traces had been found in the palaces of certain emperors. More than 2,000 years ago these emperors held public sessions, applied laws and solved the cases presented to them, but they then passed to another room to make the really important decisions. These rooms, almost always kept secret, were symbolically located in the architecture of the palace. On the outside was a cirque, a long arena where horse races took place. Rano discovered that these races contained a whole range of astrological symbols (E-6). There were twelve horse box doors, one for each constellation of the zodiac. Chariots were set off from these boxes around two obelisks, which symbolized sunrise and sunset. Each chariot represented a star or planet moving through the sky, the importance of the star or planet being indicated by the number of horses pulling it. The color of the chariots was linked to a season of the year, but all the symbols had been lost in the mists of time. The color of the chariots was the only thing that was retained, but it was associated with different levels of society and, by extension, political parties. One still-unexplained element is the asymmetry of the structure, created by an off-center podium where the emperor sat during the races. Another example of this mysterious asymmetry is the City Hall in Brussels, the capital of Belgium, and some claim that it hides a secret related to alchemy.

Returning to the symbolism of the emperor's palace, if you look at plans of the building at the time you can see that the secret room was positioned at a strange angle, always the same in relation to the cirque. Nobody knows why either. The room contained a gigantic mechanism of the sky, driven by the water clock system and fed by a continuous water supply. Only the initiated had the right to enter this room. Does this mean that the initiation was linked to the mysteries of the era? Nobody knows. Perhaps the décor of this room inspired that of modern freemasons' temples, the roofs of which all have stars against a blue-sky background. It is clear that this mechanism showed the position of celestial bodies and constellations at any given time, and allowed the people in the room to prepare to make important decisions on the future of the empire.

Hadrian's Villa (E-7), which is not an emperor's palace, has the same layout. Later on, and before he became emperor, Pompey asked his friend Varro Reatinus to build a replica, but disguising it in the form of a zoological garden (E-8). At the time, it was formally prohibited to practice astrology without the permission of the emperor, but as Pompey had ambitions in that direction he made sure he did not do any astrology at home and had all the paraphernalia typical of the time built in a friend's house. It is surprising to observe that the cirque of the horse races was replaced by a pond, as if it was not so much the symbol of the chariots that should be represented as that of a space, a dimension and an orientation.

Incredibly, SAIC has access to the Vatican archives, and subject to consulting electronic documents in a room proofed against the use of any camera or USB stick, Rano is given as much access as he wants. He finds plans of these palaces and villas there, things that had never been taught in archeology studies. He observes a surprising code on each of these electronically numbered documents. Most of the documents that are of use to Rano and Susan have this code on them, and the employee responsible for the consultation computer tells him it has to do with the Jesuits. The most recent documents he has found are related to mechanical systems, 'armillary' being the exact term, installed by Chinese emperors up to the 18th century, but also closer to us in Paris by Queen Catherine de Medici, more or less at the same time. She ordered the construction of a ninety-foot tower next to her palace so that she could enter it from the street, and also directly from her quarters. There was also an animated mechanism at the top of the tower to follow the stars across the sky and to help her take the best decisions for the government of her country. This tower is still visible today in Paris at La Halle aux Blés (the Stock Exchange), although the mechanism disappeared a long time ago (E-9).

Rano was surprised that the Jesuits had built and maintained these systems over the centuries. The Age of Enlightenment cast a veil over this science and nobody would return to it later. In his research into the Jesuits, Rano discovers that the main subject at the University of Louvain in Belgium in the 16th century was astrology, and the students were taught that astrology would help them to choose their leaders better, and the ruling classes to govern better. To be good at astrology they needed to study astronomy, mathematics, physics, optics and a few other subjects linked to the greater mastery of the science of predicting the future from the stars.

Rano is amazed to learn that only one university of that era, and Catholic to boot, had used this language. Nowadays it was enough just to mention the word 'astrology' to be cast out into the wilderness.

Rano tries to understand the information on the subject of births and the descendants of the emperors and kings, but the Vatican archives can only be consulted on the basis of specific questions. You can look through them at ease without stating a specific purpose, but in this case he lacks references. He nevertheless receives two extracts, in which a queen asks her astrologer to tell her the best time to plan her lineage. Not a great result in an attempt to use to illustrate their theory with quotations!

Rano is deep in thought when his smartphone starts vibrating. It is a special model that contains two SIM cards. Here in the United States, SIM cards are still not very common. The technology is often sold by an operator and you cannot change it later. Rano has kept very quiet about this feature of his telephone. He looks at the screen and sees that the call has come through the second card. He takes a look through the blinds to check that nobody is coming to see him, turns the music down and accepts the call. He speaks in Chinese, answering in short bursts, and appears stressed and upset by what he hears.

After a short conversation he hangs up, throws the phone on his sofa bed and goes to the fridge to get a beer. He sits down and tries to relax.

Two years have gone since he met Chang Soung in the hall of the American embassy in Beijing. Despite his good academic results and his parents' good social standing, he was having difficulty getting a visa to travel to the United States to continue his studies. For most Chinese, the United States is the ultimate dream, the consecration, and those who manage to get there work so hard that they always find a well-paid job in line with their qualifications. Chang approached him at the bottom of the staircase in that great hall that was built to impress the Chinese. He made his request three times, and was rejected each time. Chang had asked him to have a drink with him, saying that he was also having trouble getting a visa. Rano had accepted, glad to be able to express his frustration to someone. These refusals were a real frustration for him and his family and the delay was starting to jeopardize his year abroad. He either had to give up and look for work in China or take a chance and continue to persevere at the embassy.

Chang tried to relax the atmosphere, and got Rano to drink more than he normally would. He asked him strange questions about his family, leisure pursuits and friends and ended up telling him more about these things than Rano knew himself. More and more surprised, and despite the effect of the alcohol, Rano lifted his head, which he had rested on the Formica of the old table of the bar where they had met. He looked at Chang in bewilderment, not knowing where he got his information. Chang told him that he worked for the government and he was charged with surveillance of the best Chinese people. Rano had been identified as very promising, and Chang had decided to help him. He told him he could get him his visa provided he agrees to provide certain services in exchange. Rano started to see the mist clearing from in front of him, realizing that Chang had never made a visa application for him and that he was trapped in one of those obscure systems where the government negotiates visas in exchange for information. Rano should have known better. It was not right that his applications should fail one after the other, nor was it normal that he could not get a visa first time round given the excellent references he had. Rano had heard these stories, but thought that they were just rumors. In any case, he was not stupid and knew full well the kind of regime he lived under. Now that these rumors had materialized in him … It was considered shameful to rebel against the regime, although after the four beers he had just drunk − for someone not used to drinking alcohol − he really could not care less.

He adopted a passive attitude and listened to Chang telling him what the government wanted in exchange for getting him his visa.

All in all, it was quite delicate, and also almost normal. During his stay in the United States he should pass on any information on recent military or space activities involving state-of-the-art technology.

He had been a real mug!

He had signed the document that Chang put in front of him, relieved to learn what was asked of him, because his specialty was archeology. In his work he would be very far removed from knowing about these subjects, of which the Chinese are very fond when it comes to espionage.

One trillion Mao Tse Tungs, is that what they would give him! He wanted to disappear under the cushions of his sofa bed, disappear forever, and never have been born. Initially, he had looked the other way and thought that nothing had changed for him, and continued to write cryptic reports after the calls received on his second SIM card. However, after he had moved to San Diego his compatriots quickly detected that he had changed city because they could locate his SIM card, and he had difficulty in giving convincing explanations. They had also found out from his college that he was on detachment at SAIC.

Rano dared not imagine the fuss that must have been made on the other side of the world in the basements of the Chinese secret services. SAIC, what a boon for them!

Cursing himself, the Chinese now blackmailed him about his grant, and even about his father's job, which he ran the risk of losing if Rano did not send back information of interest.

Rano got up and banged his head against the fridge, furious with himself for having signed the piece of paper that day.

On around ten occasions he had almost confessed everything to Susan, but decided not to for fear of being sent back to his country under armed escort.

This time, the phone call came with an ultimatum. If he did not send any information within a month his father would lose his job.

If they only knew what he knew! The spectrograph, the theory about the microtubules, the X-37C Shuttle, its launch dates, or the full-scale test at the Great Pyramid …

He knew all that, even if he did not know the details, which were reserved for people with ECE clearance, but he had found out about the launch dates and the deadlines for all the teams, and Rano was no fool; he knew that the Space Shuttle program had been abandoned and that the Americans had launched a military shuttle whose missions would all be top secret. A child could have reached the same conclusion, but the public knew absolutely nothing about this project, code name 'Icarus'. Rano knew that his nation had an inferiority complex, in line with the arrogance of its government, which believed that anyone outside China was one of their slaves and their only objective was to make the world submit to their will. However, the Chinese knew they were behind in terms of inventiveness. They are good copiers, but are not so good at inventing things. Their space program is thirty years behind schedule. If they could imagine just for a moment what he and Susan were working on, i.e., making Man more of a visionary, his family would immediately find themselves in the depths of the government's jails, in the heart of the Empire, and that they would use all their cruelty to force Rano to give them a lot of information about the Icarus project.

What can I do? he wonders.

Disheartened and full of remorse, Rano goes to bed early, putting off the cruel decision for tomorrow.

Chapter 16

June 27th 2010, Huntsville Space Center, Alabama

Susan wakes up early at 6 a.m. Although many Americans get up around 4 a.m. to get to work by five to avoid the endless traffic jams, she is now in the small town of Huntsville in Alabama. Alex is still asleep. They have been going out together since the day on the surf beach and Susan has now moved in with Alex, although she has not told SAIC, which continues to pay her rent. She feels it is wise to cover her tracks in case they break up one day, and anyway they want to keep their relationship under wraps at work. Rano and her other colleagues are in the picture, of course, but everyone keeps quiet and it is no big deal.

This is the second time they have come to Huntsville, the site of NASA's oldest base and the place where the new X-37C military shuttle is being developed. Alex is responsible for getting everything ready to put the spectrograph on board. His previous job stands him in good stead and his colleagues on the ground are impressed by his attention to the small details of its stowage.

Susan's presence is not a problem. Her working days do not have anything to do with SAIC, and as a researcher she does not have to account for how she is using her time to anyone right now. She left Rano behind in San Diego and flew with Alex to the small town in the heart of Alabama, where legends about the Ku Klux Klan still abound and there are more tornados than tourists. In reality, they were in the back of beyond, but that is understandable; NASA wanted a deserted and discreet place to carry out its first rocket launches.

Susan has already visited the Space Museum, with the surprising inclusion of a submarine, and also, behind a dark room, the spacesuit used in the film *2001: Space Odyssey* by Stanley Kubrick, the filmmaker who some people say shot the Apollo missions. Following the publication of the high-resolution photos of the Moon, showing each LEM on its surface, several urban legends went into the garbage, much to the chagrin of the conspiracy theorists, who were thirsty for mystery.

She also visited the Von Braun Center, a kind of big covered stadium used for conferences or exhibitions. There was a mushroom growers' convention going on at the time; it is incredible how people can spend their time doing things that can sometimes seem futile to others. The place was full of stands presenting mushrooms, and it all reminded her of another exhibition she had seen one day in Paris, entirely dedicated to the Barbie doll. She would never have thought that that toy from her childhood was so well-known in Europe, and even less that grown-ups could make Barbie their favorite pastime.

Today she was going to sign up for a visit to the NASA facilities. A small train would leave at around 9 a.m. and she did not want to miss it. She was hoping to catch a glance of the new shuttle. Alex did not want to talk about it, and Susan did not press him on the subject; like the rest of his work, it was classified information. They quickly found a way of not talking about a particular subject whenever they got close to a classified part of the project. Rather than give Susan evasive answers or suddenly change the subject, Alex had decided to tell Susan that she would be the first to find out when the project was declassified. He hoped this project would soon enter the public domain, because its implications affected too many humanitarian uses, and if it fell into the wrong hands it could lead to some rather undesirable consequences. His view was that in 2010 the US government had lived through enough horrors to not feed any more fires that could threaten the country. Moreover, SAIC, like many companies in the military-industrial area, ran the risk of being detached from the government in the future. In the UK the old DERA had already gone, and that body, a through-and-through military research organization, had to come to terms with its privatization and now earned a living in areas that had nothing to do with secret projects and huge budgets.

The French had invented another system to safeguard their industrial jewels Thalès and EADS. They set up a fictitious private company that competed with these two for every tender, thus keeping a handle on the budgetary slippages of the two giants, which are surely still attached to the freemasons. In short, Susan and Alex are enjoying a perfect love, working happily at the same place, or, more precisely, in the same building without being in the same office.

Susan is drying her hair in the bathroom of their small motel on the town's main avenue – the only one worthy of the name – when Alex appears at the door. He seems upset and self-conscious.

"Susan, I've wanted to talk to you about something for a few days now, but I don't know how to start."

"What do you mean? What's wrong?"

Susan finishes drying her hair while Alex paces nervously at the door, although not without admiring Susan's figure in the process.

"Right, I'm finished. Now, what were you saying?"

"I said I had something to tell you."

"OK, come on … what are you waiting for?"

Suddenly, thinking it might have something to do with their relationship, Susan swallows and goes on:

"Is it about me? Something that's my fault? Have I done anything wrong?"

"No, no, it has nothing to do with you. Well, at least I hope not."

"What then? This is really not the best time. It's ten after eight and I want to be at the entrance to the center at nine."

"It's about Rano."

"Rano? What has he done? Are you jealous, is that it?"

"No, no, not at all … believe me, that's got nothing to do with it …"

"What is it then? His work isn't good enough? You know full well that he doesn't cost you anything, and I think he does good work for our thesis. He's a real library rat, and his passion for armillary mechanisms is amazing. Soon we'll have restored not just a monument but knowledge that our society is completely unaware of. We're incredibly lucky to have this opportunity and I wouldn't have been able to do it on my own; all that compilation, research and the rest. I'm not letting you take him off me to benefit from his work! Quite honestly, I don't think Rano is surplus to requirements."

"No, you're on the wrong track, Susan. I didn't want to talk about his usefulness to your project, nor to ours, but it still has to do with his work with us."

Susan keeps quiet while she puts her shoes on and ties the laces, sitting on the edge of the bed.

"In fact, I didn't dare raise the subject with you, but my boss has told me to. In his building there's a guy in charge of security. I immediately thought of you and feared that they were going to stop me seeing you outside work, but that's not the problem at all. It's about Rano … at the moment they have nothing against him, but they wanted to tell me about something that happened two weeks ago."

"What, they saw Rano eating his offerings to his Buddha?" says Susan, making a feeble attempt at a joke.

"No, but you're not far off. You know that he always waits so that nobody can see him removing the offerings. The fact that he put his altar in his office is quite normal, that's not a problem, and considering the size of his Buddha nobody can really say anything to him. But … they've told me that the sensors located all over the buildings record every coming and going to within around four inches, thanks to the passes that we have to carry. You know if they catch us without our pass we immediately get a lecture from the head of security, and if happens again there's an inquiry."

"Yes, I know, I remember the time I forgot my pass when I went to the restroom and was caught. I'll never forget the face of the security guard who passed me in the corridor. . Six-and-a-half feet of muscle shouting at me, but with no button to stop him. They took me to the control center and I could only leave when the director came by to reassure them. Jesus, it was really frightening, and since then I always make sure I have my pass on me when I leave the office."

"Exactly, our passes are tracked by very sophisticated sensors. More and more companies deal in sensitive issues … information, drugs, precious metals and who knows what else. SAIC has taken the technology even farther. In addition to surveillance of incursions into prohibited zones, it has installed algorithms to detect any sudden changes in our movements. I already told you that they even analyze our urine after we go to the restroom. Since they know who is where, they can immediately associate a detected drug with the last person who went to the restroom."

"And tomorrow they'll tell me I'm pregnant, is that it? I understand, so Rano is pregnant." Susan's ironic response and her nerves are starting to show.

"Look, Susan, don't joke about this, it's serious. Their algorithm has detected a change in Rano's behavior for a few weeks now. Quite simply, they do not know what he's up to. They told me that he moves around the office much more than before, and that he's constantly going to the corner where his altar is. He often waits until you've left the office."

"Yes, I'd noticed he was staying longer and that he seemed more absent-minded, but it didn't seem to have any effect on his work. What else did they tell you?"

"They'd just like you to speak to Rano, try and find out what's going on. You shouldn't find it too difficult."

"You're spooking me, you know? Every time I enter their building and I see those two hulks with their dark glasses I get shivers up my spine, and anything else they might find out really freaks me out. Have you ever seen them smile?"

"No, now that you mention it. Seriously, could you do that for me?"

"Sure, don't worry. I'll do it as soon as possible. .... Oh, shoot, it's a quarter to eight, and I've only got fifteen minutes to get to the space center!"

"Don't worry; you know it's just a stone's throw away. I'll throw some clothes on and drive you over there. I'll have breakfast afterward."

"Thanks, honey!"

Chapter 17

June 28th 2010, SAIC, San Diego

Susan knocks on the door of Alex's office and waits to hear his voice before entering. Even though they know each other well, Alex works on top secret dossiers and has to observe extremely strict rules. His office has even received its own 'pass', its locks and walls have been inspected by the security personnel and he has been allocated a safe to put any sensitive files in every time he leaves the office. Naturally, nobody is allowed to enter his office when these dossiers are out of the safe. It is all very procedure-based and might appear excessive at first sight, but one can never be too careful.

Susan is quite happy to respect that rule and patiently waits for Alex to organize his papers. He calls her in, and she tells him she has spoken to Rano, who has told her that his father has fallen very ill and he is feeling on edge, and he also prays a lot more as a result.

Alex considers this a suitable explanation and asks if Rano would like to return home. Susan had suggested that, but Rano said that getting a visa is too complicated and he does not want to run any risks. He speaks to his mother every day on Skype, and she can get by on her own for the time being.

Alex tells Susan that he will have to tell his boss, but he thinks that this explanation should bring the matter to a close.

He gets up from his chair and walks over to the window. He has picked up two metal balls, which he restlessly turns in his hand. He looks at the military buildings on the other side of San Diego bay. He knows he cannot see inside because, like all SAIC buildings, their windows reflect everything. What is more, his window is bullet-proof and, naturally, impossible to open. The air conditioning has to do the job of renewing the air supply.

"I have another delicate thing I need to talk to you about."

"Ah, I'm pregnant, is that it? Have SAIC's sensors tested positive with my pee?" smirks Susan, wondering what the security people have found now.

"No, you dope, it's something that concerns you this time, but related to work."

"Work? They want to stop us working together?" is Susan's immediate reaction. That means that she would have to return to San Francisco, and not see Alex again.

"No, but it's something that could affect your relationship with your college. You know that the next phase of the project involves sending the machine we're working on to the ISS, and then loading it on the X-37C again to take it farther out into space, to the other side of the Van Allen belt (S-3)."

"Yes, I know that, except that I've had to guess half of it … you know that sometimes you only have to fill in the gaps to find the missing pieces. I read the newspapers like everyone else, and know that the old shuttles are out to pasture in the museum, but I also know that there's a replacement craft, theoretically reserved for military missions. I've seen three different models on the Internet, and the biggest ones can carry six people."

"Yes, that's it, more or less. I've been told that I should travel to the ISS, and my training needs to start early next month. The question now is … are you coming with me?"

Susan opens her mouth, but no sound comes out.

Alex waits a few moments before continuing.

"Yes, I know, it's my fault, I should have talked to you about it earlier, but I didn't want to take you on a mission that could put your life in danger and ..."

"Hey, are you crazy! Go into space! I wouldn't miss the chance for anything in the world!"

"Susan, listen ... you have no obligation to go any farther in this project. I spoke to my bosses and they think you should accompany us. Your vision and the contribution you've made to the project have been decisive, and it's highly likely that you can help even more by being with us. Every minute up there means millions of dollars and nobody really knows where we're going or how to get there. We'll probably have to make a lot of changes as we go along. Having you there alongside the machine could make a difference to the success of the operation, if it *is* successful. SAIC has been very bold by directly linking the Ark of the Covenant with the Great Pyramid, but I've had several telephone conversations with Jacques Vallée and he's up for the challenge. This mission is going to cost a hell of a lot of money, and they want to combine a number of key elements of this forgotten science that we want to revive. But, it's definitely not a pleasure trip, and you know the risks involved in space flight as well as I do."

"Alex, I would much rather be with you. If that damn shuttle decides to explode in full flight, I want to take that great journey with you instead of crying my eyes out down here in the sunshine. Just imagine, we're at a historic moment in the evolution of the human race, and we're probably going to make a loop with ancient knowledge from many thousands of years ago, and rediscover knowledge from all kinds of unusual sources."

"OK, but there's another problem. If you come with us you'll have to be vetted, obtain clearance, and follow the same training program as me. You'll also have to stop being a researcher and you'll be employed by SAIC, which will put the brake on your thesis. Think hard about what all this means."

"Alex, if I am going to spend my life with you, the rest is not so important. Rano and I have worked really well and I don't think my college is unhappy with our discoveries. Can you see me pouring over old stones in Cistercian abbeys in the future? What discovery could I make that would be more important than the one we've made, although, sure, it still has to be confirmed. Just realize, being able to carry out this research at your side, travelling into space, all this is almost unreal for me. How could you think that I might have said no?"

"I don't know, I've no idea what's going on in your head, or about your career aspirations. We've never talked about it, and you know I'm pretty clumsy at expressing my feelings. I'm frightened of losing you and I always look at the options from the negative side."

"Oh, Alex, I love you. I have no ulterior motives. You're thirty-one and I will soon be thirty-three … don't you think it's time for each of us to get hitched up, as they say?"

Alex moves away from the window and approaches Susan. He takes her in his arms and gives her a big hug. What she just said went straight to his heart. He has always found it hard to talk of plans for a lifetime, fearing that he would be rejected. Susan's proposition reassures him; he has finally found someone worth creating a future with.

"Thanks for saying that. You know how much I appreciate it. I'm going to tell my boss that you're on board. Rano won't be needed up there, but he can stay in the project as long as he likes. If necessary, he can support you from the ground."

Alex leans over the face he loves so much, and hugs her tenderly.

Chapter 18

August 28th 2010, Marshall Space Center, Huntsville

Susan has the jitters. They are putting her spacesuit on her. In two hours from now she will be up in Space. The precautions are almost a waste of time, because they will make the entire trip in a pressurized capsule and she won't be doing any space walking, but they have to be ready for the worst, such as a pressure drop. For example, a meteorite could penetrate the outer shell, the pressure would fall to zero in a few seconds and the temperature also fall below zero. No living being could survive those conditions for more than five seconds without irreversible consequences. Susan got her clearance – the supreme 'Cosmic Top Secret ECE' – at the same level as Alex without any difficulty. She was surprised how easily they gave it to her but Alex explained that possession of the document did not mean that she would have access to all the government's well-hidden secrets, visit the top-secret places at Base 51 or talk to little green men and experience all those other urban legends. He tells her that having clearance does not allow just anything. You are only authorized to gain access to the confidential information that is strictly linked to the project you are working on, according to the 'need to know' principle. If your work does not require certain classified information you will not be authorized to see it, even if it is classified at the level of your clearance. Working with classified information is no picnic. Even if it stays in your office, it must be put away in a safe every time you go out, there has to be a special lock for the door, and it is even worse when the information needs to travel. It must be put in a double envelope, and the courier who carries it must co-sign the documents, which must then be sent back by the recipient once the documents have been received and the second envelope opened. The mystery soon becomes a chore, and many people soon realize that it is better if you do not have to work with confidential data. In any case, quite often these secrets get out anyway, either through people saying too much at the coffee machine or when they are transferring data.

Some of the best-kept information is in the form of drawings, or, more precisely, anything that cannot be spoken out loud. Worse still, if you transmit these documents to people who do not have the required clearance, the punishment can be very severe. Alex has heard that people with top secret clearance 'benefit' from a kind of discreet surveillance, and that incoming and outgoing mail is systematically checked, going as far as reading the content of USB sticks, DVDs or hard discs. However, there are still plenty of gaps that are easily identifiable in their surveillance protocol. Everything exchanged from hand to hand is very difficult to check. Real spies use a 'letter box' system, placing documents in original places and telling their contact to come and pick them up after receiving a discreet signal. Everyone has seen this in spy films.

Susan is awakened from her thoughts when she is asked to hold her breath. They are in the process of pressurizing her spacesuit. God, she would rather be lost in her thoughts; that way she could forget her jitters. Well, in a few minutes she will join Alex and the others to board the minibus that will take them to the launch pad. No civil rockets have been launched from Huntsville for years, but as their mission is more military than civil, they will fire off into Space out of the sight of inquisitive eyes. Susan has already been inside the new shuttle several times, and it is very different from the old ones. Here, the craft is designed for the transport of goods or satellites and is remote-controlled, i.e., without any crew, or a minimum crew like a normal airplane. It can still carry some freight with a small crew on board; the layout can be changed to carry half a dozen people, seated like in a private jet, one either side of the aisle. In this case, the luggage hold is reduced to a minimum. The layout is similar to the bigger version of the shuttle, but Susan has no idea about layouts or if there are different sizes of shuttle. During her 'tourist' visit to the space center they were shown the old installations, shuttle simulators and the impressive swimming pool that allowed the astronauts to train for work in Space in a state of total weightlessness. She also saw the old Saturn V rockets that took the Apollo missions to the Moon. Those rockets were gigantic, with enormous engines, and she found it difficult to believe the tiny proportions of the capsule sitting on top of that immense structure.

Nowadays the launch vehicles are smaller, first of all because they use boosters located on each side, not stages stacked one on top of each other, and also because the loads are much lighter. Manned missions no longer escape the pull of Earth's gravity, and the Space missions that people now watch as a matter of routine never fly very high. One hundred and twenty-five miles is the altitude for orbiting satellites, and 22,500 miles for geostationary satellites. The ISS orbits at an average height of 220 miles above Earth, and it is estimated that a rocket can only escape from the gravitational pull of Earth when it is over 558,000 miles out into space.

They have finished harnessing her up. What a drag, two hours for an astronaut to get dressed! She reaches the corridor and walks towards the exit. Here, all the buildings are identical, wide, in dark gray prefabricated concrete with large painted numbers identifying each one. Thank goodness there is greenery all around to brighten up this rather oppressive military atmosphere. She finds this atmosphere difficult to forget; half the entrances to the buildings are guarded by military personnel.

Their bus is waiting, and she looks for Alex among the five astronauts who are already waiting outside. Everyone carries their helmet, but they have a kind of fireproof hood that prevents you from seeing their hair. Susan worries how she is going to look like up there when she takes off that horrible hood. They are in luck; the weather is excellent. She finally reaches Alex and touches his arm. He turns round and stands next to her. He is well aware that she is nervous; he is too, but Susan is also the only woman in the expedition. Luckily for her, there is another woman already on the ISS; they will be able to have a good session of 'girly talk' if they want. Alex would like to take Susan's hand in his, but that is a waste of time with their spacesuits; she would not feel anything and they would both look ridiculous. To ease the tension, Alex tells Susan that astronauts usually pee on the way to the launching pad. The bus stops half-way and all the astronauts get out and pee on the rear wheel. When Susan asks him how she is going to do it he just says that this 'tradition' is specific to launches made from Cape Kennedy.

They are called back to the bus and it continues on its way. The launch pad is not far away and they arrive in no time at all.

Susan lifts her head and looks at the Atlas 5 rocket that will take them into space. This rocket still uses the technology of the V2, designed seventy years earlier by Werner von Braun, as do all other rockets, in fact. It was originally used as a ballistic missile. Their X-37C spacecraft (T-5) is lighter and smaller than the previous space shuttles. They now walk towards the elevator that will take them up to the access door, where they will then enter what looks like the inside of a private jet, but one that points skywards. It makes her think of those weird boats that are used to evacuate oil rigs in cases of emergency; they are amphibious and almost vertical. Going inside, it is so dark you have the impression that you are entering a kind of movie theater, but one in which the floor is inclined ten times more than usual.

Here the cabin is completely vertical and they need to climb a ladder embedded in the floor of the Shuttle.

Susan's seat is the fourth of six. Alex will be just in front of her. The front two are for the pilot and copilot, and she finds it strange that they are still called that. Behind them, two engineers from the technical team of the Icarus project. Once everyone has settled in and the last checks have been made, the auxiliary personnel leave the craft and the heavy cabin door closes behind them. The silence is impressive, although punctuated by radio conversations between the pilot and the control center. Susan curses the distance that separates her from Alex. There is no way she can hold his hand, or give him a kiss before takeoff. Damn it! Despite her sudden hate of the shuttle's designer, she has to stick by the protocol, check her belts and connections and activate a number of buttons to her left, beneath a window that this crewed version has. To her right is the aisle, then the other wall. The first countdown can be heard. There will be another soon after, the difference being that if the launch is cancelled after the first countdown the cost of resetting the shuttle goes through the roof. So, there is no alternative to being patient. At least her big gloves have the advantage that they stop her gnawing her fingernails. The second countdown starts, much shorter this time, and the whole craft starts to vibrate violently Her seat starts to shake as if it had been bought in an Army surplus store. She knows that she is going to have to resist up to 3G, which is really not that much, and these G are neither positive or negative but from the front, as if you were driving a dragster. Positive G are the worst because they drain the blood from your head and the brain stops receiving oxygen. Negative G forces are better, because they make the blood flow to your head. During the Shuttle's takeoff the blood is pushed to the back of the head, and that is easier to bear. Even so, Susan feels her head three times heavier than usual, and realizes she cannot move it from her headrest. From where she is sitting she cannot see her colleagues because they are all aligned in front of each other. The view is extraordinary, however; she can see the curve of Earth as the shuttle climbs out of the atmosphere. The feeling is fairy-like. She sees the dark night above and the blue sky below. The play of light where the two colors join is incredibly beautiful, like gold dust. In the distance she makes out a thunderstorm and sees lightning rise above the clouds towards space. These streaks of lightning are called 'Blue Jets' and can reach the stratosphere. NASA fears that one of these Blue Jets will hit one of its craft one day, and it invests a lot of money on research into this little-known phenomenon. They have been observed to reach a height of fifty miles. Even bigger lightning strikes can occur higher up, called 'Elves', and they resemble the 'hats' of jellyfish. They are red and spread from the mesosphere to the thermosphere, a zone at an altitude of between fifty and sixty-two miles. They can reach a diameter of 250 miles, but only last a fraction of a second. Between these two types of lightning there are also other kinds of explosions, also red, which look like the arms of a jellyfish.

The moment comes when they can finally open their helmets, by lifting the visor. Not a moment too soon! She is starting to turn into a red fish! As soon as she lifts the visor she moves closer to the window to admire the view, and immediately thinks how beautiful the world is. She knows that this is the standard reaction, that nobody who has been able to admire the curve of Earth from Space ever gets over the impression it makes on them.

Her fascination is cut short by Alex, who, like her, is admiring the view and has also stuck his nose against the window. Turning his head, he sees Susan, but has to twist his neck in his helmet, like a hermit crab that wants to get out of its shell. Now that they have almost reached the altitude of the ISS he knows they will have to wait for quite a while before it reaches the exact position of the ISS and locks into it. They will orbit Earth several times in the meantime, each orbit taking around ninety minutes. It is August and the weather is generally good in the northern hemisphere, which means great views of the continents. The windows are quite big; you get the feeling you are in a jetliner. Alex told her that if the shuttle has to cross the Van Allen belt, lead shutters would hide the windows to protect the astronauts from the bombardment of neutrinos and other harmful cosmic particles. They would be exposed to around a billion neutrinos per second per square millimeter. These neutrinos go right though us, and only exceptionally come into contact with electrons, neutrons or protons in our body. So, we do not really know the consequences of such a collision. Some astronauts have reported flashes of light in their eyes, and it is believed that this is due to collisions of neutrinos.

As a precaution, and because the number of particles is much greater outside the magnetic belts that protect Earth, future space missions will be planned to protect astronauts from this potential hazard.

Susan is completely overawed by the beauty of the continents that slide beneath her. The stars too; there are so many more of them than she thought. She had already observed the sky under good weather conditions in the desert, and is reminded of the nights spent in Sardinia with Rano. However, nothing had prepared her for the sight of so many stars up here outside the atmosphere.

Alex tells her that he needs to check the conditions in the cargo hold, where the spectrograph is located.

Their spacecraft is not very big, about three times smaller than the old shuttles. NASA realized that it is not a good idea to transport satellites or supply packages at the same time as astronauts. The X-37 range was therefore designed to launch small satellites, most of them military, carry out espionage missions, or transport astronauts to the ISS or other unknown destinations.

Time drags on for Susan. She has already seen Earth pass before her eyes several times. The craft is silent, because the engines have stopped. From time to time a positioning pipe is activated, making the same noise as a hot air balloon when the burner is ignited. These twenty pipes are positioned all around the Shuttle and allow it to be steered in any direction, or even turn on its own axis. A firing of these pipes for a fraction of a second produces effects that last for a long time, because hardly anything is holding the craft back. Susan is annoyed to find a choice of video games on the console on the back of Alex's seat, just like on a normal airliner. Everything is laid on to de-stress the passengers. When they are not working, there are several relaxing and enjoyable activities for the crew. She even finds a game in which you have to destroy invaders' spaceships! "That takes the cake," she says to herself, despite trying out the game for a few moments.

An announcement tells them that they are approaching the ISS. She cannot see it from her porthole, but through the cockpit she can make out a point in the distance that gradually gets bigger. They need to put their visors back on and make sure the spacesuit is airtight. Once again, the entire docking procedure will be computer-controlled, and the pilot will only take over the controls if there is a problem. The docking procedure has been done before, and the first missions did it without any difficulty, so everyone feels confident.

Susan is amazed at the ease with which their craft clicks into the steel monster which, now they are docked, seems enormous to her. It is much bigger than a Boeing 747 or an Airbus A380!

A dull sound and a whistle indicate that the two craft are locked into each other. They can open their visors again, and soon she will be able to enter the ISS.

Chapter 19

August 28th 2010, on the ISS

Alex and Susan have got to know the insides of the ISS. It only measures 240 square yards, but up there it is best to speak of cubic feet because there is no real floor, wall or ceiling. So, 14,210 cubic feet is available for the activities of the occupants of the ISS. They listen carefully to the safety instructions and carry out some exercises to be followed in the event of an emergency. After more than four hours of procedures and explanations, they are given some free time. Alex's machine is still in the X-37C. It will be operated from there, and in any case it is too big to pass through the hatch.

Susan gets the team together to give some explanations so that everyone can understand the experiment better and optimize the conditions under which it will take place. The occupants of the ISS, who they have met, will also be informed, at least as far they can be. While waiting for the meeting planned for the next day, she would like to have a few moments relaxing with Alex. Up here, the word 'tomorrow' means something else; rather it means less, because effectively you reach 'tomorrow' every ninety minutes when you see the sun rise each time. They need to keep a check on their watches to know when to try and catch some sleep. The custom is to let people who want some peace and quiet go into the Tranquility module. This module, recently attached to the ISS, has one end in the shape of a diamond, each face being a window. It is, therefore, a fantastic place to observe Earth turning below. There are no experiments carried out here, it just has air conditioning and garbage treatment equipment, toilets and sports equipment. Tacitly, the rest of the crew stays away from this module when they know that the people in it are off duty.

"So, you don't regret coming?" Alex asks Susan.

"You must be joking! Just look at the view. It's hard to believe. You have no idea how happy I am right now. Remember that I'm an archeologist, because I love our Earth, our history, the human race, and just imagine what it means to me to be able to see Earth beneath me."

"Yeah, I can imagine. I'm pleased you're happy. Not only that, the flight was great. We just need to get used to the lack of gravity. Maybe we could learn not to crash into each other, I already have bruises all over my body. I almost prefer the big spacesuit I had in the shuttle," jokes Alex while trying to grab Susan by her arms, but at each attempt she drifts away from Alex as if she were a soap bubble carried along by the wind. They finally manage to hold on to each other and find a place inside the module. It is really strange and disorientating, because it is impossible to sit down. They float around all the time, their bodies in continual motion; it is impossible to just lie down and rest. After a few moments of clumsy movements they finally use their legs to settle in a corner and curl up together. They are touching each other's shoulders and, hand in hand, they watch the blue planet in its majestic procession below them.

"Alex, do you realize how lucky we are? Just think of where we are. Living such a moment, such a beautiful view in the company of the person you love is amazing!"

"Yes, it sure is … and we didn't even ask to be here. I only had to push a little for you to come. In fact, my bosses had also suggested it but were afraid that you'd turn it down. You know, it takes me back to when I was young. Once when my family went skiing, my brother and I found a path that started just behind our chalet. A twenty-minute walk took us to the foot of a rocky crag. We used to go there and sit, and watch the whole valley from there. We were also under cover in case it snowed. The isolated tranquility of the place, where other people never came, the fantastic view, and the admiration I had for my brother made it feel like time stood still. We could stay there for hours without saying anything, or at least we had the impression that time stood still. I've hardly ever felt that since then, but here I'm back there again, and so happy to be able to share it with you."

"I didn't know you had a romantic streak in you, but I know that where we are now creates all kinds of extraordinary impressions. Have you noticed how our eyes are almost capable of distinguishing each light source on Earth as we pass over it at night?"

"Yes, I have. It's incredible how extraordinary our eyes are, created by Nature. On Earth we can't see things beyond the horizon due to the curve of the horizon, at around fifteen miles. People say you can see a lit cigarette at five miles. I have often made out cars on the roads from the air, at around six miles high. Here, though, we're 125 miles away and we get the impression we can make out every little light."

"To come back to Earth, speaking about work … are you ready for the start of the operation?"

"Yes, I've met all the crew of the ISS and I already know the other SAIC people who are with us. I think I can get along fine with all of them. True, as a woman I have to make an extra effort when it comes to telling them how to carry out their experiments, especially because I arrived towards the end of the project. I need to brief them tomorrow, and I think you'll be able to launch the experiment in two days' time, because we have to wait for our orbit to take us over Cairo. Rano has permission to represent me there in case he needs to give any extra information or decide on some improvised measure. Do you have any news of the preparations down there?"

"Yes, it's all going well. I checked it out during the flight. The Great Pyramid will be closed to the public the day after tomorrow, which will give them time to install the material in the container inside the

King's Chamber. I doubt if we'll be able to aim our ray of light at the duct that leads to the outside of the chamber, and even less so on the right axis. But, these new microwave military GPS they started using in 2002 can work miracles. They're accurate to less than half an inch. My colleagues are very confident. You'll accompany me, and you'll see Earth much smaller; well, actually you won't see it because the windows will be covered by the radiation shield. We'll have exterior cameras, though. In any case, we're not here to admire the scenery, but to coordinate the experiment."

"OK, shut up and hold me because I feel empty far from my Earth. I want to feel your vibrations."

Alex is quite happy to do that and our two astronauts in the making admire the planet below them, in silence.

Chapter 20

August 30th 2010, Cairo, Egypt

Rano had arrived in Cairo the week before. He is staying at the Manial Palace in the heart of the city. This old botanical garden built on an island in the Nile was wrecked by the Russians at the time of the construction of the Aswan dam. They basically set up camp there to accommodate their engineers. Years later, the *Club Méditerranée* redeveloped the site and restored a bit of harmony, with the holidaymakers believing they were staying in beautiful recently-built bungalows while in reality they were in refurbished construction site shacks. In 1994 the garden was reclassified as a museum, but the government – and the Americans – usually accommodate their VIP guests there. Rano is there with some other members of the team who, like him, do not have Top Secret clearance. It is an incredibly peaceful place. Indeed, as soon as he leaves the front entrance to the Palace the noise of the city assaults his ears in an endless din of engines, klaxons and bells. Once you have got used to that you have to take on the taxi drivers. They hang around in front of the main entrance to the Palace, waiting for the tourists to come out to take them to their own homes or to an archeological site. What they really want to do is take you to some factory that makes papyrus, wooden or leather objects and get their commission in the process. Rano realizes that have to get mentally ready to deal with them, because when you refuse to pay what they ask for they scream at you as if you had killed someone in their family, but you should not back down. They accept what you offer, will insult you and walk away in a temper, but next morning welcome you outside the Palace with a big smile, offering their services to you again as if you were their best friend in the world.

Today, however, Rano will take the bus provided by SAIC.

In a few minutes it will take them to the plateau of Giza, at the foot of the Great Pyramid.

Eight of them are staying at the Palace. Rano knows that there are about fifty other people already be there. What a big team, he thinks, as the minibus winds its way through the noisy traffic of Cairo. He notes, with amusement, the small police kiosks at crossroads, where officers make a note of the license plates of the taxis that transport the tourists. He has learned that this decades-old system makes it easier to detect taxis that rip off their customers, thus ensuring a certain level of security for tourists in Cairo. The traffic in this over-populated city is incredibly dense.

They pass in front of crazy stores, filled to the roof with old bicycle tires, broken clocks, or unidentifiable mechanical parts. They finally leave the city and approach the plateau. A line of children going to school crosses in front of them, all wearing the same blue and white uniform; a little touch of order in this dusty city where most public buildings seem to have been abandoned.

Rano makes out the pyramids and, farther on, what remains of the Sphinx. The pyramids seem bigger than in the photos. The blocks at the bottom are almost as tall as him. In front of the biggest pyramid there is a series of military tents hiding the entrance. They pass by a group of unhappy tourists who want to go inside the Great Pyramid. He imagines that they have been told to come back the next day, and that they can visit another site free of charge. That is not much of a consolation … entry to archaeological sites in the Cairo area is free in almost all cases.

Rano gets off the bus with his colleagues and collects his bag from the back of the vehicle. Then, after looking up to the top of the mass of stone, he goes inside the maze of tents and comes across a horde of technicians and security guards. He can enter about half of the tents, but others are guarded and marked with a "Restricted – Authorized Personnel Only" sign.

Indeed, it is never openly stated that these areas are restricted to people with Cosmic Top Secret ECE clearance, because according to the system that manages secrecy, those who do not have the clearance will never know that the project exists and that it involves such a level of secrecy. People without the clearance simply do not know about it because they are refused access to that particular place. If it is about a document, they will not be surprised because they will never see it and not be aware of its existence.

It all seems quite complicated to Rano, as he realizes that the tents have air conditioning. Now that's luxury!

He takes time to find the person he needs to touch base with, and finally does so. He knows that he will not sleep tonight. The connection with the shuttle is planned for 03:15 hours. They have already started to arrange the material inside the pyramid. Rano knows that the Ark of the Covenant is somewhere in one of these tents, or that it may be taken there at the last minute. He should not really know that piece of information, but Susan told him after Alex told her. The grapevine is very permeable to the notion of secrecy. Probably only ten people really know what is going to happen tonight. The others are quite happy to move boxes, connect up equipment, and check clearances or passes. Rano has to attend a briefing at 7 p.m. and then be on standby until 6 a.m., when a debriefing session will take place. The only thing left for him to do is go back to the hotel and sleep, but sleep is the last thing on his mind at the moment, because he is as tense as a harp string. Everything was OK in the hotel, but as he approached the site on the bus he got more and more tense. He thinks again about his problem in SAIC linked to his change of attitude, the lie about his father's health, and the information he has sent the Chinese embassy over the last few weeks. He feels incredibly guilty and trembles when he recalls how nervous he was when he placed the envelope in the trees behind the hotel. The sun had gone down and he acted as if he was just going for a stroll around the vicinity, taking great care to start his evening strolls in the weeks leading up to this trip. He received a piece of paper under his door one day with a plan of the wood behind the Palace, and a red cross where he would find a trash can. He was told that there would be a flat stone at the base of the trash can, which he should put back in place after putting a letter in it. He saw that a white spot had been painted on the bottom of the stone, allowing the other agent to walk past the trash can without stopping, checking from a distance whether it contained a message or not.

No electronic communication is allowed, no e-mails or phone calls, and phone calls even less.

If anything untoward happens he should go to the nearest Chinese embassy and ask to speak to the person in charge of plumbing; this is the code used to ask to speak to the information service there. With his heart freezing, but with the aim of saving his family, Rano had already placed two notes in the trash can informing on the progress of the project and what he knew about it. Each time his heart pounded wildly, his throat fluttered and his stomach twisted; the first time he even vomited as soon as he got back to his room. He started to panic when he heard no more from the embassy, or when the cans had been emptied by the cleaning staff, and feared that his family would be mistreated.

However, he noted that the stone had been turned each time, awaiting another possible note from him.

Rano knows that from tomorrow he could do the same in Cairo, in the compound of the Manial Palace itself. He tells himself that the Chinese secret service is everywhere. He has been told to leave his envelope in a crevice in the perimeter wall, still using the stone but in reverse. This time, he sees a white spot hidden by the crevice, and when he leaves his message he should turn the stone so that it becomes anonymous but hides his envelope. Swearing at Mao Tse Tung, he just wants this adventure to finish and then go back home. As long as he is with the Americans he will be in the pay of his country's intelligence service, and he will not be able to deal with that stress for long. Once back in China, there will always be time to apply for a visa again through the normal channels. Surely they will leave him alone now.

In any case, they continue to put pressure on him, threatening to harass his family if he does not continue to transmit information on the project.

Rano's thoughts are interrupted by a security guard who comes up to him and asks to see his pass. A routine check, he tells himself. Hell, that's all he needs right now!

Chapter 21

August 30th 2010, on board the ISS

Susan has called a meeting of all the people involved in the experiment. They are in videoconference with SAIC headquarters. Thanks to the company's satellites there is a continuous link between the ISS and SAIC. The official function of these satellites is to relay data collected by commercial airliners. Sensors take the temperature and other characteristics of the mechanical parts, engines and pumps of the aircraft and send them back to McLean, where they are analyzed in real time to detect any possible defects and intervene as soon as possible when the aircraft lands somewhere. These satellites, of course, are used for other missions that are more discreet and sensitive.

They are together in the Russian module Zvezda. There is more space here. Susan has connected the laptop she has been given to the screen set on the rack in front of her. She knows that astronauts cannot, under any circumstances, take their own laptop or their work computer on board; the electronic material taken to the ISS or used on the spacecraft has to fulfill extremely strict security requirements.

Susan starts her presentation with images of ancient conquerors, emperors and kings, each one illustrated by their ability to achieve great things in a very short space of time. Some of them conquered the known world – and sometimes the unknown parts – in less than twenty years.

What was it that drove these outstanding people?

She explains that observation of the sky and stars over thousands of years led the ancients to identify correlations between the position of the stars, the birth of a baby and the future ability of an individual to reign or govern. That was not enough in itself, however; wanting to govern is one thing, but good decisions also needed to be taken. They had noticed that children born when Venus was rising, and when Venus had completed a certain part of its journey across the sky, were good at taking clever decisions and making choices that were often fair too. It was too much of a coincidence to be mere chance. They no doubt began to understand this over 10,000 years ago.

They had noted the cycles of Venus, its brightness, its distance from the sun, and probably learned to procreate on a date that would allow a baby to be born under optimal conditions when Venus rose. They built special megaliths for these occasions, allowing them to know immediately if the baby had been 'well born'. Some, such as the Sardinians, would have taken this practice to the extreme, building tens of thousands of megaliths just for this purpose. It is also possible that the practice actually improved the human race in the long run, or rather improved its actions, allowing it to see what the best choices are in different areas, not only in terms of conquests but also in things such as urban planning, animal breeding, culture and science.

So, the first Pharaohs, Alexander the Great, Genghis Khan, Julius Caesar, Hannibal, Cleopatra and the Queen of Sheba may have all been born according to this practice.

The French researcher Michel Gauquelin dedicated his life to collecting statistics on great figures of history born in more recent times with the aim of collecting their dates and times of birth to see if there really was an influence of the position of Venus and other planets near Earth on the baby's chances of becoming a great figure later on in life. Always based on statistics and blind studies, he concluded that each of the planets leads to different characters. All the research committees that have tried to belittle his results, grouped under the heading 'the Mars effect', really should admit that there was an effect of the planets on the future character of babies born when the planets were in specific positions in relation to their birthplaces. His statistics show that the angle of light of a star in relation to the place where childbirth takes place on Earth is very important. He identified a window of around 10 degrees above the horizon as the ideal position for benefiting from the effect of the star or planet. Beyond that angle, the effect is no longer felt. In contrast, this effect returns after the planet has passed its highest point in the sky, although it is not as strong. Basically, when the planet sets, and when it is at its lowest point, hidden under the horizon, the effect is felt once more. This demonstrates that it is not a case of photons but of other particles capable of penetrating matter such as neutrinos, which would be responsible for the changes made in the baby's body, or possibly inertons.

Alex then shows them diagrams of how the Sun's light reflected by Venus is strangely polarized, and how this polarization becomes negative when the maximum elongation of Venus approaches. He explains that the spectrograph has been designed to reproduce the range of colors of photons from Venus, and to reproduce their polarization. He presents the technique used to produce negative polarization, a real challenge for the SAIC engineers. Until then, nobody had been able to produce negative polarization. This characteristic was discovered while observing the light from Venus, but nobody could explain how it was produced. Alex and his colleagues thought of drilling tiny holes in the polarizing filter, of a diameter almost equal to the length of the wave emitted. The machine would then emit several wavelengths and use a number of different polarization filters. Then, regarding the transformation of this particular light into the particle that will modify the baby's brain, well, that is the great unknown factor, which is why they had decided to let Nature do its work and take the machine to the other side of the Van Allen belt. The photons will pass through this very strong electromagnetic zone, then into the ionosphere and the magnetosphere. The first stage is, therefore, purely technical, and focuses on the Ark of the Covenant. The Ark was the first objective of the Icarus project for SAIC, and the relation between it and conquering and visionary babies only appeared very recently as a result of Susan's research and imagination.

Given that the mission had been planned some time ago, SAIC decided to maintain it, the presence of the Ark of the Covenant justifying it completely. As a precaution, know that it is known that the light from Venus can have an effect on the brain, it was decided that it was useful and reasonable to have Susan along during the experiment if unusual results appeared, or so that she could draw conclusions from the information collected.

This first stage, therefore, consists of producing a ray of light as powerful as possible and directing it towards the Great Pyramid on a very precise axis, because it needs to penetrate the duct that leads from one external surface of the pyramid to the inside of the King's Chamber. The Ark of the Covenant will be there, placed inside the one-piece granite sarcophagus. The chamber will be made airtight and filled with hydrogen. A powerful low-frequency generator will be regulated to the Earth's frequency, i.e., 440 Hz. This is the frequency that should be captured and amplified in the great gallery, filtered by the 'portcullises' at the entry to the King's Chamber, and set to resonate inside the sarcophagus (E-10). Although the fans located in the ducts will have been removed it is still not sure if the ducts are in a straight line. That is the place where the transformation of the photons into these (still unknown) particles would take place. They would penetrate matter, but would also be diverted by layers in the upper atmosphere. Will the linings of the ducts contain reflecting material, allowing the wave to bounce and reach its destination, like a light bundle propagates itself in fiber optics?

These unknown factors continue to worry the SAIC team, but the basic elements are too clear so as not to attempt the experiment. A surprising fact is that the ducts did not end in the King's Chamber when it was discovered. They stopped just over three inches from the stone face. Their presence was guessed at through fissures. This means that the builders of the pyramid knew that the wave that would propagate itself in the ducts could penetrate matter.

When Susan takes over the presentation, Alex moves away and goes to the Unity module for a bit of peace and quiet. The last few hours have been exhausting, and he finds it hard to understand why Susan looks so cool and refreshed.

One of the men in the team comes up to him. He was in the shuttle, but he had never seen him in San Diego. He introduces himself as a backup technician.

"How's it going, not too nervous?" he asks.

"No, I'm OK. Everything seems to be under control. I'm more worried about those guys down there. Nobody knows how the Ark of the Covenant will react. Building that pyramid was a serious affair, and some people have observed that there was an explosion in the King's Chamber, but they don't know why. If, as they think, there was hydrogen in there, you can just imagine the effect of such an explosion. Anyway, I'm talking too much and I don't know if I can tell you any more. Do you have clearance?" asks Alex.

The man pulls a pass out: "Cosmic Top Secret ECE" and quickly shows it to Alex.

"Don't worry, I'm not here as a technician, I'm from headquarters and I've been working on this project since before you were born."

"Wow, you still seem quite young to me!"

"No, young man, I'm fifty-nine years old. Let me introduce myself; Paul Smith, ex Stargate project (P-11)."

"Ah, I thought I'd seen you somewhere before … the photos of the project team, right? If I'm allowed to know, why are you here for his experiment?"

"That's exactly what I wanted to talk to you about, and very discreetly. Even if you don't have the clearance level, I should fill you in on certain important points. Tomorrow's experiment has several facets, and you know people are only told on a need-to-know basis. Now, however, we're arriving at a critical moment, and it's important to try and get all the odds on our side. I'm sure you've heard of Ingo Swann and seen the photos of the Stargate team?"

"Yeah, I saw him there. He's the one who fine-tuned the Remote Viewing method during the Cold War, right?"

"Exactly, but what very few people know is that he also set up a second Remote Viewing method that used the technique of astral projection. You know, people who claim they can travel around the world with their spirit, or explore other worlds."

"Yes, I know. I have a friend who is really interested in that. He told me about the Monroe Institute, created by a master of the technique."

"That's right, and the Stargate team attended courses there. Ingo is no longer involved, but from the moment he started to use the technique he began to see flying saucers or aliens entering his field of vision. SAIC's MIB service kept track of him at the time to see if he could help us to learn more about the UFO phenomenon, but he couldn't handle the stress and we had to stop our attempts. We still believe that this gift of remote viewing interferes with the UFO phenomenon, which we still don't understand completely. You must know of SAIC's involvement in this area; in fact, we took it over from NASA. Military units such as the US Air Force report all incidents to us, as do the Pentagon, NSA, the CIA and the FBI. Don't repeat what I'm going to tell you, but I'm just telling you so you realize what's at stake. We control absolutely everything that is done, said or observed about UFOs. Nobody knows as much as we do. The other day in McLean you saw Jacques Vallée. Well, he's our 'thinking head'. He wanted to come along, but was frustrated when he was told he was too tall, so I've taken his place. This experiment is crucial for both of us in our understanding of the UFO phenomenon. Jacques' idea is that the light from Venus, and surely the light which will be produced by the activation of the Ark of the Covenant, will allow mankind to make easier contact with what hides behind the UFO phenomenon. He thinks that, beyond the precognition produced by the light of Venus, he can find the capacity for entering into contact with the alien phenomenon. However, I'm not using the term 'alien' accurately here. We don't believe in aliens as such, but in an intelligent force that can manipulate matter at will. We don't know the purpose. Is it what some call God? We don't know. What is sure is that this force is omnipresent and seems to have limitless power. We wonder why it has fun making small craft in the form of saucers appear, together with the little green men who stroll through our fields picking lavender. We've been thinking crazy things for sixty-five years! We hope that this machine, with the help of the Ark of the Covenant, will allow us to understand the whole thing better. The most delicate aspect, as I'm sure you know, is the human aspect, which we don't know how to manage very well because we don't know what will happen. We have around fifty people down there on the ground, but they will all be outside the pyramid at the time of the experiment. From what we know, the pyramid was designed to function as a hermetic unit, without any human intervention except for the supply of liquid to generate hydrogen, but that was no doubt done through some still undiscovered ducts that ended in the Queen's Chamber. We don't think there were people inside the pyramid when it was 'working'. This means that the effect we are seeking must have gone beyond that, or that it was aimed at the other duct – the one on the northern side – but we're still completely in the dark about the purpose. We're basically walking on eggs and need to be pay attention to the slightest visible sign of the external effect of the experiment. All our personnel have had a strict medical examination and have signed a discharge clause. We're paying them well enough for them to do that."

Alex listens carefully to Smith's explanations and his comments about secrecy.

"What do you think will happen?"

"Until a few months ago we didn't know too much, but thanks to the information provided by Susan we think we're on the right track. This business of microtubules in which the molecules are modified by particles emanating from the light of Venus that allow a person to acquire precognition immediately made us think of our research into contacts with the UFO phenomenon. Previously, we looked on the side of quantum physics, imagining the entanglement of electrons between certain human beings and the aliens, but just look how Susan's theory has changed things. Our original idea was biased and limited in scope. Biased because we were still focusing too much on a phenomenon linked to 'entities', and limited because quantum entanglement only involves two particles at a time, but it appears that the ones contacted are linked to an unlimited number of unknown entities. So, on the one hand, we have people such as Travis Walton, Betty and Barney Hill, Anthony Wood and Chris Miller who are interesting 'targets' for the phenomenon, and on the other, people like the Japanese researchers from the OUR-J group or Pierre Berthault (alias Pierre Vieroudy) who were able to provoke the phenomenon at will (A-43). I won't hide from you that we want to master this type of communication, but also to understand the internal structure of what makes it all happen. According to the evidence, it covers an enormous amount of knowledge, including inventions. It's easy to imagine the interest of this project if it succeeds."

"Yes, but I still don't get how you think you'll be able to control the phenomenon from there ..." replies Alex, who is wondering just how far Paul Smith is going to give him confidential information.

"Well ... eventually we would like to find a person who can 'converse' with this universal consciousness. You'll have heard of people like Margrit Coates who speak to animals. We're sure they aren't really communicating with animals, but with this universal consciousness. Unfortunately, this is still in one direction, even in 'double one direction'. Let me explain. Not only does an animal not know it is giving information, a person can gain access to the animals' information stored in the universal consciousness without the animal being aware of it. However, these people do not go higher than one stage in this consciousness, and they speak to what lies above the animal's consciousness."

"Do you mean that this universal consciousness is intelligent?"

"Yes, of course, otherwise it would not have created these incongruous apparitions over the centuries! We have understood that it is capable of using locally-available minerals to materialize a vehicle. Observations have revealed incandescent material escaping from a flying object, a kind of molten metal, but each time with a different composition. A spectrogram at Hessdalen in Norway showed that the metals present in the rays of the specter corresponded to metals present in the ground nearby. It could, therefore, be a case of an intelligence that can manipulate material, but not create it."

"But … what would be the relationship between this intelligence, precognition and people who speak to animals?"

"Imagine that our memory is not contained in our brain or in our body, but in this universal consciousness, whose location we still need to discover. Let's say that it's everywhere. Every person would have their memory located within this consciousness, and have easy access to it. After training, some people are able to leave their zone and reach the zone of another person or animal. Thanks to the Stargate experiments, we even think that we can connect to the memory of an object or a location. For example, we have observed that access to different zones is achieved through a name, an address, a date, coordinates, and if this 'access code' is modified later on the contact with the memory zone is interrupted. A good example is the embassy that the United States wanted to build in Moscow. They asked the 'remote viewers' to travel in time to follow the construction of the building and see if the Russians were installing microphones inside. This was right in the middle of the Cold War and around the time of Watergate. They were able to follow the construction until a certain date but then there was nothing, they couldn't see any farther. What really happened only became clear when the real building was examined. Indeed, the Russians were placing microphones there and the Americans decided to move the embassy to another building. That was the day when the Americans decided to stop construction work on the embassy, because the status of the building as an embassy had disappeared overnight. If they had asked the remote viewers to follow the construction using the address of the building they would no doubt have been able to continue their séances."

"Are you saying that there are several access codes to an information zone, and that once you start you need to continue to use the same access code?"

"Yes, exactly, and access to that memory zone will be blocked if that code disappears at some time in the future, but if you used another code you would surely be able to continue. You can use these codes to travel in the past, the present and the future. We have also learned that information is distributed within this memory by the association of ideas, not by images of objects. So, if you access the zone related to a steam locomotive you'll easily be able to perceive images of tunnels, slag heaps, and even hear the whistle, but you won't see the image of the locomotive itself. You could also present it as if this memory contained a complete replica of our world, a theory consolidated by astral voyages. If you remember, this method was also used by Ingo Swann. The most surprising thing is that this memory contains everything that concerns the past, and even more surprisingly … the future!"

"The future?"

"Yeah, sure! Think of Susan's research, which you're quite familiar with, if my information is correct. It is precisely through the reading of the future contained in this universal memory that oracles, prophets, and, later, emperors could make their predictions and take the best decisions."

"But how can we accept the notion that the future is already written somewhere?"

"The future is not written as such. It is the 'most likely' future that is written, or maybe even endless possible futures. They could be modified on the basis of events that take place on Earth and in the Universe, and each time the variety of futures is modified to adapt to these changes. The more the future approaches us, the greater the probability of something happening. That's why when they talk of the Holy Spirit in the Old Testament they say it is a gift acquired at birth that allows us to see the near future and, therefore, govern better. You know, what Susan has taught us is really intriguing and interesting. While we were just researching in one direction, she showed us that Man has tried to master this ability to read inside this universal consciousness since ancient times. Something we do not know yet is why some people can read the future, while others can speak to animals and some see UFOs."

"What do you do about ghosts and possessions?"

"We don't know. That sort of thing seems much more difficult to verify. And although the examples I've just mentioned show that we have increasingly strong evidence about the reality of the phenomenon, there's nothing to prove that ghosts really exist. As for possessions, they seem to be associated more with people with hysteria and personality disorders."

"What about the people who speak other languages when they are possessed or in a trance?"

"Despite the number of cases and reliable studies, direct testimonies almost always show that the facts have been amplified or embellished to give greater glory to a personality who is adulated by his or her admirers. Take the example of monks dug up intact from their tombs after centuries. A simple check shows that their faces were reconstituted with wax with the aim of sustaining the myth of the living monk. How sad and disappointing is that? As you say, though, we prefer to confine ourselves to domains in which it is easy to demonstrate a telepathic phenomenon between a human being and this universal memory."

"What would you like me to do specifically?"

"There are three of us here who understand the full scope of the phenomenon. The others are mere technicians. Nobody knows what might happen, and I can't count on the technicians to analyze the situation. I have plenty of people down there on the ground aware of the psychic problem, but I would like to count on you two and Rano to see what happens at the precise moment of the experiment."

"But what do you want Rano to do? He doesn't know anyone on site, and he doesn't have the right clearance ..."

"That's not a problem. What I want him to do is just observe, and pick up anything my men might not detect. Of course, if they have the opportunity to observe something clear-cut and visual with physical results, they can do the job on their own, but if the consequences of our experiment are more 'subtle', then there is a real advantage in having an external observer who has good background knowledge of the experiment."

"Ah ... I see that Susan has finished her presentation. People are starting to come out of the module."

"Right, let's leave it there, and let's keep this to the four of us."

Paul rejoins his team and Alex goes back to Susan. Everyone is going to be rather unoccupied until the next day, when they will re-enter the shuttle to move further away from Earth and cross the Van Allen belt. Susan's presentation was also planned to keep all these people busy. Although it looks gigantic from the outside, the ISS only has limited living space and it is very crowded in there. As the spectrograph had been left inside the shuttle, it was not even a case of checking it out or preparing the experiment. From the time of the Apollo missions, when the astronauts had to stay in isolation chambers after their return from space in a kind of quarantine, people were trained to be alone and not have a lot of things to do. Deep-water divers are familiar with this too, as they sometimes have to stay in decompression chambers for up to eight days with their fellow divers, completely isolated from the outside world.

The evening takes place between the discovery of meals in tubes, straws used for almost all foods – often reduced to stewed fruit or soups – and, later, vertical sleeping bags! As there is almost no gravity everything floats around and it is impossible to lie down and stretch out. ISS passengers are given complete freedom ... they can sleep in small compartments allocated to them, attach their sleeping bag wherever they see fit, or even sleep without being tied down. They need to know that there is always some noise and that the lights are always on. They have ear plugs and blindfolds, and the virtual night is the same for everyone, set at the Greenwich Meridian. In the morning, ground control chooses some wake-up music and broadcasts it over the loudspeakers. The selection of music is not that unusual ... Spandau Ballet, Cat Stevens, some classical music and even the soundtrack of *Top Gun*.

ALAIN HUBRECHT

Chapter 22

August 31ˢᵗ 2010, on board the X-37C Shuttle

The SAIC team has settled back into the shuttle after saying goodbye to the personnel on the ISS. There is no take-off as such this time, just a simple detachment from the ISS, firing the secondary pipes to move the craft away from the ISS and positing it correctly before reaching its high orbit beyond the Van Allen belt. The protective shields are in place but will be removed once in high orbit so that the 'crew' can observe the scene. They will use the ion engine to increase altitude. This new-generation engine consumes ten times less fuel and, thanks to the atomic battery, the propulsion unit also weighs ten times less than a standard configuration. The engine is coupled – how is highly confidential – to an inerton generator (inertons are gravitational particles that can cancel out the gravitational pull of planets). From now on the ion engine will propel the shuttle without having to fight against inertia.

Susan is sitting in the same seat as on take-off. She feels less stressed now, but is still very excited. Alex seems calmer and Susan is a little sad that she cannot share her excitement with him. She hears the dull thud of the separation from the ISS and feels the spacecraft draw away from it. Every time a secondary pipe fires there is a sound like a small explosion. The firing never lasts long, one second on average. After around thirty minutes of maneuvering, they are ready to start the ion (and inerton) engine. The noise created by the ejection of the ions is like a whistle; inertons do not make any noise. They are ejected depending on the position of Earth and the trajectory of the spacecraft. Although ion engines have been used for several years in satellites and space missions this is the first time that an inerton generator has been used on a manned mission, although very few people are aware of this. The pilots have naturally received special training, and understand that it is a new way of flying the shuttle. They are sworn to secrecy, just like the pilots of the B2 Stealth bomber before them.

The other passengers realize something unusual has happened. They do not feel any acceleration, as no movement is perceived when the inerton generator starts up. However, given that nobody had previously been a passenger on the X-37C and had not taken part on more than one space flight, they have no reference point and can just feel the strange way in which the spacecraft moves. The impression is even stranger because the windows have been covered up.

The pilot finally tells them that they have passed through the Van Allen belt and that the shuttle has reached its programmed geostationary orbit. Susan sees the protective shields slide up the windows and realizes that they are upside down; to be more precise, the shuttle is on its back. This is quite normal, as the cargo hold needs to be facing Earth. She unclips her safety harness and moves alongside Alex, who has already put her in the picture about part of his conversation with Paul. From here, Susan knows she cannot do anything particularly important, and that everything depends on Rano down on the ground. She casts a glance at Alex and moves to the back of the compartment, where the control panel of the apparatus is located. It only rains one day a year in Cairo, and luckily today is not that day. The X-37's powerful zoom camera gives them an incredibly good view of the pyramid, although unfortunately in infra-red because it is still night-time in Cairo. She can hear the hum of the variable pitch motors of the spectrograph that positions it based on data from the GPS. On screen they see an image from a camera inside the King's Chamber. Around ten cameras have been placed in there, many of them capable of taking more than 1,000 images a second, and one that can even capture 10,000 images per second. It is the kind of camera used to film atomic explosions.

Paul and Alex are next to each other and Susan does her best to see both of their screens. Paul has a soldier's broad shoulders, which does not make it easier for her. Luckily, thanks to the lack of gravity she can float upwards and see the screens from there. She notes that the sarcophagus has been moved to a spot between the ends of the two ducts. It will, of course, be put back in its place after the experiment, but the SAIC people are sure that it was originally in this position.

They are told that the filling of the chamber has begun and will be completed in around ten minutes. They decide to start the frequency meter two minutes before performing their final experiment, which will only be triggered when the computer indicates the perfect position of the shuttle vis-à-vis the pyramid. She also hears the micro explosions when the positioning pipes carry out the delicate task of aligning the craft in the right position, coinciding with the best position of Venus in a period covering 200 years, just when it rises and its reflected light is most strongly polarized.

Susan cannot resist resting her hand on Alex's shoulder. She knows how important this moment is, but feels that by making physical contact with him she will remember the event with even greater pleasure. That's it...! They receive the green light from the ground. Alex makes a final check of all the variables, throws an approving glance at Paul and waits for him to press the blue button in front of him.

Their eyes are glued to the screen showing the King's Chamber.

Chapter 23

August 31st 2010, Pyramid of Cheops, Egypt

Since his arrival, Rano has got to know some of the men better. He knows who Jacques Vallée is, and also Russel Targ, the man who started the Stargate project. They are both tall and thin, and therefore easily identifiable. They are among the few people on site wearing civilian clothes, with the SAIC employees all wearing dark blue overalls and the security personnel black overalls. There is nothing on their clothing that says 'SAIC', however; the operation must not be identified by visitors. Rano spoke to Alex the evening before, who told him about Paul's request. The instruction is to remain discreet and only contact Paul and Jacques Vallée if he observes something really out of the ordinary.

He enters one of the tents full of giant screens linked to the cameras inside the King's Chamber. Other camera are located on the faces of the pyramid, their lenses focused on the outlets of the ducts.

Rano wonders why the Americans did not reconstruct the conditions of the experiment at home on one of their military bases, but he soon realizes that hardly anyone knows what they are doing here. They are simply carrying out orders. He dares not to disturb Jacques and Russel, who are not paying any attention to him anyway. He asked Alex about the site the evening before while he was on the line to him, and Alex replied that since nobody knew what the experiment was going to produce it would be better to reproduce it in the original place so as not to leave out any essential elements.

It is freezing outside but the tents have good heating. In any case, with all that computer equipment there it might be that it is already cooling the air rather than warming it up.

He looks at his watch and notes that there are only fifteen minutes to go before the experiment starts. He then hears a series of beeps telling personnel to evacuate the hazardous zone.

Rano shows his pass giving him access to the tent with the screens and, being short in stature, tries to weave through the crowd to get a better view of the screens.

Hi-fi microphones have also been placed in different places inside the pyramid, but it is only the sound recorded by the one in the King's Chamber that is broadcast in the tent.

Just over two minutes to go …

The tent falls silent and the only thing heard is the hum of the frequency generator in the King's Chamber.

There it goes … on the left-hand screen showing the outside of the pyramid the imposing south face of the pyramid is seen. A pallid blue light illuminates it, as if an enormous spotlight had been connected to the exterior. The central screen, which Rano focuses on, shows nothing, at least not yet. No ray of light is penetrating the chamber.

Everyone holds their breath, and suddenly a bluish halo seems to invade the King's Chamber. Some micro flashes streak through the mist, which gets denser and denser. Gradually the bluish light becomes denser between the two dishes. The scene in the middle of the image is clearly visible, enlarged on the right-hand screen. The halo, carried by the ionized hydrogen that is filling up the chamber, links the two dishes with a clear ray of light of a diameter of around four inches. These are the particles emitted from the light from the spectrograph bouncing back and forth between the two walls to create a concentrated 'hyper ray' whose density increases second by second. The system is in the process of concentrating all the particles on the same plane, just like a laser beam. So, the principle of the 'maser' defined by Chris Dunn seems to work, although he does not see other phenomena taking place. The ray's intensity increases and saturates the video cameras, but fortunately these cameras automatically adjust their filters and they continue to film the scene. Chris Dunn had observed that the inner faces of the sarcophagus of the Great Pyramid and the giant sarcophagi of the Serapeum are completely flat and perpendicular. It is difficult to explain why they would have taken so much trouble at the time of shutting away a mummy. If, on the other hand, it was to obtain certain very specific vibratory phenomena such as those that take place in a maser and a laser, it is easy to understand their interest. The parallelism of the surfaces makes the hydrogen vibrate in exactly the same way so as to have an influence on the particles.

The lens suddenly swings through ninety degrees to reach a perpendicular position, crossing the ray. The room falls dark again and only a weak halo of light remains, similar to the one seen at the start. Nothing more happens. The people there look at each other warily, not knowing what to think. Did things go as planned? A simple glance at one of the screens shows that the south face of the pyramid is still lit up by the shuttle.

The SAIC people confer and decide that the experiment has been a success. They contact the shuttle to tell it to stop sending light.

Rano tries to pick up everything that is going on and hear what the coordination team personnel are saying. He cannot speak to Susan or Alex at the moment because the frequencies are being used for commands and exchanges with the control room.

He decides to stay in the tent as long as possible, or to follow Jacques Vallée if he decides to leave.

He hears that a teleconference will be held with the team in the shuttle and only then will a decision be taken on what has to be done. It is important to decide if the shuttle should stay up there or return to Earth.

ALAIN HUBRECHT

Chapter 24

August 31st 2010, on board the X-37C Shuttle

"Hi! Paul, Alex and Susan, can you hear me?" asks Jacques Vallée. In front of him, a big screen shows the three people he wants to talk to. He is in a secure truck parked alongside the tents. The truck is set out like a Faraday cage: no windows, no telephone landline and no GSMs anywhere, i.e., the classic layout of a meeting room classified Defense Secret.

"Yes, I'm sure you've realized that we stopped the experiment after the lens of the Ark of the Covenant tipped. We haven't observed anything since then. The process of concentration and alignment of the particles was stopped, as planned, by our engineers. Did you see anything from your side?"

"No, nothing special. We continued to send the ray of light until you asked us to stop," replies Paul. "What do you think happened? Why did the dome tip?"

"That was planned, don't worry. We can't explain everything for fear of eavesdroppers. We thought the Ark contained received particles, thus allowing the amplification – perhaps by 1,000 – of the natural effect of the particles. Now we really don't know what we have to do. No version is clear enough to explain what the ancients did with this reserve of particles. We suspect that it should reach the brain or the body of the people who want to benefit from it, but we don't know how to proceed.

"I have an idea," says Susan, who did not dare to speak before.

"Go ahead …"

"Good morning Monsieur Vallée, it's an honor for me to speak to you, even at this great distance. I've thought about this long and hard, and I wonder if the pyramid is not a system that means you do not have to wait for the planet to rise to benefit from its influence, and even more so at the moment of birth. Paul tells me you've received a copy of my thesis. If you've read it, you'll have seen that Man understood that a birth at the moment when Venus rises could mean that the newborn baby had the gift of precognition. My studies have not revealed traces of the use of the light of Venus at another moment in the life of our ancestors, no doubt because it was not possible. After it reaches adult age, the brain would not be as receptive to the waves coming from the planet. They were happy just to observe the position of the stars, knowing that they continued, despite everything, to have an influence on their behavior but not their abilities. Why didn't the Egyptians envisage the construction of a machine capable of improving adults' capacity for precognition?"

"I'm listening, but I don't understand the connection. What are you trying to explain to me?"

"I don't know what your objective in this experiment is, but you know what interests me about it. I understand that you believe the Ark to be a condenser of light from Venus, or of the particles the planet sends us."

"That's right, but initially we only thought we would make use of it to try and re-establish communication with the so-called 'alien phenomenon', a communication that would only be created by the presence of the Ark and its contents."

"No," replies Susan "I think you need to use what you have stored and expose it to volunteers, and then see if they have better precognition after."

"What makes you think that?"

"Just look at the Bible. The apostles received the Holy Spirit at Whitsun. Remember where it happened … just in front of King Solomon's temple, where the Ark of the Covenant was kept. I know that you thought of the Great Pyramid because of the rumors that the Ark would have been captured from the pharaohs and therefore came from Egypt, and that stories tell us of pharaohs who went into the Great Pyramid to 'recharge their batteries', or – as we now understand – by means of something that was located inside the Great Pyramid."

"But that doesn't tell us what protocol we need to follow now to become exposed to the action of the Ark."

"At Whitsun, it was reported that there was a loud noise and the apostles were then surrounded by flames. We would probably say 'sparks' nowadays. The least we can say is that the Ark does not release its contents quietly. I know that, in principle, the Ark was no longer in the temple at Jesus' time, but it is very difficult to know where it was at the time, or even if it still existed. The Roman general Pompey went there to see it once, but could not find it. Nothing proves that the episode of the apostles took place before his arrival, and maybe it was hidden from him, when people knew that he was going to make a visit. There are texts that describe how to build the case that protects it, but there is no clue as to its exact content. The classical texts talk of the Tablets of the Ten Commandments and different cult objects, but the instructions for the construction of the case seem to indicate that it contained something rather strange, dangerous and very heavy. Given that you did not have the drawings, I wonder what you put in place for this release."

"As you saw on the video screens, we planned to stop the charge after a particular moment. We invented a system to store the particles that takes them to a tank in the form of a torus, and the reflecting walls of the tank are cooled to absolute zero. The particles spin around endlessly, minimizing any losses. We stopped the charge after observing that the torus had filled to almost 90%. That's the maximum we would reach with the volume that was sent to us. We believe that the ancients did not have any means of cooling something to absolute zero, but they surely knew of other methods that are now forgotten. Engravings found in Egypt show that they used electricity."

"OK, I see that, so I imagine that if you know how to capture these particles in your torus, you also know how to get them out."

"That's true. We can focus them in a highly concentrated manner, or disperse them all around the Ark by using the other face of the dishes."

"If I were you, I would do it in a secure environment, and be prepared for anything. Again, the Bible says that just before the Ark was activated, two men dressed in white came down from the sky. I don't want to joke about this, but I think you should be ready to expect anything. We might even be talking of angels or astronauts."

"We don't expect to see any astronauts or angels, but we do hope to provoke phenomena that will help to us to understand UFO apparitions better."

Paul decides to intervene in the conservation.

"Seeing as some UFOs have had psychic effects on the environment, such as the deactivation of nuclear missiles, the death of men or the destruction of fighter jets, it would be wise to release the particles in a controlled environment."

"Yes, you are quite right. Our plan was to take the Ark back to the Wright Patterson base where we have quite a lot of people, but maybe that's not the best solution. It's probably better to take it to Base 51, where we'll be out of reach of eavesdroppers and far from centers of population. If anything weird happens we'll be in a confined military environment."

"Can you access Base 51 as easily as that?" asks Alex.

"No, the place is highly secret but we have ways of getting in. I need to fill in some documents and I think we can get in there next week. I am going to ask for the Ark to be transported there. I'll try and get you access permits, but don't jump for joy too quickly, the procedures are fairly strict."

"OK," says Susan. "So, should we return home now and then fly straight to Las Vegas?"

"Yes, I think that's the best plan. We can't afford to waste time. The contents of the Ark won't last forever; to tell the truth, we have no idea how long. Have a good flight home. If there are any changes I'll contact Paul Smith. See you soon!"

ALAIN HUBRECHT

Chapter 25

September 5ᵗʰ 2010, Ambassador Strip Inn Hotel, Las Vegas

Alex, Susan and Rano are staying in a hotel just a short distance from the airport from where they will fly to Groom Lake – the other name of Base 51 – the following morning. This base does not officially exist and it is where secret American prototypes are tested. Rano will not be able to accompany them because he is not an American citizen, so he will wait for them in the hotel.

Alex and Susan no longer try and hide their romance and have reserved a room together. The descent from space went well, with no technical incidents or bad weather to delay them. They landed at Huntsville the evening before. Paul did not accompany them as he had things to do elsewhere, but he will rejoin them for the flight tomorrow morning.

It is 6 p.m. and they have just unpacked their suitcases. Susan heads straight for the shower, the first real one since the morning of August 28ᵗʰ, when they took off in the shuttle. She lets the water run down her neck and feels it on her spine, warm and reassuring. Eight days of stress, eight incredible days, an amazing adventure for her, but her muscles and nerves are now showing the strain.

The minutes go by slowly as her body relaxes. Leaning against the glass, she does not realize that Alex has come into the bathroom and is watching her in silence. He hands her a towel as she comes out, happy to see that her body, finally relaxed, has become more fragile and wanting tenderness. She can become a real woman again, not weaker than her man but more sensitive. Above all, she can reawaken her hormones and her genetic programming, which means that she will want to make love to someone who she feels secure with. Alex does not think like her. He does not understand the twisting and turning paths of thought that women often follow. What he sees is the most beautiful woman in the world, never-ending curves behind the glass where drops of water glow like pearls and fall to the floor. Alex moves towards Susan and then the bed that is waiting for them in the next room. Rano will have to have dinner on his own!

Rano, however, had other reasons to be worried. Just after he reached his room he received a call from reception saying that a package had arrived for him. He went downstairs quickly, not taking care to check if anyone in the hall was behaving suspiciously. He picked up the parcel, which looked quite ordinary but had no postmark; it had been directly deposited at the reception desk. Back in his room, he opened the package anxiously to find a pile of photos of his family in China. He could see his father and mother, clearly photographed in their home with a telephoto lens. He then found a piece of paper folded four times. He unfolded it and began to read. "We are OK. We love you with all our heart and hope that everything is all right. We hope to hear from you as soon as possible. Don't disappoint your father. You know he is in poor health." The message was clear: they were putting even more pressure on him. This simple message started to weigh him down. He thought he was in the clear after sending them information on the mission in Egypt, which included everything he understood of the experiment.

But no, they wanted more. When would they leave him alone? With a heavy heart, he put his overcoat on to combat the cold of the Las Vegas night and found a call box. He reluctantly gave information on the planned movements of his colleague and Alex, explaining that he did not know anything more at the moment.

He did not go straight back to his hotel and turned off towards the casino in the Luxor Hotel, just a stone's throw away. Ironically, this hotel is well-known for its replica of an Egyptian pyramid that reaches a height of just under 350 feet, i.e., almost three-quarters the height of the original, with a reproduction of the Sphinx at the bottom. Rano tried to console himself for not going to Groom Lake the next day by gambling a few dollars, but what he was really trying to do was forget his problems with his country's government.

Around 11 p.m. Rano's lifeless body was found on Las Vegas Boulevard. A police car had been called by tourists who had found him. A quick check made it clear that he had been run over, but there were no witnesses at the scene. Susan was awakened at 2 a.m. by a call from the County Police Commissioner. After asking her if she knew a certain Rano Saret, she was told of his death and was asked to go to the mortuary in the morning to identify the body. After a moment of panic, and then hesitation, she explained that she simply could not postpone a meeting in the morning and that she needed to go to the mortuary immediately.

"Alex, wake up… Alex!"

"Uh… what's up? Have you seen what time it is?"

"Alex, something serious has happened. We need to talk!"

"What could have happened? We only just went to bed!"

"I got a call from the police. Rano is dead!"

"What?! You can't be serious!"

"I am serious! He was hit by a car!"

"But where? He was in the hotel restaurant this evening."

"Apparently he went to the casino in the Luxor Hotel across the road. You know, the one with the enormous pyramid."

"Holy shit! This could compromise the entire experiment today!"

"Yes, I know, and I've thought about that, but let's not panic. I need to go and identify the body in the morgue, and have asked to go there as soon as possible so we can take the flight with the others. If all goes well we'll be there on time, but I'm still worried. Apparently a hit-and-run driver ran him down and then made off. Anyway, the Chinese don't need to be taught how to cross the road!"

"Should we warn the others?"

"No, I don't think so. Rano wasn't going to come with us anyway, because he doesn't have the clearance and wasn't on the mission. We don't necessarily have to tell the security service of SAIC, although we'll have to tell them sometime because he was on a temporary contract in San Diego."

"Oh my God, waking up in the middle of the night when I was sleeping like a baby, and now this! For Christ's sake! Can you get me a glass of water and an aspirin?"

"Sure, honey,

Alex's eyes followed Susan as she walked to the bathroom, or rather the curve of her buttocks, which her tiny nightie had difficulty hiding. He already felt better, and by the time Susan came back he was fast asleep again.

Chapter 26

September 6th 2010, at the mortuary in Las Vegas

8 a.m. Susan arrives at the Las Vegas mortuary in the northern part of the city. Luckily, the city is not so big and the traffic is not too heavy at that time of the morning.

"Good morning, I have come to identify someone."

"Ah, yes, we were waiting for you!"

"Waiting for me?"

"Not me personally, but there are some other people who are here to see you."

Puzzled, Susan follows the guard through some corridors until she is asked to wait in a room. The room has a glass window and Susan soon sees the same guard reappear pushing a stretcher, accompanied by a person wearing a white coat. Behind them, a police officer and two civilians. Susan immediately recognizes the very specific look of SAIC's security personnel.

The sheet is lifted, and Susan sadly confirms that it is her colleague.

She nods her head and the man puts the sheet back down on Rano, who she will never see again. He was not really a friend and she did not know him very well, but they had travelled together a lot and almost slept under the stars, so she had vivid memories that would stay with her for a long time to make the loss of Rano even more painful.

She is lost in her thoughts when the door opens and the two civilians come in, followed by the police officer.

"Ms. Susan Gomez?"

"Yes, that's me. What a terrible thing!"

"Unfortunately, we fear that as well as being terrible it might be criminal."

"What do you mean?" replies Susan, still shocked.

"Not only failing to stop, which is a crime in itself, but we have good reason to believe that he was run over deliberately."

"Someone killed him on purpose? But nobody knew he was here, and that young man never harmed anyone in his life. Does it have anything to do with the casino he went to?"

"No, we don't think so. The case is really strange. He had a lot of money on him, so it could be money he was given in exchange for the chips he won at the tables. Looking at it that way, even the presence of a large sum of money can be explained. But we're almost certain that it was a hit-and-run driver that got him."

"What? Please explain, I'm not with you. How do you know the money didn't come from the casino?"

"The notes from the casino all have invisible markings. It's something they do to avoid lucky gamblers being attacked when they leave the premises. It's possible to trace the banknotes for a few days, and I won't tell you how they associate them with each person but they do a good job. Anyway, these particular notes were not marked, and the way in which your colleague carried them wasn't exactly natural, and we think he only walked ten yards with them. They were placed on him when he was lying down rather than standing up."

"What are you saying? Your story doesn't add up!"

"This country's law obliges us to send his belongings to his country of origin together with the body, because he wasn't resident here. That money will be returned to his parents."

"What sort of money are we talking about?"

"There were 50,000 dollars in an envelope, just an ordinary one like millions of others, with no marks on it. It's true that you won't break the bank with that sort of money here, but where he comes from that could solve any family's money problems."

"But this is crazy, it's like a fairy tale. OK, so a hit-and-run driver runs him down, no doubt drunk, and leaves a stack of money on the body as an apology! Maybe he'd just won that money in the casino."

"Good try, Ms. Gomez, but we just told you that banknotes from the casinos are invisibly marked, and these did not carry any marks. Our big problem is that we know where those banknotes came from."

"Well, there you have the solution!"

"Not quite, because this complicates the case even more. These notes come from China, and were withdrawn from a bank just two days ago."

"China?"

"Yes, and unfortunately collected by an agent, from the Ministry of Foreign Affairs if our sources are right. Miss Gomez, this is almost an affair of State, but because the victim is not a US national the matter is out of our hands. Nevertheless, I'm sure you will agree that the affair is more than suspicious."

The man who was talking to Susan turns round and asks the police officer to leave the room.

When they are alone again, he continues:

"We know about the mission you are working on. We were already familiar with your dossier, and those of Rano Saret and Alex Bergen. We have also contacted your mission director. You understand that this identification of the body was just a front for the police. What they want is to avoid negative publicity in Las Vegas as far as possible, and they certainly don't want to scare the tourists away. So, they will leave us alone and there will not be any official follow-up to this murder, but as far as we are concerned we are faced with a matter of espionage. Last night Alex's boss confirmed to us that they had already had a discussion about Mr. Saret. Were you aware of that?"

"I ... um ... well, no, I don't think so, I don't remember. We knew that he had been on edge for several weeks because his father was seriously ill."

"We have collected information from China. Rano's father was not ill at all, that was just a pretext to explain his nervousness. We think he was spying for his country; it's quite common. They are 'sleeping moles' programmed through blackmail. They are identified as soon as they have a problem, in his case his application for a visa. They pay off their debts and give them visas, and then the poor guys owe favors to their country for the rest of their life. Most of them never have to do anything in exchange and die of natural causes with a clear conscience. In this case, the thing is serious, very serious, because we are talking about a classified Secret Defense mission."

"But Rano didn't have access to it. He wasn't given clearance, and he wasn't going to accompany us today as a result."

"Hey, come on! Didn't you talk to him? Was he was blind or deaf to everything that happened around him? It seems they were stupid enough to let him into the tents in Egypt, and we are told that he attended the retransmission of a very important experiment."

"That part of the experiment was not classified. Very few people were in on the classified part."

"That doesn't stop you both being part of it!"

"No, but it is true that I was in on the secret."

"Yes, we know. It's not up to us to judge the decisions made by people in high places, but your colleague, as cold as he now is, has still got us into a real fix. What information do you think he could have transmitted, and what part of it could put the rest of the experiment at risk?"

"I have no idea. I'm not up to date with everything that goes on, but I believe that Rano had no idea of the reason why the experiment was classified. He and I joined the project for completely different reasons, and I've only officially been in on the classified part for a few days."

"We're going to let you go now. We know you have to catch a flight. We're going to find out more about his family and his contacts over there, to try and find out how he used his time in those last few hours. If you see anything abnormal, let us know. For a start, you can bet your bottom dollar that his apartment in San Diego will be inspected with a fine-tooth comb."

"Do what you have to do. Honestly, I don't see that he could have passed on any sensitive information, but you are right to make inquiries, you never know ..."

"Well, have a good trip, and take care."

Susan takes her leave of the two men, who join the police officer again. She goes outside, happy to get out of that atmosphere of death. She feels completely exhausted. Rano a spy! She never suspected anything of that sort.

What will Alex say? It's true, Alex had been told of Rano's strange behavior, but the matter seemed to have been sorted out at the time. Well, as they say, moles can spend their whole life inactive and never carry out any operations. Perhaps that's the case with Rano. Nevertheless, this business of the banknotes and a sick father seem to indicate that something bigger was going on.

Susan looks at her watch and realizes she has just enough time to jump in a taxi and get to the airport, specifically to the terminal of 'Janet'.

ALAIN HUBRECHT

Chapter 27

September 6ᵗʰ 2010, Groom Lake, aka Base 51

'Janet' actually belongs to the US Air Force. It is a company that ferries employees to and from Base 51, which officially does not exist. A few years ago one of the workers there filed a lawsuit because he said he had been over-exposed to chemicals and demanded compensation. The government dismissed him, saying that the place he referred to did not exist.

Susan catches up with Alex in the terminal, and they board after meticulous checks by a number of armed men. They had been told not to take their cell phones with them; they would not be able to use them anyway after arrival. Before take-off Susan has time to explain the situation with Rano. Alex is still confused, and wonders what will come of it all.

The plane finally takes off for the short flight, with the shutters of the windows in the down position, and they remain that way for the rest of the flight.

On arrival, they are asked to wear special glasses, not unlike welders' goggles. The lenses are thick and are ground in a strange way. You cannot see either side, and in front you only clearly see what is very close to you. Everything beyond a distance of three yards becomes blurred. They have to wear these glasses to get on a bus – which also has opaque windows – and, when the bus reaches its destination they enter the building where a preparatory meeting has been arranged.

"Pleased to see you," says Jacques Vallée as they enter the meeting room. The last time he saw them was when they were in space.

Paul is already there, and several other people are sitting around a table. They remember, just in time, that you should never ask who is who in this kind of meeting.

One of the unknown people starts by talking about Rano's death. It is clear to them that he was murdered and that he must have been blackmailed. Precautions have been intensified as a result, but he advises everyone to be very careful about what they will carry, write or say about the experiment in the next few days. Jacques then takes over and thanks everyone for the work done so far. He explains that, after reflecting long and hard, they are going to proceed with the release of the particles stored in the Ark in a deserted area of Groom Lake. Volunteer soldiers will stand at different distances around the Ark to evaluate the real potential of the particles. Jacques will be in the front row.

Susan and Alex will not be allowed to take part in this exposure, because they will be needed in the analysis phase of the effects. The Ark is already in place and Jacques suggests that they all go outside immediately. Several cameras, radars and other measuring equipment have been placed around the site.

They go back to the bus, put their special glasses on again, and ride for a good half-hour before stopping in a completely flat and deserted area. They should not take their glasses off, thinks Susan, who would nevertheless like to preserve a bit of her femininity.

She gets into an armored truck with Alex, similar to the one parked next to the pyramid a few days before; these trucks like Faraday cages that are protected against all kinds of potentially harmful waves.

From there, they will be able to see the progress of the experiment on screens. Jacques and the other volunteers take up position around the Ark, which is standing on a kind of wooden pedestal. The men spread out in a radius of one hundred yards, with Jacques standing around two yards away from the pedestal. The cameras film everything, including the faces of the volunteers. They are all wearing biometric and EEG sensors. Once wired up, a thick black cable comes out of their suit and runs to another truck near theirs.

It takes a good thirty minutes to get it all ready. The poor guys must be dying of heat, out there in the blazing sunshine on a salt lake. They had considered doing the experiment at night, but decided on the daytime to be able to make out any strange manifestation in greater detail.

The time is near. A countdown takes place. Three…two….one… zero!

Susan's eyes are glued to the main screen, but out of the corner of her eye she also watches the screen to her side, focused on Jacques' face. The lid of the Ark opens silently, the discs rise and immediately afterwards a spherical bluish light appears around the Ark. The halo expands almost instantaneously to reach a diameter of at least twenty yards, although it is not visible on all the screens. The light is not in the visible spectrum; well, it is, but it is polarized in such a way that it is invisible to the naked eye. At the moment the halo reaches the volunteers their bodies seem to turn blue. A strange phenomenon occurs, sparks seem to emerge from their clothes and hair, but on closer inspection the phenomenon seems more like a kind of rainbow. Not really sparks, more like when sunlight is reflected on a mirror from a distance. A flash of light is seen, like millions of small flashes coming from their bodies. It only lasts for about a second. The halo dissipates after reaching its maximum size, with an effect a little similar to the start of an atomic explosion. The volunteers do not seem to have suffered, or even felt, this phenomenon of strange reflections.

Susan now looks at Jacques. He seems lost in thought, but he is probably concentrating very hard. The other volunteers behave differently, but their behavior seems to be clearly related to their distance away from the Ark. Those more than 20 yards away act normally, and look like they want to get back into the shade and freshen up while the others seem, like Jacques, lost in thought.

Paul picks up the microphone and talks to Jacques.

"Jacques, Paul here. Everything OK?"

"… Yes, everything's fine, sure. It's incredible. The experiment has been a success. I felt new sensations inside me."

"Jacques, you should come and see what our cameras have captured."

"Right away. Get the champagne out!" jokes Jacques as he finally starts to move.

The other men follow him and they all head for the trucks. Jacques comes into their truck and takes off his suit and disconnects the hundreds of wires attached to his body. The specialists will look at the measurements later, but Jacques is keen to see the video recordings.

"Look, on this screen connected to a camera equipped with a lens array, you can clearly see the particle field coming out of the Ark and moving in the form of a sphere to around twenty yards away. Now look at this other screen, a shot in the visible spectrum. You can clearly see your bodies start to shine with a thousand sparks, as if you were covered in diamonds. We think this has to do with negative polarization and the density of the particles stored."

"Yes, I saw that out there, and I confess that my brain took a blow. At the time I even panicked a little, I felt something unusual, but very strong, inside my head. It went away very quickly, but I soon realized that I was not thinking in the same way. Even as I speak to you now, I need to make an effort to communicate with you. As I talk, I am assailed by messages from my subconscious, as if I were planning my life for the next few months. I tell myself I must think of this and that, plan something and cancel something else … When I look at an object, so many impressions come to mind. For example, if I see this microphone on the table I can tell you who used it before. It is as if I could read the history of objects, and if I look at you, Susan, I receive different and blurred information from you but if I think hard about something I receive information that is relevant. Right now, I can see the stress you felt this morning in the morgue, but because I am thinking about your friend Rano."

"Wait a moment! I feel something is going to happen now, outside, right now. Let's go outside!"

Jacques has already opened the door and descended the steps of the truck to look into the sky. The others follow him, forming a group behind him.

"What can you feel? What's happening?" asks Paul.

"I don't know. As I said, all these impressions are new to me and words cannot describe them. Even so, I'm certain that something is going to happen. I'm sure of it. It's as if someone has just telephoned information to my head. I haven't had time to hear the conversation, but I have a memory of it. It's a bit like when you say 'I know what I know'."

Even as he gives these rather chaotic explanations, Jacques turns his head in all directions. "Are those outside cameras still filming?" he shouts at the technicians. "Yes, they are," says Paul. "We have rotating turrets, phase change radars and very high-speed cameras, and they are all still connected, of course. The smallest insect flying over the lake would be filmed from all angles."

"OK, good, I can feel it, I can feel it, but I can't perceive anything else."

Susan looks towards the mountains behind them.

"Over there, I can see something!"

Everyone turns round. At first they do not see anything, but then, as Susan continues to point in the same direction, about half a mile away they can make out a small fuzzy thing suspended in the air approximately 300 yards above the ground.

It is very small, very faint, but there is certainly something unusual that can be seen against the clear blue sky.

Paul looks through his binoculars.

"It's moving, that's for sure. Even with the binoculars it's very faint. I can see metallic reflections and dark areas, but the rest is blurred. It looks like it's coming this way."

A solider runs towards them carrying pairs of binoculars. The team picks them up and tries to make out the shape in the sky.

The object continues to approach, but still looks shapeless. It is strange. Forms can now be seen, but they change all the time in a way that is difficult to understand. There are some bulges, but they seem to change place continuously. The colors are strange too. Some parts seem to be metallic and reflect the sun, while others are dark or white, rather vaporous and apparently without substance. At a particular moment two small objects emerge from the first one and start to spin around it, like birds playing.

Jacques remains silent. He watches like the others, but a smile can be seen on his lips.

The objects have come closer and are now around twenty yards away, but even so it is impossible to make out what they are. It is as if the observers were all short-sighted. In life, nothing is blurred, except perhaps clouds or fog, but these things are not mechanical at all, and certainly do not show any signs of intelligence.

Here, it is true that the phenomenon is on them. It would be really surprising that a natural phenomenon unseen until then should be manifested now that the experiment has taken place.

Nobody is using their binoculars now. Everyone is looking at this extraordinary apparition of an impossible object.

It approaches, flies over the group and moves towards Jacques, stopping two yards above him. The two smallest objects do not resemble anything. They are just hazy spheres that continue to spin around the main object. In the meantime, the other volunteers who were within the twenty-yard radius have moved closer to the object. They also seem to be hearing something; they look like people who are busy doing something, whose attention is monopolized by some sort of intellectual activity.

Silence reigns. Behind them, the hum of the generators of the trucks can be heard, but no other noise. The swivel cameras turn their lenses silently, following the movements of the objects.

"Everything OK, Jacques?" asks Paul.

"Sure, fine. Don't worry. I'm trying to listen, to understand what's going on. This thing doesn't say anything, but I feel new sensations in my body and brain. It's like learning a new language. At the start you don't understand anything but you can see that the 'foreigner' is trying to communicate with you. What's most surprising is that I can feel the intentions of this object, or messenger. They're completely peaceful, but I tell you, I can't understand anything it's trying to say."

The objects then start to move again, and slowly move away in the same way as they came. The cameras record their departure, and they will later see that the objects disappeared into thin air at exactly the moment when they could not be seen with the naked eye. Disappeared, faded into the background, as if they had evaporated!

Jacques and the others are back in the truck. He looks at the sequences filmed during the experiment with Paul, and also the arrival of the objects. They save everything on external hard drives, together with the biometric data recorded.

The twelve other volunteers who were in the close-up zone need to have a medical exam before they can go home. They have to remain on call, and they are asked to return to San Diego to meet the project team.

They will stay on SAIC premises and will not be allowed to leave. They have become ultra-secret 'prototypes' until further notice.

Alex and Susan take the evening flight back. Despite their fatigue, they insisted that they wanted to join the team in San Diego the next day. The Janet Airlines plane lands at Las Vegas, and they have just enough time to take a connection to San Diego. The taxi drops them off at Alex's place at 11 p.m.

"Well, I'm quite happy to be home. Do you realize what we've been through in just one week?"

Alex falls on the bed, throws his shoes on the floor and stretches his arms out.

Susan continues. "Yes, it's all quite incredible, and we're probably at the start of something that none of us has any idea about. Think of that object that appeared right over our heads; it's something that theoretically should not exist. It had no form, made no noise, and seemed alive with those two other small objects that flew around it. But nobody understands what it wanted from us, not even those who were close to the Ark. When I think about it, why didn't we stay at Groom Lake to continue to observe the phenomenon? I imagine it'll come back again, and that we could try to interact with it."

"No, that's out of the question. SAIC may have a lot of power and access to many places, but they don't run the show at Groom Lake. You can't even spend the night there. Don't forget that we have all that footage, so we can go through it tomorrow at our leisure. I know that Jacques Vallée's team is interested in UFOs and that you're more interested in what happened inside his brain and his new ability, but – as everyone understands – the two are inevitably linked. I wonder how they will manage the priorities."

"Ok, let's stop talking about this. Come over here" says Susan, who had changed clothes during their conversation and was now wearing a really sexy little nightdress.

"You're kidding! I'm exhausted and you want to fool around!"

"Shut up, you clown. You know full well that we've been sleeping like soldiers for a week, now it's time for you to pay me some attention."

"OK, then, come over here, and show me how much you love me."

Chapter 28

September 7th 2010, SAIC, San Diego

Susan and Alex arrived at SAIC very tired, but happy to have had some time alone together again. As soon as they arrived at the place where the meeting was planned an unusual level of activity suggested that something important was going on. Checks had been strengthened, and there were more men in suits and ties than usual. When they finally entered the room Paul Smith and Jacques Vallée were already there, sitting at the end of the room as if they were going to give a press conference. They nodded at them and sat down in two free seats.

In ten minutes the room fills up and the doors closed twice. As usual, no windows, cell phones or visible telephone lines. There are not many people there, maybe fifteen at the most. Jacques starts with a summary of what happened the day before for those who were not present or in the picture about the project in general. He then explains who the key people are in the project, and who people need to report to in the future if new elements emerge.

Alex is mentioned, as is Susan, much to her surprise. Alex will be responsible for interpreting the measurements made in the Ark and by the photonic sensors, and Susan will be in charge of coordinating questions related to the sensorial experiments for the people who were within the range of the Ark.

Others are responsible for examining the other recordings while Jacques Vallée and Paul Smith will deal with everything that has to do with the abnormal apparitions. Susan realizes she has been given a good role, but does not really know why she has been chosen. The 'irradiated' soldiers are accommodated on site, on a specially prepared floor. Susan is allowed to visit and interrogate them without restriction.

Jacques then presents his view of the situation. Since Man has existed he has observed unexplained manifestations that are strange and often resemble flying forms that sometimes land, and humanoid forms may emerge from them. Between this kind of encounter – of the 'third kind' – and the other extreme, which could be a mere point of light, there is an enormous range of manifestations. Some are mortal while others are absurd, as when the humanoids resemble the local people and even speak their language, more or less. The flying forms, when they are described in detail, sometimes correspond to techniques used at the time of the apparition: flying chariots in ancient times, flying ships two hundred years ago, flying saucers sixty years ago and flying triangles twenty years ago. A French researcher by the name of Bertrand Méheust has also drawn a parallel between fictional stories and observations made several years later, as if something thought up at a particular moment in time would materialize some time later.

Jacques projects a list of things on the screen:
- Unexplained apparitions
- Technology related to the era
- Fiction prior to an apparition
- An infinity of forms and behaviors
- Frequently manifested absurdity
- Certain people are 'attractors'
- It is possible to 'believe' in these apparitions

He then traces a line that divides the screen in two. Above the column he just filled in he writes, not 'UFO' as everyone expected but 'Consciousness', and above the second column he writes 'Holy Spirit'. The silence in the room suddenly becomes heavier. These are two terms that SAIC employees are not used to seeing in their dossiers. People seem to wonder what is coming next, and it is easy to sense a slight unease on the part of those present.

"Yes, I know, you are wondering where I'm going. Most of you have come here to hear about an interception of flying saucers and, no doubt, alien technology, but we cannot keep the secret under wraps any longer. You who are here need to know that our future, thanks to the experiment of the Ark of the Covenant and – I must pay tribute to her – the discoveries of Susan Gomez, will never be the same again. We have great ambitions, and what we expect to discover and master could lead to the greatest turning point in the history of the human race. Given that Man almost discovered it more than 2,500 years ago, it was necessary to start again and rediscover things, and we are only at the tip of the iceberg.

"I need your help, all of you. I cannot guarantee that we will find anything, nor what we will find, but what I do know is that the little we have discovered makes it all worthwhile. Let me finish this second column first."

Jacques calmly adds the following lines:

-   Hunter-gatherer > Farmer-breeder
-   Apparition of the fear of the unknown and of totems
-   Sorcerers/shamans discover precognition/clairvoyance
-   Observation of the stars
-   Great leaders and the discovery of Knowledge
-   Epoch of megaliths
-   Apparition of the Mysteries and Astrology
-   The Antikythera mechanism
-   Emperors and policy-makers

- Apparition of the term 'Holy Spirit'
- Announcement of the Messiah
- Monotheistic religions and holy scriptures
- Age of Enlightenment: loss of Knowledge

"Let me explain. One year ago, this second column was not present in my study. We had no idea of the interaction between it and the first column. In front of you is a leaflet that summarizes the explanations in each category that appears in these lists. On the left, we have the characteristics of something that we have been trying to understand for decades, and on the right the history of Man's knowledge throughout history of a notion that I will call 'Holy Spirit' to make things easier. I was really blind to this, because I presided over the creation of the Stanford Research Institute team, precisely with the objective of implementing the capacity for precognition. How could we have ignored the relationship between the UFO phenomenon and the capacity of precognition? Well, it's quite simple, we were missing the most important pieces of the puzzle, and Susan's research has given them to us. However, there is still one element missing: why?

"Since life has existed on Earth an underlying will seems to make it evolve in very precise directions. The diversity of species and forms of plants and animals all seem to be organized and evolve better than if evolution were only based on chance or Darwinism. I think that this 'will', this intelligence that manages evolution, is also seen on the column on the left, through interaction with our consciousness.

"The column on the right shows how Man has been able, over thousands of years, to detect and master the ability of a person to connect up with this consciousness, and more particularly to capture information related to our immediate future. The two columns have something in common. They interface with a notion of consciousness, more precisely universal consciousness, even though I believe that our consciousness is also encapsulated in universal consciousness and not in our brains, as we have been led to believe."

One of the people in the room suddenly asks: "Excuse me, but could this will that governs the evolution of life be none other than an ability to read the future?"

"Yes, we have considered that option, and if it were so it would simplify our research considerably, but it does not explain the left-hand column at all. We could also have added, either in the left or the right column, the visions of inventors such as those of Nikola Tesla (P-13). This allows me to focus on our only explanation for the left-hand column, which is to lead us to foresee possible technological developments and, indirectly, inspire our scholars and other inventors. Take the case of Jean-Pierre Petit, who produces an enormous amount of scientific papers on the basis of observations or other supposedly alien manifestations (P-9)."

"That's exactly it, you said yourself that certain apparitions look like imagined images from science fiction in earlier years!"

"No, that's not possible, because if it were, seeing something that will appear years later doesn't explain how the thing will materialize. If, according to our research and Susan Gomez's, Man can read the future within a universal consciousness but he cannot, as far as we know, materialize things in our universe on his own."

"Nevertheless, you said yourself that in the left-hand column, on the last line, that it was possible to create these apparitions!"

"Yes, I grant you that, but it's a short cut. It is possible to make these things manifest themselves on demand, but not really to create them from scratch."

"What do you know about it?"

"Not much, to tell the truth, but to date we don't have proof that this is possible, and seeing as the induced phenomenon behaves exactly like the one observed by the entire population, we suppose that we are speaking of the same phenomenon. You are right, however; we shouldn't be so sure. Let's come back to the follow-up to the experiment and our research. We already have a medical report and the measurements taken on the affected people, myself included.

"The physiological parameters were not modified, neither during or afterwards. No measurable perturbation was recorded on site, despite the light effects. The video recordings show exactly what you saw for yourselves, and the recordings in other spectra do not show anything else. We didn't have enough time to include an action detector in our protocol. In any case, we now know that the particles captured and released by the Ark are not in the known domain, which is why we continue to believe that the axion particle (11) is the best candidate. For those of you who were not there, I will show you a film of the experiment and the way the light phenomenon approached."

Jacques stands back and leaves the screen clear. It shows a well-made montage of what happened in the X-37C, in the Great Pyramid and at Base 51. The light spheres are shown from a number of angles, and also with high enlargement and in slow-motion.

"As you can see, the light spheres that did us the honor of appearing on the sites seem to move like groups of animals, or as a family. They are not military formations, although the spheres were observed making maneuvers that are almost military. We see that they do not have different forms, regardless of the zoom factor. The spectral images show a rather banal composition, made up of chemical elements that can be found in the surrounding areas. The most distant cameras show that they disappeared into thin air, not gradually over the horizon.

"We can conclude that we have not made more progress on this level, except for the opening of the Ark and the appearance of the sphere at the same time. I would like to think that the link exists, and that what we induced with the light from Venus has to do with these spheres, but in what direction, and with what purpose? That is still a mystery."

Susan decides to speak up.

"Have you observed, either in your case or in the other soldiers, any signs of psychic powers or precognition?"

"Yes and no. Some have already contacted me, and I confess that I saw certain things, but it's difficult to explain. In general, our thoughts are different. Our ideas seem more original, and I wonder where they come from. We all use a notebook that Paul gave us, also consisting of pages divided into two columns. In the left-hand column we write down what comes to mind when we are not expecting something to happen, and on the right, the ideas that seem to be linked to our own reflections, to things that evidently emerge from our own intellect."

"Can I ask you to describe, in as much detail as possible, what characterizes the visions or perceptions that you write down in the left-hand column? I think it could be useful to find very specific discriminating factors, and perhaps deduce certain links to our bodies."

"Yes, that's a very good idea, I'll get the information and we'll keep you up to date. In any case, you are responsible for the protocols linked to sensorial observations. We'll organize it this afternoon. Any other questions?"

"Major Convens here. Can I ask if you are going to carry out any mind concentration sessions to recreate the phenomenon of the light spheres?"

"Yes, that's planned, but we need to think hard about it. In principle, it won't tell us anything new. Like the thousands of observations already made in the world and what we saw yesterday afternoon, we can never do more than observe. We would like to go beyond that."

"Could we try to capture one of them, or bring them down with missiles?" asks Major Convens.

"No," replies Jacques Vallée, lifting his hands. "We certainly don't want to do that. We start from the idea that the phenomenon is peaceful until otherwise proven. Nevertheless, we are open to any suggestions."

The meeting ends and another one is called for two days later. Susan will see Jacques this afternoon. The people disperse or continue to talk in small groups. Alex suggests to Susan that they go for lunch near the beach. It's a beautiful day and he needs to do something like that to wind down. He also wants to talk to Susan to ask her if she has any idea where all this is going to end.

They drive along the tram lines, and have to cross a kind of no-man's-land of partially abandoned buildings where people live in their cars or sleep on the sidewalks. It's not very pleasant, but that's America too. When they see the baseball stadium in the distance, at a crossroads indicating the start of the city, they see a cyclist lying on the ground, clearly unconscious. He is a black Rasta, like many other people in the neighborhood.

Alex slows down and sees that he is bleeding from the head. The front wheel of his bicycle is twisted. The poor guy, no doubt under the influence of drugs, probably didn't see the car arrive and the driver clearly disappeared fast. There are not many cars around, and this is not a very busy route at any time of day anyway. Alex parks the car on the sidewalk and walks back to see if he can help the man. He is half-way there when he hears a scream behind him. He turns round and his blood curdles: two men have grabbed Susan. One of them is in the front seat of the car and the other outside, probably to drag Susan out. Alex is confused by what he sees… what do these guys want? Steal the car, or their money? Their behavior doesn't seem to fit that. Just to be sure, he throws a glance at the black guy and realizes that he has stood up. "Shit!" thinks Alex … "this is something planned, and they will have a hard time getting out of this situation." He starts running towards the car, but to his great surprise the man on the sidewalk opens the back door and makes a sign to Alex to get in. Alex makes as if to speak, but the man behind the wheel suddenly points a gun at him and tells him to shut up. Alex backs off, more worried that something might happen to Susan, who looks terrified. The Rasta gets in the other side and the car turns round and heads for the hills.

"What do want from us? We're not rich. Take the car and leave us here," begs Alex.

"Take it easy, smart ass. We know who you are, and if you behave yourselves nothing will happen to you."

"But we don't have any money, I swear to you, and our families are not rich either. You must have made a mistake!"

"Oh, no, man! Your name is Alex Bergen and the girl who has just wet her pants is Susan Gomez," he says, with a strong local accent.

Alex wonders what is going on, not understanding anything. What could they want from them?

"If you're not smart, you'll soon be meeting your friend Rano," the driver laughs.

Alex's blood freezes, and his eyes meet Susan's, also as cold as a Siberian lake. Rano! The Chinese!

Alex is gutted to hear these words He hoped that was all over and that the doubts about Rano were just bad rumors, but here was the nightmare taking shape in front of him in the form of these three Afro-Americans. They must have been hired by the people who murdered Rano, who obviously forced him to 'squeal'.

The car continues and finally approaches a wood. They drive around for a while before taking a small track into it. The driver goes very slowly because the track is very bumpy. After a few hundred yards they see a small house. The shutters are down, but another car is visible at the back. They cannot read the license plate from where they are. The driver tells them to get out and go inside the house.

Once inside, they are taken to the living room. There are only two chairs and a small table. They are told to sit down. It is very dark. Their hands are tied to their backs, a door opens and some other men come into the room. They are blinded by a pocket flashlight, but as soon as one of them opens his mouth it is clear that they are dealing with the Chinese.

"Don't be afraid," he says, "we don't wish you any harm, but we need your help. If you cooperate, we will let you go and you can return home free."

"But we don't see how we can help you. My colleague is an archeologist and I work in the field of photonics!" says Alex, trying to gain a bit of time.

"Don't waste your breath, we know perfectly well what we want and we also know that you can help us to obtain it. We want to speak about the Ark of the Covenant, or did you not suspect that anyway?"

"We have no idea where it is, or even if it works."

"Oh, in that case it's very simple. We'll keep you hostage, and you will ask your colleagues to give it to us."

"They'll never do that. We're not one of them; we're simple researchers, I tell you. We're not worth anything to them."

"We'll see".

Right then, the men put hoods on their heads and take their personal belongings from them, including their cell phones.

Jacques Vallée is having lunch with Paul Smith and a few other senior SAIC people when a security guard comes in and whispers in his year. He is wanted in the security room for an urgent matter. He takes his leave and enters the security room with its walls full of screens. A security team and two men in civilian clothing are there, the last two dressed in the usual style of SAIC: crew cuts, ear clip-ons and dark glasses, and certainly not smiling. Jacques immediately realizes that there are serious reasons for interrupting his lunch. They explain that they have received a phone call warning that Jacques will not see Susan Gomez and Alex Bergen again unless they hand over the machine where and when they are told. The two civilians ask Jacques what 'machine' they are talking about, but he tells them that he cannot reveal that information at the moment. He tells them to act as if they were going to hand over the machine, making the excuse that it has to be brought from somewhere else and they will have to wait until the next day.

One of the men explains to Jacques that if it is a case of national security there is no way that high technology can be exchanged for the lives of simple researchers. Jacques, however, is already thinking of something else and only listens to them half-heartedly.

He tells them to do what he says and to keep him informed, but he hopes to contact them again very soon.

He returns to the senior management restaurant and asks Paul to follow him. Away from the others, he explains the situation. Jacques says that it is the ideal moment to test the effect of the Ark. He offers to volunteer and wants to try something before calling in any soldiers. He asks Paul to be his guide during the experiment, and Paul immediately realizes what Jacques wants to do.

"You want to see where the hostages are, right? At the time of Stargate we carried out similar missions, with more or less success. You're right, it's worth a try, it's now or never, but let's get going. We need to find an isolated room without too much noise around it. Theoretically, we just need a piece of paper and something to write with."

"OK, follow me" says Jacques, "I think the office they gave me will do the trick. You know, I'm really keen to see what comes out of this. I didn't expect to get ahead so quickly, I had prepared a kind of protocol in my head but we have an opportunity here, or rather an unfortunate event. How long do you take to identify a hostage cache by Controlled Remote Viewing?"

"It depends on the people and the missions. Usually several hours; sometimes even several days."

"That's not good enough. At the most, we have half a day, and even then I'm not sure they will accept the time I've asked for. I give us an hour, no more!"

"But that's crazy, you've never done this, and the last time was over thirty years ago. Let me have a go, I was very good at it in the Gulf War."

"No, either I'm going to do it or we give in to their demands. It's not a matter of putting their life in danger. If I remember well, your success rate was not total, and on more than one occasion you focused the search on the wrong places."

"Yeah, but at least we had some results," replies Paul. "I also remember that you didn't get great results at the time, and that's also why you left the team and its research pretty quickly."

"I know that, but the situation is different here. Either the experiment works or it doesn't. I don't want any half-measures. Don't forget, we're talking about less than twenty-four hours, I've hardly had time to get back and last night I was too exhausted to look at anything. Ah, here we are! Come on in and sit down. I'm going to lower the blinds to make it darker."

Jacques organizes his papers; he is anxious, realizing that he will soon find out if the project, which has already cost a fortune, will throw up some success.

Paul is sitting in a low armchair, while Jacques is at his desk looking at a blank piece of paper, mechanically turning a pencil between his fingers.

"OK, let's go, I'm ready," he says.

"Right, you have already drawn a vertical line to divide the sheet into two, that's fine. Relax, and stop turning that pencil. Breathe in deep twice and exhale slowly. Now, empty your mind, try to see the dark, only the darkness behind your eyelids, and be attentive to any thought or form that comes to you, like a shooting star crossing the night sky. It will disappear as soon as you see it, but that is precisely what you have to note down in the left-hand column. What you are going to do is intellectualize or construct your thoughts, identify it and write it down in the right-hand column to get it out of your head."

"Yeah, yeah, I know all that. Come on, let's begin!"

"OK, let's go. ..." Paul starts a camera to record their conversation and film Jacques' sheet of paper. "Three forty-eight p.m. September 7th 2010, San Diego, SAIC offices. Paul Smith as monitor and Jacques Vallée as the subject of CRV. The session aims to identify the place where Susan Gomez and Alex Bergen, kidnapped today at noon, are being held hostage."

"Stop, don't bother continuing ... It's amazing! Everything's coming to me at once. I'm battered with flashes!"

"Hey, come on, that can't be right... you were always lousy in your tests!"

"No, seriously, I'm not joking! As soon as I closed my eyes I could see dozens of images of Susan and Alex, like what they say happens to people on their deathbed as they see their life pass before them. There's no time to make any notes, it's all happening too fast, but I can remember almost everything."

"What did you see, then? Turn to the camera to catch this historic moment on film for posterity. It's clearly the effect of your exposure to the particles from the Ark yesterday."

"That's for sure. What's crazy is that I have had no doubts about anything since then. Deep down I thought that the experiment hadn't produced any results apart from those light spheres, but now, what I've just felt is exceptional. You'd just finished stating the aim of the session and I shut my eyes when I started to feel a flow of sensations. Everything was there, smells, feelings, images ..."

"Come on then, tell me everything, and don't forget that we have to free the hostages!"

"Yes, yes," says Jacques, turning towards the camera. "Look, I have just received a lot of information in my head about what happened to Susan and Alex. First I saw two people arguing inside a car, then the poorer neighborhoods of south-east San Diego, then a man, a black man, lying on the road next to a bicycle. Then I felt fear, heard some screams and knew it was Susan. Then I saw them in the same car, but with three men, all black. I immediately knew they were under the control of the attackers, and then I saw some trees and the car driving down a dirt road. They got out of the car and went inside a house. They are tied to chairs and two Asians are speaking to them. Then it all goes dark and the flow finishes."

"Incredible, I can't get over it. Did you see where the house was?"

"No, but let me shut my eyes again, I am going to ask myself where they are right now. Wow, this is unbelievable, as I speak to you I have an aerial view in my head, I can see the trees, the road, the house… wait, a bit farther on… yes, I can see a freeway, I know where it is, and in the distance there's a freeway junction …. Right, I'm sure I can show you where that house is on a map."

"Do you realize how much information you have just received? We have never got anywhere near that kind of amount, nor at such speed!"

"Hey, calm down, nobody's saying I'm right."

"True, I might be getting over-excited, but you know how to sort out the type of precognition information we are after, and I'm counting on you to get it right."

"Yes, you can count on me. I'm sure it's true. I am absolutely convinced that these images and sensations are from precognition. Let's see if they are accurate."

"Wait, what if we try and see if we will be successful in saving them?"

"What do you mean?"

"Well, seeing as this went so well, let's try and look into the future to see what's going to happen! Have you forgotten what Susan has contributed to the project, all those references about emperors in the past who used their power to check – in the future – that their decisions were good ones? And her references to the Holy Spirit quoted in the Old Testament?"

"OK, so what should I do?"

"Let me think for a minute … yeah, it should be simple. Ask yourself if, by going over there, we will come back with Susan and Alex, safe and sound of course."

"Right, just a moment, let me take a breath…. Wow, this is great, just great!"

"So, what can you see?"

"Everything, absolutely everything!"

"Come on, I can't wait to hear it!"

"Listen, it's difficult to explain. Since I said to myself that I wanted to know if we would come back with Susan and Alex I have seen them here with us, in this building. I felt that they had been saved. They were happy, and inside of me I felt that it was a scene that had not been played out yet, but I lived it, just as I'm looking at you now. Then I thought of their release, and I saw armed men dressed in black, no doubt a SWAT team or something like that, surrounding the house, then I saw them kicking down the doors and throwing flash bombs inside. It took place as if in a sketch, a bit like a trailer for a movie. What was strange was that certain areas in the scene were blurred."

"Did you hear anything? Voices, for example?"

"Yes, I heard the noise of the explosions, the doors crashing down, screams, but no words in particular. The colors were also different from those in the previous session. Hey, do you realize how efficient this thing is, this particle that penetrated me yesterday? Do you realize that if the ancients used the Ark more than two thousand years ago, they were able to see into the future just as I can right now. Those who were born at the right time in the cycle of Venus would have been particularly gifted. Indeed, the Ark was a way of not having to wait for that good moment from Venus."

"No, not really, because they had to wait for Venus to be in the right position to charge the Ark. No, the difference is that the Ark was able to give an adult this capacity for precognition, of premonition, whereas otherwise the change only works on a baby at the time of its birth."

"Yes, we need to measure all that. Anyway, let's call Security. I want to see if what is going to happen fits in with what I've just seen."

Paul stops recording and carefully slides the memory stick into his briefcase while Jacques contacts Security. Five minutes later they are in the control room on the first floor, talking to the head of the reaction force. They use Google Earth to locate the house, and what Jacques sees certainly corresponds to what he saw in the session. He can even provide other information to make a precise description of the layout of the house, the number of people inside, their weapons, and the rooms where the two hostages are being held. Using this information, which they trust in the light of where it comes from and the person who provides it, the reaction force gets on the road while the project team meets in a nearby room in the building. Jacques and Paul give them a summary of the last two hours.

It seems clear that the project is a success, but not yet in the sense that SAIC expected. Jacques suggests setting up two teams, one to study the gift of precognition and the other to try and better understand the phenomenon of the spheres. He proposes Paul to lead the first group and himself the second. With the help of the soldiers who were exposed to the radiation, Paul should first try to understand the extent of their new ability, and also in the past, the present and the future, and then discern the notion of existence, which seems more related to an abstract notion rather than a physical presence, followed by the phenomena of death, survival and telepathy. They will also try to see how far it is possible to receive more information – perhaps advice – or descriptions of inventions like those experienced by Nikola Tesla, and perhaps many others.

For his part, Jacques will also work with the exposed soldiers to create multiple protocols to try and make the light spheres or other objects appear, to see if it is possible to interact with them, and then see the extent to which – and how – they interface with the notion of precognition. It is an ambitious program, true, but in the light of the initial results, quite realistic and achievable.

Jacques looks at his watch; he is worried that there has been no news of the release of the hostages yet. He shuts his eyes for five seconds and tells everyone that the house is surrounded and that the assault will take place very soon.

Content with his 'live' demonstration, Jacques collects his papers and heads for the security room on the first floor, accompanied by Paul. Once there, the people are told what Jacques has just seen, and the follow-up is heard in real time by radio.

The operation will only last three minutes. The SWAT team is highly trained for this type of attack. Each one knows what he has to do and it only takes two minutes to capture a house, especially if the layout of the place is known in advance. Two helicopters with silent blades and engines had been detached and are very close by, ready to intercept any runaways if they try to escape.

The crooks have no chance to put up any resistance. Susan Gomez and Alex Bergen are taken to SAIC immediately, while the reaction force remains on site with the five crooks to check the place out and not overlook anything important. These people usually try to commit suicide to prevent any links being made to their bosses, and the slightest piece of evidence found on site could either betray them or induce them to speak. One hour later Susan and Alex arrive at the security post, happy to be safe but still shaken by what just happened. Jacques tells them everything, and feels a pinch of pride when he sees Susan's eyes moistening. She is finding it hard to believe what he is saying, but is also relieved to see that her theory had a firm – and now demonstrated – basis. It is as if the weight of a year of non-verified estimation was suddenly lifted from her shoulders. The emotion is too much for her; she breaks into tears. Alex holds her in his arms while the others turn away discreetly.

While Susan is getting over her emotions, news arrives about the kidnappers. They are clearly linked to the Chinese government. The three Afro-Americans are just hired henchmen told to watch over the comings and goings of Susan and Alex in order to prepare an ambush. They do not know anything about the other two men. They do not want to say anything, but the car found near the house had been rented by the Chinese embassy. The American government will call for their immediate expulsion and there is a good chance that this episode will cool relations with China even more.

They all want to concentrate on their research subjects and Susan, now back in the conversation, asks if she can join one of the teams, preferably Paul's, as she knows that he will head the work on the phenomenon of precognition or, as she calls it, universal consciousness. Jacques accepts quite happily, pointing out that she has improved their understanding of the phenomenon so much that they cannot refuse her request.

Obviously, clearance is no longer as important as it was. The value of the people involved seems to be the priority over inquiries into good conduct, and Susan will receive her clearance almost immediately.

Chapter 29

September 23rd 2010, the desert near Phoenix

Susan looks at the immensity of the desert that unfolds before her. The heat is brutal and the temperature is around sixty degrees out of the shade, but luckily they have tents and generators that pump out cool air. They have already been here four days in these tents that make up a small village.

The previous two weeks were productive, and the decision was made to transport Paul's team to this remote place away from eavesdroppers. For once, they did not have to report to the US government.

She turns a spoon in her cup of instant coffee. Behind her, Alex emerges from the tent, bare-chested and wearing shorts. Susan is wearing desert camouflage pants and a matching shirt, with high-top combat shoes adapted for the desert. They are very light and let the air through, while protecting their feet from the salt and sand as well as the heat. She may as well accept the situation; there is no point in worrying about her looks. Given the environment, she realizes that things have been organized in the best possible way to deal with the extreme conditions.

"Sleep well?" she asks Alex without turning round.

"Mm, not too bad. Apart from the view, we could be in a three-star hotel," he jokes.

"You ready for today?"

"Yep, why not? There's nothing to lose, and the results so far are pretty encouraging".

"Don't you think we're going too fast, that we're cutting corners?"

"No, not really. You know, in wartime people work miracles in terms of timescales, and aren't we in a similar situation here?"

"Don't exaggerate. I know we're being accommodated, fed and are working under conditions identical to those of soldiers at war, but the comparison ends there. There's no hurry and there are no enemies."

"You mean 'we don't have enemies any more'. You seem to have forgotten our Chinese 'friends' very quickly, people who didn't hesitate to kill your assistant and kidnap us!"

"Yes, but the expulsion of their fake diplomats has taught them a lesson this time. Anyway, please answer my question: don't you think this is all going too fast, that it could be too much for us?"

"No, not really. Jacques seems to have his head screwed on, and Paul too. Just look around. Do you see anything badly done? And what about our experiment protocols, aren't they good? Personally, I'm impressed by these people's professionalism, meticulousness and their innumerable procedures that lead to clear and successful decisions."

"Yes, I agree there. Just look at the results since the day we were kidnapped, the same day that Jacques demonstrated his psychic powers. An apparently infallible ability, easy to put into practice. With Paul and his team we've worked on different forms of precognition, made comparisons with telepathy, carried out tests to modify the future, and compared the results with the predictions. Do you remember when they stropped that secretary from driving home because they saw she was going to have an accident on the way? Clearly, the fact of seeing an event occur in the future does not mean that it will occur. It might happen if nothing unexpected takes place in the meantime. A mechanical part that breaks through wear and tear is not unusual, nor is the fact that another car might crash into you, even the likelihood of a horse winning races is not unforeseeable. Indeed, only a premonition allows you to do unexpected things, or actions that bring chance into play like a lottery or tossing a coin in the air. Everything else is the result of all the parameters present at moment t-1, and they are also the result of moment t-2 and so on. Obviously, the farther you go into the future, the greater the degree of uncertainty."

"Yes, all that's very logical, but haven't you made any progress in the analysis of the types of information?" asks Alex, going back into the tent to get dressed and, probably, to make himself a coffee. Susan waits for him to come back, but has picked up a pair of binoculars and is looking at the horizon.

"Yes, and that was also a very important and difficult thing to understand. When Jacques had those visions the day of our kidnapping he saw almost everything as if it was in a movie, but that's not always the case. In what happened to us he already knew something about the 'target', that is, us two, and it was easy for him to see everything that was around us, as well as identifying our location or finding us in time, either in the past or in the future. It gets more difficult when you don't know the target, a bit like a dog that has to follow a scent. If it has nothing to sniff at it's harder for it to know what to look for."

"What do you mean?"

"It's like those experiments where you have to guess what's on a photo inside an envelope. If the experiment is just done single blind, it's possible to connect with the consciousness of the person who put the photo in the envelope, provided that person is known to the one who has to guess the contents of the envelope. If it's done double blind, that is, nobody knows the contents of the envelope, it's more difficult to get the information. You have to project into the future, to the moment when you open the envelope, or connect with the consciousness of the photo inside the envelope, without having a direct view of the photo. In all these cases it's been demonstrated that you need to access the memory structure of the individual, the object or the memory of the future, and things don't happen in the same way. At that moment, the information is distributed through the association of ideas, shapes, colors, and very scattered elements appear in the head of the clairvoyant. And it's very difficult to put it all back together afterwards."

"You mean that it's easier to see a scene through people's eyes than through a photo?"

"No, but there's something of that .... If you know how to connect with a person you can see everything around that person, and better if you see what he or she sees. But if you have to connect with an object or a photo you get into a less rich zone of universal consciousness, or a less efficient one, and the information needs to be recreated as a kind of puzzle, linking the different elements related to the photo or object. It's like there's a hierarchy – the more memory we have, the better we can restore structured information."

"Are you saying that an object has memory?"

"Yes, just like a photo, but not so much. Our memory continuously filters the information it receives and only retains what's essential. This process of notation still contains different interpretations, but yes, it's exactly the case that everything is related to consciousness. Every living being, plant, pebble, object, molecule or atom is linked to this universal consciousness, in which they store what has marked their existence, so to speak. We've also confirmed this notion of function, which is also associated to a specific zone in universal consciousness. Let's take that case of the American embassy in Moscow. It's a building, and you can interrogate its memory by connecting with the memory of the molecules that made it up, but you can also connect with the memory of the embassy. If you use this type of connection, you only have access to the period of time when the building was an embassy. The same applies to living beings. Even though their soul survives after death and exists before they were born, if you want to link into that soul after a person's death you are trying something that is impossible. We still focus on the notion of soul, but that is not our priority. We've also made progress on a notion of 'access code'. Each entity maintains, in its memory, the access code of any other entity it has entered into contact with. That's why some people ask to be able to touch an object that has belonged to someone else in order to gain access to information about that person. Another thing we've discovered is that when we set out to look into the future, we can only obtain information about particular persons, not general events such as a war, unless that person has been directly affected by that war, perhaps due to the amputation of a limb or an early death. But … nothing in the vision will allow you to associate that to a war. We wonder about the practices of the ancients, because we know that emperors used their psychic powers to decide whether to wage war or start other great undertakings. No doubt they decided on the basis of their own future, knowing whether they would still be emperors in the future. It would not be possible to know the outcome of a future war, but they could make out the status of one of its commanders. But hey, tell me about yourself, you've also made great progress in the last two weeks."

"You said it! Jacques is on the verge of a nervous breakdown! Not a day goes by without him congratulating us all as if we'd found unexpected results, and then the next day an avalanche of results starts coming through. In our team, everything is unexpected. Don't forget that we have no precedents, not like your team with the entire Stargate legacy behind it."

"I know you tell me all this every evening, but our working days are long and I have a problem remembering everything. Tell me again what you plan to do today."

"Susan, can I get me a coffee and a sandwich first?"

"But first make love to me, and take your shirt off!"

Alex goes into the tent, mumbling something, and takes his shirt off. Susan follows him silently, and leaps on him with such strength that they fall onto their mattresses.

"Hey, come on, Susan, be serious. People are waiting for us and anyone can come by at any time."

"Chicken! First of all, it's not 8 a.m. yet, and you know very well that we start work at 8.30. What's more, we've been here four days now and nobody has come to our tent without letting us know before."

"Yeah, but once is enough!"

"So, we're not allowed to make love? Come on, you big softy. Relax! Look, seeing as you've thrown your shirt away, I'm going to massage your back while you explain your program to me."

"OK, OK, you're right. I get tense and I almost forget to breathe. Mm… that feels good, I'm feeling better already. What were you asking me about? Ah yes, our program… Today's going to be a great day."

"Go on…"

"You know that we've carried out a number of experiments here in the desert over the last two weeks. If you joined me this week it's because things have gotten really interesting and I wanted you to be involved. We started with concentration sessions together, like the OUR-J team did ten years ago in Japan, with great success. The results have exceeded our wildest dreams. We were able to reproduce what had happened since the first day of exposure, but this time through our own will. I showed you the films shot at the time, both during the day and at night. We counted up to eighty spheres at the same time, and also fusions, fragmentations and other shapes, plus other amorphous objects that change their appearance constantly or emit red or green light, other metallic objects and also – believe it or not – objects shaped like flying saucers. It's clear that this 'armada' is linked to the same phenomenon, but we have not yet understood why it takes on a certain shape one day and a different one the next, nor what affects their number and behavior.

Today we've planned something else. For the first time we're concentrating on interaction with these objects. We've asked them something very specific, which will prove – if they do it –that we can interact with them."

"So what have you decided?"

"We've asked them to land and allow us to approach them."

"Wow … but isn't it dangerous to get too close to them?"

"Listen, honey, if you find me in your bed tonight it's not dangerous …. No, seriously, the guys who will approach them will be soldiers packed with sensors and video cameras. So far the videos have not shown us anything specific, the objects remain blurred, inconsistent and there's no way of seeing their mode of propulsion."

"Can I be there?"

"No, you'll have to stay here and observe what happens on the screens. I'll be there, about half a mile from here."

"What time is the experiment planned for?"

"11 a.m."

"If I understand it right, the soldiers who were exposed to the particles stored in the Ark will concentrate hard so that the objects will come to them at a particular time and place?"

"Yes, just as the OUR-J group did, and also Pierre Vieroudy. They had to concentrate their minds for much longer, almost a month, before they saw any effects. Here, we saw that just one concentration session was enough. In England, Anthony Woods also achieved results quickly, but he wasn't aware of it. The thing was always out of his control, because he is always in a state of great excitement."

"Well, that's really strange, and something else we'll have to study later on."

"Right now, our 'guinea pigs' are focusing on an encounter of the third kind, so to speak. If the objects do land, those who were exposed before will approach first. They'll carry special cameras and other instruments like gravity meters and magnetometers. Then Jacques will come along to see if the objects react differently."

Susan has stopped rubbing Alex's back and has put her arms around his waist, squeezing up against his back and enjoying the pleasure of feeling his skin against hers. Alex looks at his watch and says it's time to join the others. They finish getting dressed and reach the command tent. The guinea pigs are already there, together with Jacques and Paul, who had been there since Monday. Behind them is the usual battery of screens, which other members of the team are busy adjusting.

They can feel the tension rise. The screens are not showing anything except the blue sky and the whiteness of the dry lake.

They learned a long time ago that periods of concentration can easily be desynchronized from the moment planned for the apparition. The guinea pigs and Jacques do not, therefore, have to do any exercise of this kind for the time being.

Time passes, and everyone keeps busy as they wait for the time of the rendezvous.

At 2.45 p.m. two trucks carry the personnel for the assignment to a place just over half a mile away. The scene is a little surrealistic, just a little more and you would think you were on Mars.

At last, everyone is in place. The soldiers are wired up like astronauts, bristling with antennae, sensors and cameras. Jacques prefers to concentrate on his physiological sensations and is wearing a simple khaki suit, a helmet and polarized sunglasses.

At 11 a.m. sharp, one of the soldiers points towards the North. The whole group looks in that direction and sees a flotilla of spheres arriving. They seem to slide on a cushion of air in silence. The curves they trace as they approach are perfect and it seems clear that they are trying to transmit a message of beauty.

At a distance of fifty yards they start to descend and come to a stop just five yards from the group, floating about four and a half feet off the ground. One of the spheres breaks away from the group and approaches them in a sort of undulating movement. It also starts pulsating slightly.

It winds its way through the group of men and moves towards Jacques, coming to a halt one yard in front of him. Even at this distance, it is impossible to perceive the slightest detail on the object; it is as if it was only made of light. From the side, the object becomes opaque after half an inch of a blurred zone, looking a bit like fog.

Jacques tries to open his mind and empty his spirit to try and perceive some kind of telepathy, but nothing happens and the only thing he perceives is whiteness and silence. He extends his arm and opens his hand, the palm facing upward, in the direction of the object. The sphere moves and settles into Jacques' palm. He feels no weight, no sensation of hot or cold, no electricity, just a sort of swelling in his hand. Seeing the sphere so close, he tries to see if there is a mechanism, but it is impossible to distinguish anything. Nevertheless, he detects some current-like movements within the luminosity of the particles, a bit like long waves at sea. Jacques really feels that the object is alive. He feels empathy with it, a sensation that is difficult and even annoying to try to explain, like a love for something he does not know. However, in a fraction of a second it disappears to give way to another object which, after Jacques got over the shock, is an Ankh (E-11), the one all the pharaohs held in their hands and that Thot presented to Seti in a rather unconventional manner on an engraving, leaving a hint of a still unknown function of this utensil. Another engraving shows it at the top of a column of Djed, another object of Ancient Egypt that is still the subject of great controversy. For the moment, the object in Jacques' hand is inert, black, and measures around eight inches. Jacques lifts his eyes from the object and looks behind the soldiers; the other spheres have ascended and are leaving towards the north.

"This is incredible," says Jacques into his microphone for the people in the control tent. "Did you see what happened? We received an object, one that looks like an Ankh!"

Jacques turns the object over and over, his eyes wide open, with the soldiers forming a circle around him.

Sure that the spheres have disappeared completely, the group gets back in the trucks and returns to the main camp. Jacques holds the cross like a fragile baby. The others are dying to see it and watch the trucks get bigger as they approach.

Jacques gets out and goes inside the control tent. He clears a table and puts the cross on it. Paul approaches first, but the table is soon surrounded by everyone present. Alex and Susan also crane their necks to have a look at the object. Jacques explains that it is the first real artifact that is not alien but has come from a world unknown to men.

Cameras are placed around the table while Jacques tries to understand why he received this kind of present, because it is a present in the very best sense of the word. Paul asks him to concentrate on the future, and to see how he will handle the object. Jacques stops, closes his eyes for a few seconds, and everyone soon sees a smile forming on his lips.

"My friends, I think we are going to have some fun!"

"What did you see, tell us," says Paul impatiently.

"I understand what this object is for. If it works, I can tell you we have an incredible discovery here, yet something ridiculously simple and close to us.

"I'll talk more about the object later. First of all, I want to check out what I understand, and anyway there are too many people here for me to speak openly about it. Well, with the naked eye I can't make out any opening or hidden roughness, no screws, no buttons, nothing. The object is completely smooth and it doesn't look like it can be opened. I suggest we break camp and return to San Diego. We need to take stock and make some decisions. Everyone back home, then, and see you tomorrow!"

Chapter 30

September 24ᵗʰ 2010, the desert near Phoenix

It is six a.m., and Susan has not slept well all night. Alex kept moving and it was very cold, despite the thick Army sleeping bag. She has dreamed a lot, mostly about flying. She saw herself overflying Base 51 and seeing futuristic forms of aircraft on the tarmac, while flying saucers danced a kind of aerial ballet in the sky. Susan joined them and played as you play with a cat or a dog. Like the day before, she wakes before Alex and goes outside to look at the sky. Although realizing the importance of what she is experiencing, she still feels a twinge of annoyance when she thinks about the minor role she is playing at the moment. It is different for Alex; he is always busy around the cameras and recorders, deciding whether to use such and such a filter or to change a certain setting. So far, however, nothing outstanding has emerged from these recordings. It was as if it had to do with different physics. The optical phenomena have been clearly seen and recorded, but do not contribute anything that they cannot see with their own eyes.

Susan wonders if other planets apart from Venus, and also the zodiac zones, also exercise some influence on the brain, and no doubt the microtubules. She knows that the ancients took the position of Venus into account to plan their offspring, but then they also took a whole load of other things into account, but she cannot grasp this at the moment. It seems clear to her that the ability to read within universal consciousness, or the gift of the Holy Spirit, was the first thing to be researched, but in that case what were the other planets and constellations useful for? For her, the other stars must have been less important, even if they did have an influence on the character of a newborn child in one way or another, for example in the form of a combative spirit or intelligence. She was sure that there was an influence, probably beyond what Gauquelin had detected, and some people were surely capable of studying the characteristics of the light from the planets and constellations of the zodiac. Gauquelin had not, however, observed the influence of the constellations. That is strange and annoying, she thought, because it had been demonstrated that Orion emitted light with some of the characteristics of the rays from Venus. There were some good subjects for study in the next few years, she thought, but not for her, preferring to concentrate on the notion of precognition. What a beautiful mystery, surely related to the realm of the divine and the reason behind the universe. Most of the myths of antiquity have one goddess of love and another of war linked to the planet Venus; Inanna for the Sumerians, Ishtar for the Assyrians and the Babylonians, Ashtoreth for the Canaanites, Anat for the Ugarits, Seshat for the Egyptians, Artemis (or Aphrodite) for the Greeks, Tanit for the Phoenicians and Venus for the Romans. She is often represented with a child on her knees, as was the Virgin Mary later on. Not only that, apart from the ancient Incas and Mayans, who also worshipped Venus and attached a high value to the planet in astronomic calculations and astrological decisions, there is hardly any trace of Venus elsewhere in the world. It is almost as if a people in the Mediterranean zone of influence and a Nordic one, for example the Celts, had discovered the exact influence of the planet in order to make a kind of accurate astronomical monitoring to take decisions that were later called 'astrological predictions'. The existence of this same principle in Central and South America could lead one to think about the existence of ancient cultural contacts. Coming back to Egypt, specifically to the zodiac (1.2) found in the temple of Denderah, the Seshat is represented alongside beings that personify awakening, consciousness and enlightenment, and in a zone of the zodiac dedicated to wisdom; the other zones are linked to instinct, rigor, rationality, fairness and culture. Could all these be character traits linked to the stars themselves? Regarding this temple, there is a papyrus called the 'Westcar papyrus' that tells how King Cheops (2650 B.C.) destroyed a very ancient temple on that spot before the Flood. The temple was famous because it contained the books of Thot, which describe the science and techniques of that era. It is interesting to note that the person who knew where these books were was called Djed, as in the Pillars of Djed. At the time the place was called the Inventory of Heliopolis, a building that was probably a center for astronomy and astrology. These sciences and techniques that King Cheops wanted to learn about were, therefore, more than likely linked to the stars and astrology.

Susan is not really sure where she is at, everything has happened so quickly. Her life is now linked to Alex's, and they seem to get on well. Since she met him their infrequent arguments have always been about dumb things, never anything serious, and she really likes his nature. She also loves his body, feeling good as soon as she approaches him, when she touches his skin. She had never felt like this with a man before. Sure, they had only been together a short time, but they had already experienced such incredible things, been 'promiscuous' in space and in the desert and they had also lived together for quite a few months, which is always a good test of a relationship. No, she loves him and does not want to lose him. She will have to adapt her life plans to his, without giving too much ground because she also has her own ambitions. Until otherwise demonstrated, she believes that her work is more interesting than his adjustments of photons! Except her archeological missions, she can also allow herself the luxury of working anywhere, while Alex must always be near his machines. Well, it is true that these archeological missions will not be easy to cope with; they usually involve long stays abroad, and Susan is not too keen on that as far as her relationship with Alex is concerned. She tells herself that after all these discoveries her future might not lie among old stones so much. She would be happy to work for SAIC with Alex on machines that modify the powers of the brain, although she knows that it is not always a good idea to work with your partner; few couples manage to survive the experience.

On that thought Susan decides to go back inside the tent and shake Alex. She wonders how he manages to get up on his own to go to work. That is a question that all early risers ask themselves; miraculously, the people who get up late do not arrive for work later than the others. What sort of justice is that?

"Alex, wake up! I'm hungry and I want to have breakfast with you."

"Jeez, do you have to shout right in my ears just to tell me that!?"

"Come on, stop acting like a child and get dressed. It's beautiful outside. By the way, did you sleep well? I didn't!"

"Oh, so sorry, honey. I slept like a log all night."

"But you didn't stop moving. Anyway, are you ready for today? We're leaving this morning when everyone is ready. Do you still need your equipment for all these experiments? I get the impression that they don't capture anything."

"Give it a break … It's true we haven't captured anything significant, but we're getting a new machine this morning, if it didn't already arrive yesterday evening, that can measure gravitational fields. It comes from the Ukraine, and is completely new. A guy called Volodymyr or something has fine-tuned it and we want to test it on these objects. Perhaps we'll finally understand what they're made of or how they move. We're more or less sure that they're made up of molecules found in the immediate environment, but we don't know how they move or how they change shape. This obviously requires a certain effort, since their default appearance is a light sphere, something plasma-like."

"Yes, but since we're going to break camp this morning, you won't be able to use it now. In any case, you should get up and get dressed. One or two pieces of toast?"

"Two, please."

"Tell me, what do you expect from all these measuring instruments you carry with you everywhere you go?"

"Well, SAIC hopes to discover all kinds of new technologies such as stealth, invisibility, anti-gravity and who knows what else; basically, all the technologies used by flying saucers. Even if we don't capture one, many people think that by studying them we'll learn how they work through inverse logic. Some people believe that these technologies can't carry heavy loads or escape from the pull of Earth's gravity, so they're not very useful for non-military applications."

"These experiments that Jacques has been carrying out for weeks, do they go in that direction?"

"No, not at the moment, but given the strangeness of events we won't stop placing our equipment and trying to get valuable information."

"Anyway, we're getting out of this desert today, and I won't be the last to complain."

"Hey, honey, come in the tent and put that toast down. There are more important things to do right now ..."

ALAIN HUBRECHT

Chapter 31

October 4th 2010, SAIC headquarters, McLean

Susan and Alex are driving along SAIC Drive in McLean, a street lined with buildings that all belong to SAIC. They are big with reflecting windows, with no rough bits or embellishments. They park the car and head for the reception area. They receive the usual identity checks and later, once at the meeting room, more and stricter clearance checks. Jacques has invited the cream of SAIC and they can feel proud to be part of 'his team'.

The room is not big, but from the heads of the other people present, with haircuts very different from those usually found in the company, they understand that the attendees are not just SAIC people. Out of modesty, they sit at the back, even if there are only three rows of seats.

Jacques, as usual, starts off:

"Good morning, everybody! Thanks for coming here today. I know you are all very busy but I felt it was necessary to get you together and bring you up to date on the results of our work. As well as the people heading the research – me, Paul Smith, Alex Bergen and Susan Gomez – I would like to welcome the members of the Jason project. Until today we haven't brought you in on our research, but our progress in the last few days means that we need to do so now. We have been out in the desert near Phoenix for the last three weeks, while Paul Smith stayed behind in San Diego. We tested the results of our exposure to the particles of the Ark on UFOs while grading the performance achieved in the field of precognition. You will find the tables in the documentation we sent you. You will see that the document and everything that is said about it is classified COSMIC TOP SECRET ECE, and I would stress that point. What we are working on no longer has anything to do with improved technology but with an authentic revolution in our understanding of our history, the world of knowledge and human development."

Jacques summarizes the events of the last few weeks and shows some films, for example the loading of the particles from the Ark in the Great Pyramid, the release of the particles over Base 51, and the reception of the cross of Ankh. The people present remain silent during Jacques' presentation, but a mad rush of questions breaks out in the coffee break and Jacques has difficulty calming the people down. He finally shuts them up by explaining that what he has said is nothing in comparison with what comes next. Everyone wants the break to be short so they can listen to his explanations.

"Now that you have the facts, I'm going to tell you about what we discovered last week. We carried out some precognition sessions based on this object that we received from the spheres, and what emerges is nothing less than dynamite. Some of you will have heard of the Book of Enoch, an apocryphal text quoted in the Old Testament. One of the oldest references to the Book of Enoch is found in two fragments collected by Alexander Polyhistor around the first century BC. According to him, Enoch was the father of astrology, and he learned everything from angels. Reading between the lines of the first chapter of the book, called 'The Fall of the Angels', we deduce that these 'angels' were astronauts that arrived on Earth thousands of years ago, maybe following a mutiny against the commander of their spacecraft. In order to end the mutiny, the commander decided to leave them on the first habitable planet he found. These astronauts have also been called 'watchmen', and each one would have taught men their specialty. Among these 200 watchmen was Barakiel (aka Rakiel), who was responsible for matters of astrology. We don't know when this arrival of alien travelers on Earth took place. Some signs indicate that they were contemporaries of Noah, but as the book is a collage of different stories, like the Bible, the story is not closely related to the episode of Noah.

"Some Egyptologists think that these watchmen were the first pharaohs, and their deductions date them at over 20,000 years ago, and that they lived for 1,000 years.

"After reigning for just over 10,000 years, they could only reproduce by mixing with ordinary mortals, and their descendants would only have lived for 300 years, although they still managed to reign for around another 10,000 years. Anyway, their blood was no longer present in the last pharaohs, whose life span was 'only' that of normal human beings. We contacted one of the Egyptologists who challenges the official theories, and he strongly advised us to visit the Serapeum (E-12) to learn more about this vision of history.

"We are going to send a team over there in the next few weeks. In relation to this, Peter Tompkins (P-14), who worked in NSA, researched some strange monuments built in Ireland 1,000 years ago. There are around one hundred of them, and they defy history and science because nobody can say what they were used for, a bit like the nuraghi in Sardinia. Peter believes that we should focus on an explanation linked to precognition. We will also go over there and see what they are all about.

"Well, without guessing the results of this future research, we think that they will be linked to the origin of our spheres. In other words, those 'astronauts' who came down to Earth thousands of years ago subsisted outside their 'carnal envelope', and in their capacity as 'watchmen' they continue to watch over the human race. They cannot have any lasting physical existence but can materialize themselves, or rather gather molecules together, for a short time and take on the appearance they want. As a rule, they do it as easily as we might decide to take a walk, without any particular aim, and some of them have their 'favorite' human beings while others keep a close watch on our warlike impulses. In the Cold War, for example, they learned of our progress with nuclear missiles and showed us, from time to time, that they disapproved by systematically defusing our nuclear warheads. These beings have nothing to do with 'God', or what we call 'God', but they come from a civilization that is rather more advanced than ours. They have taught us how to get closer to 'God' by communicating more easily with universal consciousness, and therefore how to read the future.

"They are the ones who built the mysterious mechanism inside the Great Pyramid, to compensate for the loss of the capacity for precognition of their descendants, already mixed in with the human race. That is where the original Ark of the Covenant comes from, together with the strange stories linked to its later use by the men who stole it from the pyramid.

"The cross of Ankh is something completely different. I can tell you that its form is purely practical; you can hold it by its handle or you can add a mirror or a glass to decorate it. This object was used by each astronaut to improve their memory and pass knowledge on to their descendants or substitutes. Rather than writing everything down in books, they handed over the object as a simple way of connecting to their space of consciousness, the one that would remain in universal consciousness after their death. It's a kind of code, if you like. It could have been anything, like what people give to a sniffer dog or, more precisely, what they give to a medium to get information on the person a particular object belonged to.

"For some unknown reason, their DNA was very similar to ours. It degraded more slowly than ours, but that was thanks to the technology developed by their civilization, of which there are still traces in the Serapeum that we will get to visit one day.

"The cross of Ankh we received is a perfect example of the accumulation of molecules in a purposeful form, abandoned in our physical world at their will. Their soul, if I can call it that, is not linked to the molecules they used to materialize themselves, but here it has 'stuck' its mark on the object and I can connect to the consciousness of its previous owner, or more exactly, to the soul that has passed it on to me.

"In most cases, these ancient 'souls of astronauts' deconstruct themselves when their mission or 'stroll' is over, but they can also abandon it, as no doubt happened at Roswell and other flying saucer crash sites. This is also the case when we see these things lose matter, like molten metal; it happens when they get distracted. In principle, when they dematerialize they do so away from human eyes, but the dissolution of the molecules happens so quickly that we see the object disappear on the spot, almost instantly.

"I have learnt from them that they used material present in the desert where we were to construct this cross of Ankh. When I had the sphere in my hand, the cross was not inside it any more, it had not been materialized; what I saw was a kind of soup of mixed molecules that looked like plasma. At the speed of thought, the being that controlled it was able to assemble these molecules in the form that we received.

"As you see, we have received information but not really technology. I think they are frustrated that humanity has not evolved too much during their time here. They have helped Man to build wonderful monuments, create machines and improve civilization, but when they no longer had descendants to control everything Man failed to maintain this knowledge and has either destroyed or forgotten everything.

"Today, with what we have received, i.e., a way of connecting with their knowledge through this cross of Ankh, we can do a lot of good for the human race, but we need to think hard about why we failed over 2,000 years ago.

"If this knowledge and technology we have developed falls into the wrong hands, those people could do unbelievable harm to their enemies or even to the entire human race. We could decide to make this technology public, but that would give enormous power to anyone with dishonest intentions. We are not prepared for that; indeed, far from it.

"We don't think this could be done before the creation of a world government, and the end of the notions of religion and country. This technology can shelter us from any problem in the future. We would have no more worries about energy or food, and pollution would be reduced enormously.

"As I speak, I don't know if we can master forms of thought, but if we succeed that would go a long way to solving our concerns about natural resources.

"Well, as you see, we could have a rosy future if we all manage to agree on things.

"Ladies and gentlemen, I propose that we all come back in two months, when a working group will be set up to think about the issue. In the meantime, we are going to send a team to Egypt to see what the Serapeum can teach us."

Jacques ends his presentation with these words. As usual, he has been efficient, clear and concise. Many of those present would have liked to hear more, but Jacques' time is always tight.

"Do you realize?" Susan says to Alex, "He gives us this information as if we already knew about it. Did you know about the Book of Enoch?"

"I think he has done really well. The subjects he deals with deserve a whole day of explanation, at least. I imagine that's the way they communicate at this level. In any case, I heard his references to two forthcoming archeological expeditions and I have a strong hunch that a certain Susan Gomez will be involved."

"Do you think so?"

"Well, unless I hear anything to the contrary it seems clear to me that you are the best person to study the relationship between an ancient construction and questions of precognition or birth."

ALAIN HUBRECHT

Chapter 32

November 9ᵗʰ 2010, Sakkara, Egypt

Susan observes the step pyramid of Sakkara. Lost in the middle of the desert, it is a witness to the history of the pyramids. The Egyptians built several pyramids along almost forty miles of the Nile, all of them linked to the river by a dual hydraulic system, one part of it on the surface and the other underground. This underground channel was a kind of reservoir, the size of a football field. There are no explanations as to how and why this enormous system worked. The Nile was also lined with quays along that entire distance, so a very good reason was needed to build this Herculean system.

Many of the pyramids have either collapsed or even disappeared, and their stones were used to build houses locally when the function of the pyramids had been forgotten.

The pyramid of Sakkara cannot be visited because the interior has collapsed, making it a very dangerous place to enter.

The construction is representative of an era when people built in layers, the result being a series of steps or terraces. There were other forms, such as a diamond or dual angle of inclination, although classical Egyptologists maintain that the techniques for building pyramids goes from the simplest to the most sophisticated, the best example of the latter being the Pyramid of Cheops.

The less classical Egyptologists – those who challenge the dates of the pharaohs – believe that the technique of building the pyramids is the opposite. They would have started with the biggest stones – those of extreme precision – and the interior mechanism is even more incomprehensible to our best scientists. Later, when the knowledge was lost, the pharaohs that came after tried to continue this work, at least partially, using the system put in place by their predecessors.

There is, however, something else at Sakkara, something just as mysterious as what lies inside the Great Pyramid.

Auguste Mariette wrote in 1857: "…this pyramid is not like the others. It does not exactly face north like the others, and does not have an entrance on the north face like them. Instead, it has four entrances, followed by passages inside, horizontal corridors, and stairs. Inside, there are rooms, cellars and underground chambers that make the whole thing look like a maze. There is a chamber twenty-five feet long and forty-five feet high – the only one of its type – on its axis, and, as a central point where all routes that lead to different floors meet, there is an enormous block of granite in its paving, cut exactly in the form of a cork, which can move and provide a passage at will to descend to a lower level whose endpoint is difficult to establish because the cellar is too small to have ever contained a sarcophagus. This pyramid is, therefore, only a pyramid thanks to its exterior shape… the more I visited it, the less I understood it."

Well, there is yet another highly mysterious structure here. In his book Mariette explains a very important element of Egyptology: that most of the monuments were recovered in different epochs by other pharaohs and other religions, often with additions or modifications made to them. Egyptologists do no insist on these different evolutions, or at least do not try too hard to clarify the question of the original function or the date the first stone was laid.

Sarcophagi or hieroglyphics have been found in some pyramids, but they were probably put there or engraved several thousand years after they were built, and were probably abandoned soon after.

Susan is not there out of interest in the pyramid, however. Turning round, she looks at the desert that stretches out before her. Farther down, at the base of a dune, is a kind of fault in the ground. A ramp goes down into it for about ten yards ... the entrance to the Serapeum!

Farther to the left, while they wait for the attendant to open the door for them, is her team of archeologists and scientists from SAIC. They have been waiting for an hour and he still has not arrived. Finally, a cloud of dust in the distance announces the arrival of a jeep with the attendant at the wheel.

Susan nevertheless welcomes him with a big smile. Getting access to the Serapeum is not easy, but receiving permission to take a team of scientists there was a different ball game, although that was child's play compared with removing the boards that block the access to the maze of corridors that had never been opened to the public, not even to Egyptologists.

The group descends the long ramp into the ground and enters a small corridor which, after a few twists and turns, ends up in a big long gallery like a subway tunnel. On each side of the galley are niches where the ground is a few feet lower. Each niche contains an enormous granite sarcophagus fifteen feet long, eight feet wide and ten feet high. Each one is covered by a thirty-one-inch-thick granite lid. The weight of each sarcophagus was calculated at fifty-four tons and the lid around thirteen and a half tons.

There is no inscription on the granite, neither on the outside or the inside. The sarcophagus is a single piece, dug with incredible precision to more than one thousandth of a millimeter. The insides are perfectly flat and perpendicular. It is not possible to pass a cigarette paper between the lid and the sarcophagus. No stonemason would be able to carve an object like that nowadays, and that is without bringing it here underground from a distant quarry.

There are twenty-four of these sarcophagi in the Serapeum. Egyptologists claim that they were designed to contain the coffins of buffalos in honor of the god Apis, but why did they oversize the inside, especially knowing the effort required to carve these 'boxes' with such precision? Particularly considering that other parts of the Serapeum, built in other eras, contain simple wooden sarcophagi and skeletons of buffalos that are very small in size.

According to Jacques Vallée, these containers were used by the astronaut pharaohs to 'recharge their batteries'. They hated being on Earth, something that also tended to reduce their lifespan, as well as their capacity for precognition. The Ankh and the Ark of the Covenant helped them to retain the latter, while these chests allowed them to renew themselves.

Susan is here with her team to try to understand if this theory will justify their stay, and if it does, what elements could be found here that are related to it?

She observes the work of men thousands of years ago with respect and admiration. The gigantic corridor, lined with rooms containing these giant chests, all so extraordinarily well made.

The team prepares the analysis, measuring and sampling equipment. In the meantime, she follows the attendant as he goes in front of her and opens the bulkheads that have obstructed these corridors for years. She discovers other corridors, equally big as the one she has just left, and other rooms with chests.

Strangely, no sarcophagus or skeleton has ever been found in one of these chests. Each chamber has grooves on each side at the height of the lids, which – turning through ninety degrees at the height of the lids – would have collided with the edges of the rooms. This shows that the lids were often handled; otherwise they would have been moved by simply sliding them on the axis of the chest, from the corridor. It is easier, however, to turn the thirteen-plus-ton lid on its own axis rather than sliding it forwards, in which case it would have fallen off the end.

Everyone knows that a tomb is only used once, so why did they design these rooms to enable the chests to be opened at will? And why design the chests with such extreme precision?

When Auguste Mariette explored the site almost 200 years ago he knocked on some walls and found that they were hollow in many places. Each time he dug through the hollow walls he discovered more rooms. Some of them contained sarcophagi with buffalos, but other strange things were also found. Sometimes there was just a skull, sometimes bones broken into small pieces mixed with bitumen, sometimes the sarcophagi were bottomless and had strange dimensions. Other rooms did not contain any sarcophagi, and left Mariette perplexed by the step pyramid.

Susan wonders how many secret rooms like this are still hidden in Egypt, and how many technologies and religions followed each other over the centuries in the same places and inside the same structures. This makes her think of Europe: early pagan sites were chosen to build churches, and sometimes even cathedrals.

Time can erases the testimony of the past very efficiently, but nothing compared to Man, who has destroyed or burned megaliths, sculptures and books by the thousands to willingly make the traces of other civilizations or religions disappear.

Few people believe that exactly the same thing happened in Egypt, i.e., that a pharaoh would order the destruction of the statues of his predecessor, change temples, or replace hieroglyphics.

It is clear that the Serapeum was used by different religions, or for a variety of activities, and it is very difficult to find out the original purpose of the place.

Fortunately, there is an element that the other occupants would have trouble removing: these fifty-five-ton chests, made from the hardest granite. Only one of them has hieroglyphics on it, but their poor quality clearly demonstrates that they were added to the chest thousands of years after it was made, as is the case in many other constructions.

Susan moves along one of the corridors opened by the attendant, using her powerful flashlight to light up the tiniest corners of this mysterious place. She visits a corridor containing twenty-eight mummies of oxen, but this section is clearly not from the same period as the one where the gigantic chests are located. The workmanship is not so good here; the carvings and the degree of precision are not to the standard that interests her. Statues and inscriptions found here and outside showed that Apis was worshipped for a long time and that this custom was picked up by the Greeks, who even continued to use the Serapeum. She decides to leave this area and goes back along the main underground passage.

She had read about this place before flying to Egypt, and the least one can say is that its history is not exactly simple. Going back to the time when the Serapeum was still in use, just before it was buried by the sand, the building was used as a sanatorium. The patients came to these underground galleries to get away from the heat of the sun and the dryness of the air. There were artisans, bakers and a vegetable market outside it. A number of small temples had been built by the Greeks, such as the temple of Astarte, goddess of Venus, where people 'voluntarily' got sick in order to find wisdom, like hermits in other places in the world. They were called 'recluses'. To earn a living, they interpreted the dreams of visitors, speaking to them through a small window that gave onto the exterior. Archeologists initially thought that these recesses were prison cells. An important fact is that half of the papyruses discovered in Egypt come from the Serapeum, although the documents are not old enough to shed light on the origins of the building. One of the best-known recluses of the Serapeum was Ptolemy, and he stayed inside a cell for over ten years.

Apparently, the recluses earned enough money to send some home to their families.

We also know that the Serapeum was inhabited by soothsayers. One of the greatest historians of Antiquity, Manethon, explains that, for the pagan cenobites of that era the configuration of stars in the sky at the birth of certain babies gave them the ability to see into the future, or to be 'inspired', and that it was quite common for them to later go into the temples to have dreams or decipher those of visitors.

The Serapeum was, therefore, a kind of 'dream factory'. The site was also used to worship Apis, the bull god, the symbol of life. On his death, he was called Osiris-Apis, and later Serapis, from where the name 'Serapeum' comes.

There was only one bull god alive at one particular time, with a life span of twenty-five years based on astronomical calculations. These data have not been confirmed, however, because the worship of Apis also involved mysterious rituals just like other mysteries of the time, and a great amount of information has been hidden or modified. This cult of the god Apis goes back at least 1,400 BC, when Amenhotep III ordered the construction of the Serapeum. Once again, the custom of re-using things may have led the pharaoh to make use of an existing installation to house his new cult.

Remembering these things from her reading, Susan finds herself in the large gallery. The chests stand in perpendicular niches and the level of the gallery corresponds to the top of the chests. The niches are arranged in a quincunx. As Antoine Gigal describes it so well, nobody is able to explain what these chests were for, and different attempts at dating them are only based on objects found on the site or on engravings made later on one of the chests.

Susan asks her team to measure the interior volume and also the quality of the surfaces and the angles. The results confirm what Chris Dunn measured in 1985, i.e., exceptional quality worthy of a mechanical precision part. Susan wonders where she had seen a similar volume and mysterious use, and her thoughts naturally lead her to the sarcophagus in the Great Pyramid, the one that contained the Ark of the Covenant.

Could it be that these chests owed the quality of their interiors to the need to capture and maintain a vibration, or wave? If so, why are they so big, while the one in the pyramid is clearly much smaller? And why are there so many of them?

It is also true that they must have closed hermetically, and that the thickness and the weight of the lid were for a very precise reason.

Susan thinks that if the lid was so heavy, it was to prevent people from moving it while the chest was functioning. A good number of men and equipment would be necessary to open it.

Her team is taking micro samples inside the sarcophagi, in the hope of finding traces of liquid or materials that would have remained attached to the granite. Someone suddenly calls her to chest number 3.

"Ms. Gomez, come over here and have a look!"

Susan runs through the gallery, goes down the steps into the niche, and then climbs a ladder to finally descend again into the chest – a space big enough to put a table and ten diners around it. Allegedly, Mariette once invited someone to have a meal with him around a sarcophagus.

"What did you find?"

"Look here, with the fluorescent lamp you can clearly see a line at this height, and the color is not the same above and below. That means that a liquid filled it up to here. Let's try and see what kind of liquid it was."

"Great … carry on. I'll see if I can find some other clues."

Satisfied with the discovery, Susan started thinking about it as she walked through the large gallery. She imagined living beings staying in these chests for a long time, otherwise the heavy lids would not have been necessary. It must have been cold, and if they were immersed in a liquid it would not have been warm either. Wow, what a way to hibernate, she thought, shivering. But that's it … they did not come to recharge their batteries, but to hibernate! If there were 200 of them they could divide the task among themselves and rule the human race for much longer than if they just replaced each other in turn. If there are twenty-four sarcophagi, it means that they could reign for eight times longer, but it would also mean that there were only around 170 of them active.

If each one spent ten years in a chest in turn, that means their lifespan increased to 2,250 rather than 1,000 years. Each of them did eight rotations, i.e., eight of them shared a chest, or it could have been the other way round. Realizing that they aged faster than on their planet of origin, they slowed down this accelerated aging process by hibernating. It was not a case of extending their lifetime, but of maintaining it.

Susan goes back to her team in the third chest.

"Have you found anything?" she asks.

"Yes, we found traces of magnesium sulfate, or Epsom salts if you prefer. This very special salt was known to the Egyptians. Cleopatra used it for her beauty treatments, and it also allows your body to float in the water, just like in the Dead Sea. It's also very good against infections."

"Keep looking to see if there are any other substances there. I think they used these chests to hibernate and extend their lives, or perhaps they aged too fast here on Earth and wanted to slow the process down."

Susan watches the man in front of her working with his analysis equipment and test tubes of samples. They even have a small spectrograph. Taking care not to disturb them, she sits down in a corner and watches, deep in thought. Something is not quite right. Why are these chests so perfect on the inside?

It is known that hibernation slows down DNA transcription, and therefore its deterioration. DNA curls up like a hedgehog and it becomes more difficult to access its genes.

But why these perfectly parallel or perpendicular walls?

Rather than thinking about the temperature of the bodies in hibernation, controlled by the depth of the Serapeum, she thinks about the vibrations emitted by the bodies. Just as the chest in the King's Chamber in the Great Pyramid captured the particles and bounced them back endlessly, like a laser, perhaps it was the vibrations of the bodies that were retained in the chest, which conserved the vibrations emitted by all the cells of the bodies better, rather than letting them go in all directions and getting lost. Susan decides to speak to Alex about it; he should be able to confirm her theory.

"Ms. Gomez, come and see. We found something else strange!"

"What is it? I can't see anything."

"Look here. We light up the granite surface with the polarized light and examine the result with special glasses, that's why you can't see anything. Take a look through these."

"I still don't see anything!"

"Turn your head and tell me what you see."

"Ah, yes, I can see a spot of light that wasn't there before!"

"That's it! The granite surface you're looking at has been treated in some unknown invisible way. We need to test several light sources to be sure, but the micro-cavities on the super-flat surface of the granite caught our attention. The micro-cavities have to be of a certain wavelength, and they are able to invert the angle of polarization of the particles that hit them."

"What use is that?"

"Well, what can I say? As far as I know, there is no filter or reflector on Earth capable of producing this effect."

"Damn!" shouts Susan as she runs out of the chest, running to the exit as quickly as she can. Once outside, she rings Alex on her satellite phone.

"Alex, it's me, Susan, I'm here in the Serapeum."

"Hi honey, you don't need to use the satellite phone to tell me you love me, but thanks anyway!"

"Shut up, of course I love you but I have an urgent question for you. The technicians have seen that the surfaces inside the chests are covered in micro-cavities, and their size is probably identical to the wavelength of a particle. They showed me that it had the effect of negatively polarizing the light from their lamp. Does that ring a bell with you?"

"Of course, it's the same phenomenon that happens when Venus gets close to its maximum elongation, the one that seemed to be present in your monuments, you know, in Sardinia, the Noriges or whatever they're called."

"The nuraghi, you dope! But what conclusion can we draw from this?"

"Let me see ... I think that being surrounded by this kind of reflector means that you can benefit from the Venus effect throughout its cycle, and not only at two very precise moments."

"Jeez! You have no idea of what that could mean!"

"No … but you were telling me that you've found something else?"

"Not yet, but it appears that the chests were full of water mixed with Epsom salts, which are used in sensorial isolation chests and make things float. Seeing as these chests are underground at a constant temperature of around fourteen degrees, I think they used this place to hibernate. A fifteen-ton lid would stop anyone from interfering with the chest. I'm sure they knew how to do it, just like turtles, bears and marmots."

"Who are 'they'?"

"Fallen angels, astronauts … the beings that make the light spheres appear, the ones that gave us the Ankh!"

"Wow, now that is something! Anyway, congratulate your team, and yourself, for having the brilliant idea to go over there. But hang up now or else the boss will scream when he sees the bill."

"Don't worry, with what I'm going to report he won't be shouting at anyone. Love you!"

Susan puts the long antenna of the satellite phone away and puts it back in her pocket, absorbed in her thoughts.

So, these beings, in addition to extending their lifespan, also regenerated their capacity for precognition! Perhaps that ability diminished as the years went by, or perhaps increased until it reached an exceptional level.

She thinks that they must have other ways of doing this on their planets, but on Earth they had to get by with the means available to them, and by applying their knowledge. Nobody on Earth can build chests like that nowadays. There are no machines to do it, or to create these micro-cavities.

With intelligence and knowledge, however, these beings manufactured apparatus and machines that no longer exist to carve stone with incredible precision, and to make complex hydraulic or chemical systems, to the extent that we now wonder how those things worked.

Susan dreamily watches the sun, already dropping low over the horizon. Farther away, the step pyramid of Sakkara looks back at her impassively. How many thousands of years have these beings lived on Earth, where had they been before, and what have they taught us?

Damn it, why was all that knowledge lost! All those religious wars that burned and destroyed the knowledge of others!

A little tired, Susan walks sluggishly towards the entrance of the Serapeum. It is getting late, but the excitement of these last few hours is masking her tiredness.

She goes back down the gallery and suggests that everyone stops work for the day.

ALAIN HUBRECHT

Chapter 33

November 15th 2010, San Diego, California

Alex goes into the 'Gaslamp Strip Club' restaurant, his favorite in San Diego. He calls a waitress and tells her he has a reservation, but out of the corner of his eye he sees Susan waving at him from a table near the window, the same table where they started their relationship.

She has ordered a caipirinha, her favorite cocktail. It is warm outside but the temperature inside is pleasantly cool. She is wearing a white top with a low neckline, the sleeves cut to fall either side of her tanned arms. Alex notices that she has bought some earrings in the form of the Ankh.

"Well, well, some earrings you got there ... it looks like your work has really taken a hold on you!"

"It's not about my work, but my life. I never did anything as interesting as this, and I'm proud of myself, because I'm partly responsible. Aren't you happy to feel involved in this research?"

"Yeah, sure, but you know me. I'm not an expert in archeology or history like you."

"Nah, I'm not talking about old stones, but what we've discovered about precognition, and also about these beings that came to Earth thousands of years ago! Don't you find that fantastic?"

"Yes, of course. It's incredible, but what will it change for you, for the two of us?"

"Oh, come on! You're in on the discovery of the thing that has had the greatest influence on the evolution of the human race, you learn that there's a place in the universe that contains knowledge about everything, and even about the future, and you're about to ask me what I want for dessert! Imagine what that can change for people in the future, for our child, if we have one someday, and for science, technology ... You're hopeless! But ... remember it was you who asked yourself one day about the meaning of the SAIC logo on the door of the Space Shuttle, remember? You're a curious person by nature, you've done some highly sophisticated technical studies, and you love progress and discoveries ..."

"Well, let's just say that it's my work. As for the SAIC logo, I was just doing my job. Maybe I got a bit too curious, but you'll agree that it's insignificant compared to what's happened to us since."

"Exactly, that's what's extraordinary, we – thanks to us, to the team – have entered a new era, and nothing will ever be like it was!"

"OK, but don't get carried away! We don't know if SAIC will pass on the benefit of its discoveries to the world, and don't forget that we're bound to secrecy. I don't expect anything, and if you look back in time there are plenty of discoveries that were filed away in drawers rather than used to save the human race. You see, I at least don't expect anything, that way at least I won't be disappointed if nothing comes of it all."

"Boy, can you be negative! The future belongs to the brave, to visionaries, that's why we need to be positive and optimistic! And then, even if SAIC doesn't do anything, we can make love under the light of Venus and have a fantastic child."

"Yeah, but don't forget we need to do it nine months before!"

"There you go, always taking the shine off things! Seriously, I believe it'll happen. I'm sure they'll do something and I am certain that something good will come out of all this. Anyway, I'm hungry and I suggest we order. The usual?"

ALAIN HUBRECHT

Chapter 34

January 15th 2011, Glendalough, Ireland

Susan finishes her breakfast. She spent the night before in the bed & breakfast in the village. She needed the second quilt to keep warm; the building is not old, but the boiler is probably quite old and has a hard time heating the rooms in winter. What a change from California or the Egyptian desert!

Susan had asked her university to open a new line of research dedicated to monuments and megaliths that seem to be able to modify their immediate environment or the flow of particles around them.

The President had his doubts at first, but a call from SAIC helped him change his mind, especially when the company confirmed that it would fund Susan's research.

The project on the spheres is effectively over for her. The project has been classified TOP SECRET and Susan no longer has the right to know where it will go. Alex continues to work on it, but he has gone back to his initial work, i.e., the development of the light machine. It is mainly thanks to Susan that he was able to follow the project after the experiment in the pyramid, but now that Susan is back at her college there is no real reason for bringing her in on the work on precognition or the light spheres.

Susan has presented a list of monuments that she wants to examine in greater detail, in the knowledge that Man could construct buildings in the past that were capable of treating particles in order to improve the skills of human beings. The director of the faculty raised his eyebrows when the project was presented to him; nobody had heard of this before and under normal circumstances it would have been rejected, but, with the support of SAIC and a few discreet explanations from them, he finally accepted without reservations. This is important, because universities the world over operate in the same way; grants are needed to pay the researchers, and the researchers who receive grants are those who publish more articles in renowned scientific journals, such as Nature. The number of times their articles are quoted is a determining factor nowadays. Researchers now seem to spend more time writing articles than actually carrying out research, apart from the vicious circle of grants from private companies that expect the research to help them market their products better.

This means that most research is focused on areas related to the marketing of new products; pharmaceuticals are a good example. That is why rare diseases no longer receive funding, and no research is done on remedies that could be obtained free of charge farther down the line. Susan is very happy that Alex's company is helping her, although she knows that SAIC expects to get something back in return. In any case, Susan will be doing what she loves doing, and that makes her feel good. Until there is evidence to the contrary, she has not heard of any negative use of their discoveries in recent months. In any case, what is sure is that Alex is in San Diego and she is back in Los Angeles, so they see each other at weekends. Either Alex comes up to her, or she goes down to him. They are getting to know each other better all the time, although Alex is less romantic, impetuous and idealistic than Susan. She thinks it is perhaps better that way; he calms her down and helps her think twice before making a decision. Alex has accepted Susan's decision, even if it means that she will often be away on trips abroad.

After returning to her room to get her overcoat and hat, Susan leaves the hotel and turns right towards the village's round tower. It is one of the last towers still standing in Ireland, and is standard in terms of dimensions and details. It is only around one hundred yards from the hotel, at the bottom of a gully on the site of an ancient monastic cemetery where some tombs can still be seen. The entrance is almost eleven feet above the ground, but the monument is not open to the public, so Susan had to ask someone from the church next door to lend her a ladder and open the door of the tower. A man is waiting for her at the foot of the tower and the ladder is already in position.

After thanking him and getting instructions on how to close the tower after her and give the ladder back, Susan goes inside the mysterious monument. It is over 100 feet high and in good condition. There are four different levels, so she can go from the top of one ladder to the bottom of the next one. There is not much space on each level to put any objects down, eighteen square feet at the most. The interior diameter of the tower is just over eight feet. The walls are very thick and give the structure a robust appearance. Eight very simple windows look out, four of them on the top level and one on the other three. At the foot of the tower there is a tiny opening of less than four inches; nobody has any explanation for this hole. To tell the truth, nobody can really explain anything about the towers. The tourist boards hide their ignorance behind information panels that give false descriptions. They all agreed on a version in which the tower was a belfry and a place of refuge against attacks by the Vikings; the monks took shelter there with their valuables during these attacks. These explanations do not hold water, however; all the round towers in Ireland were built outside the grounds of their monasteries, in the cemetery where the monks were buried. Furthermore, it was easy for the attackers to wait for the monks to die of hunger or thirst. Even though the entrances were between ten and twenty-six feet above the ground, the space inside is so small that it would be impossible to put more than six people and a few boxes in there.

The local tourist boards continue to put out their version, happily changing the interior dimensions of the towers and the scale of the people represented on the information panels.

On the panels, the walls are only fifteen inches thick instead of 4 feet plus, and the people are only thirty-five inches high against the exterior diameter of the towers, giving the impression that the towers had more space inside to stock the wealth of the monks and provisions to see out a siege.

This shows the confusion on the part of the local authorities and other historians when it comes to finding an explanation for these towers, of which there were hundreds across the landscape of Ireland in the past.

Indeed, in 1830 the Royal Academy of Ireland organized a competition to see who could provide the real explanation for the round towers. A certain Henry O'Brien presented a very detailed study of them titled "The Round Towers of Ireland, or the mysteries of Freemasonry, the Sabians and Buddhism". Basically, the study concludes that it is a phallic symbol – something this author seems to find everywhere – common to almost all religions over the centuries. Unfortunately, the competition was interrupted, no doubt so as not to offend the honorable members of the Academy, and poor Henry O'Brien saw his prize snatched away from him.

In other words, people have been wondering about the use of these towers for about 200 years. Previously, they were happy to repeat the explanations given without applying any critical spirit or observing them in a more attentive way, which led to all kinds of versions. They started by talking about shelters, then watchtowers, belfries, and – more interestingly – 'lanterns of the dead'. The notion of lanterns of the dead involves placing a lantern on top of a tower at night so that wandering souls who do not realize that they are dead can make out the light from a distance and approach it, until they finally understand that the light is above a cemetery. It is up to them to realize that they are dead and that they should get ready for the afterlife.

The reason why this idea should be taken seriously is that it is very widespread. In France, for example, there are more than one hundred lanterns of the dead, built from the 10th century onwards. In this case, the constructions are more basic, with much less variety in their shapes and dimensions. The only one that resembles the Irish towers is the one at Saint-Pierre d'Oléron, but it is much more recent and its architect may have been inspired by the towers in Ireland. This has caused some unfortunate confusion since then, because it has been clearly demonstrated that the towers in Ireland never housed any lanterns or bells, nor were they used as watchtowers.

Another hypothesis – and a well-defended one – is that of the phallic symbol, linked to Buddhism, which attracted quite a following in Ireland at the time. In that case, why in the middle of the cemetery, and why so little resemblance to a phallus? There is another interesting hypothesis: that of energy fields. Georges Prat, a specialist in vibratory networks related to monuments, developed a technique called 'geobiology'. Taking measurements in this 'science' always required a human being. Basically, it is the principle of the sorcerer's ring, but anything can be used. You can use apparatus, but a drawing on a piece of paper is just as good; you just need to believe. Georges travelled the world in search of ancient monuments and claims that the vibrations are more intense where these monuments were built. He catalogued several vibrating frequencies linked to different minerals, the most common being nickel, which gave rise to the Hartmann grid. The rarer the mineral, the more spaced out is the grid. In general, the meshing is parallel to that of latitude and longitude, but sometimes it is inclined at forty-five degrees. Georges Prat claims that a large number of ancient monuments are built where several grids cross. He says that he can also measure the vibrations from defunct or mythical entities. So, when he is standing in front of a round tower in Ireland he can measure the vibrations of a dead monk from top to bottom, then those of a Saint and finally those of Christ.

According to him, the towers were used as a chimney to send the vibrations of the buried monks into the atmosphere so that they could be part of a cosmic whole.

Susan was aware of the work of the geobiologists, but had never been able to correlate their statements with verifiable facts. True or not, Georges nevertheless hit on an interesting element. Each tower has a different height, and the height of the door also changes – curiously – depending on the tower, somewhere between zero and twenty-six feet above the ground. He also observed a relationship between the distance that separates the top of the door from the top of the tower, and the circumference of the tower to the height of the top of the door. This ratio is always the same, and strangely corresponds to the gold ratio. This ratio (1.61803399…) is the only complex one found in nature, and in innumerable places. The DNA of fauna and flora often uses this ratio to generate itself. The gold ratio is also used to create a variety of forms and proportions. It is based on the Fibonacci number (E-13), in which each member is equal to the sum of the preceding two, i.e., 0 1 1 2 3 5 8 13 21 34 55 89 144 233 377 and so on.

The gold ratio is obtained by dividing any number of this series by the previous one. So, if you divide 377 by 233 you get 1.618025, which is already very close to the gold ratio. The more you advance in the series, the more the gold ratio becomes precise.

Susan knows that this ratio was used to make towers architecturally harmonious, but something does not quite fit. Indeed, under the door the tower is filled with rubble. At the base, there is no break between the rubble and the ground, as if the earth had to 'communicate' directly up as far as the door. It also seems clear that the builders of these towers constructed the walls by filling the gap inside with rubble until they felt satisfied about something. It was only then that they put the door in and built the rest, taking the gold ratio into account. So, the gold ratio was for the appearance of the building, not the height of the door, which seems to be governed by some phenomenon that remains unknown. What mainly interests Susan is that the stones used to build the towers have a high quartz content, and also granite and basalt, which gives them interesting dielectric properties, but this also makes her think of the chests in the Serapeum. Another person carried out important research on the towers: Philips Callahan (P-1), an entomologist, ornithologist, philosopher and explorer. His work as an entomologist led him to study the reflective properties of infrared light on the antennae of moths. Later on, when he was on military service near the Irish coast he was posted to a radar station close to a round tower. He observed an analogy between the moths' antennae and the round towers, which seemed to be able to reflect radar waves.

Susan's brain starts to give off steam when people talk to her of granite and waves, or particles. She has heard all this many times before. What if these towers had an effect on the monks' brains? Were the reflected waves – optic, electrical or whatever – adjusted to improve the monks' capacity for precognition? Indeed, why put them in cemeteries?

Susan thinks of cell phone antennae, which need to be situated at a certain distance from the user to be efficient. Perhaps the towers also had to be distant from the monks in order to function. She suddenly remembers a strange piece of information: at the time, only the towers were made of stone, the rest of the monastery being built of wood. Was that done to allow the waves to propagate better?

Susan takes several photos and makes laser telemetry measurements in the tower. She also records the humidity index and the carrier wave with a special device. She looks at her watch and decides that it is time to call John Quackenboss.

This retired farmer lives in Alexandria in the United States. He read the works of Callahan and was inspired to build smaller towers than those in Ireland and place them in the middle of his crop fields. He observed that this improved the yields of his crops, similar to the way in which biodynamic culture places stones containing quartz in fields to improve their production levels.

Back at the hotel, Susan looks for John's number on her laptop, and then dials the number on her cell phone.

"Hello… is that John Quackenboss?"

"Yes, that's right. Good morning, I was waiting for your call."

"I am in Glendalough right now. I arrived yesterday and visited the tower this morning. I hope I'm not ringing you too early?"

"No, no, of course not, I keep to my farmer's routine and I always get up early."

"Well, I've seen the tower up close and taken some measurements. I also measured the carrier waves and will see if that can help. In the meantime, I'd like to know why you asked me to call you after I visited the tower."

"I wanted to be sure you were serious about your research. I didn't want to reveal information to the first person who came along. At what height from the ground did you measure the lintel of the doorway?"

"Thirteen feet eight inches."

"OK, that's good. You're on the right track. Please forgive me, but I have information I would rather not trust to just anyone, and ever since Callahan mentioned me in his books I've had all kinds of people getting in touch with me. Can you tell me exactly what you're looking for in these towers?"

"As I told you, I'm an archeologist and am trying to find constructions from the past that were built to transform matter, or to be more specific, particles. I know that Callahan thought these towers captured and stored ions, either from the rays from the sun or the sky, for the benefit of the monks and their crops. This is linked to the ionization of the ground, which also changes the atmosphere around it. The ionization of the air increases considerably at a certain height above the ground, and this height varies in relation to the ground, which is undoubtedly why the height of the doors to the towers changes too. What are your conclusions on this possible effect, since you have replicated the towers in your crop fields?"

"Well, my dear young lady, at the risk of displeasing you and seeing that a long time has gone by since I carried out those trials, I must confess that I did not really observe the effect. Other farmers have also tried to reproduce the effect described by Callahan on their crops and they have not observed any improvement either."

"OK, but do you have any idea of what these towers did, if they did anything at all?"

"You told me that you were being paid by SAIC for this research, right?"

"Yes, that's it."

"So, you've heard of the Stargate project?"

"Yes, and one of the people I have to report to is precisely Jacques Vallée, and I have also worked with Paul Smith. Both of them were involved in Stargate."

"I thought so, or at least I suspected it. I am going to give you some information that is not secret, but very few people know it, and I think it will help you with your research. When I was still farming, and Callahan had published his book that referred to my tests, I received a visit from a certain Peter Tompkins. At the time he was writing a book on alternative methods of crop farming, now called 'biodynamics. The title of the book he was working on was 'Secret of the Soil' or SOS for short, and if you look at the cover you will see that he has placed the letters 'SOS' vertically above the title. The aim of his book was to help Man to save the planet. He wrote another book titled 'The Secret Life of Plants' in which he talks of the consciousness of plants. Strangely enough, he also wrote a book on the Egyptian pyramids and another on the Inca pyramids. Peter, and don't ask me how I know, was a secret agent of the OSS, the American espionage service that was replaced by the CIA after the Second World War. He was taken on to work in the psychological warfare service. I suppose you know that the CIA started off the Stargate project. Don't ask me why either, but at the time the CIA headquarters was being built at Langley, Virginia, Peter was invited to create an enigma, materialized by the artist Jim Sanborn and exhibited in the inner courtyard of the building (T-6). This sculpture consists of several parts, and despite the fact that thousands of people have tried to understand its message, it hasn't been completely deciphered. We know that it refers to something mysterious that is buried nearby, and is also a reference to the mysteries of Egypt. Even Dan Brown mentions it in his book 'The Lost Symbol', but you know as well as I do that he never researches these things very deeply. Peter officially stopped being a spy in 1948, as he refused to join the CIA. So, there is a link between the idea that the CIA wanted to symbolize a tribute to him and the notion of waves and consciousness, which interested Peter."

"But you said you haven't been able to demonstrate an effect of the towers on plants, or their replicas. From my side, I've seen aerial photographs but I don't see any changes, either concentric or spiral, in the plant life around the towers."

"That doesn't surprise me. I think you should restrict your efforts to the effect on the monks. Look, I'll give you another clue. I happen to know Joseph Moneagle (P-8), who was also a member of the Stargate project. You probably know that the project was officially closed at the end of the 1980s, but in reality it has been classified 'Secret Defense' and it is more than likely that SAIC is still running it. Joseph no longer works on the project, like most of the early members. He's written some books, but he's the only one to focus on the extraordinary powers of the Remote Viewers of the Stargate team for time travel, and particularly looking into the future."

"You're saying that the Stargate project could see into the future?"

"Not only see, but also interact and interrogate people in the future!"

"I'm glad to hear this. I believe that they don't speak to people but to their consciousness, or rather to their memory, and there would be a protocol that they had partially implemented to interact with that memory. It's a bit like when you can't find a word. You wait, you talk about something else, and a few minutes later the word comes to mind. It's a similar sort of protocol."

"Mm … I think I see what you're getting at, but I don't know anything else in that area. What I wanted to show is that there appears to be a connection between the round towers in Ireland and accounts of consciousness and precognition, including research carried out secretly by the different bodies I've mentioned."

"Yes, I understand. I'm reassured to know that and it strengthens my idea that the towers have an influence on the monks, but I don't know how yet."

"Think of what they are made of, and ask yourself what role that material could have."

"Granite. All the towers are made of granite."

"Callahan started off on a good track, but soon switched to a system of ionization. I think his initial idea was better, which was that the tower bounced waves from the sky or the sun back to the monks, transforming them in the process."

"Yes, that's true, but what's the point of bouncing the waves back if not after transforming them?"

"What are you really looking for?"

"I'm not sure, but I've found monuments oriented to the rise of Venus, with the probable aim of impregnating babies at birth inside these monuments. It was easy to check that that baby had been born when Venus was rising, and this would be a sign that the child would have greater powers of precognition than others. Then there is the Great Pyramid, which can function as a storage unit for the wave from Venus. The ancients could then move the storage unit and release the particles in another place to the benefit of adults, but no doubt to a lesser extent."

"To a lesser extent?"

"Yes, a baby at the time of birth is highly receptive to this wave. It will still be later on, but less so, and only during certain configurations of the stars. In Egypt we also found underground chambers containing granite chests that negatively polarize the particles that penetrate them. For that to have an effect, it's probably necessary to remain in the chests for years."

"For years?"

"Yes, but other evidence, which I can't talk about now, seems to demonstrate that they knew how to do it. Anyway, at the time, or even closer to us in time, it was quite common for people to shut themselves away for ten years in a room the size of one of these chests."

"Are you serious?"

"Quite serious. Just think of the hermits in Tibet, described by Alexandra David Neel, or others in France. There are still around two hundred nowadays, living in tiny places."

"OK, from what you tell me I can see that the treatment of that light from Venus is not systematic. It is probably even different each time."

"Yes, but don't forget that there are several systems of the same type, sometimes up to 20,000 like in Sardinia, although obviously not like in the one in the Great Pyramid. I know that hundreds of pyramids were built, but I don't think they would all contain the structure of the process found in the Great Pyramid."

"On that basis, I can only encourage you to consult a geologist, and take measurements of the polarization of the light from Venus reflected by the towers."

"You've taken the words right out of my mouth, but I need more precise material than what I have with me here. Anyway, I'd like to thank you for this conversation. You've helped me a lot and I have a better idea of what to do now. Thank you very much, Mr. Quackenboss."

"John, please call me John."

Susan hangs up, lost in her thoughts. She looks out of the window at the tower in the distance.

"Hell, what are you hiding from us?!" she shouts at the tower. She realizes that it is incredible to hear the name 'SAIC' again, even in a conversation about these towers. They are everywhere, or rather everywhere where people talk of precognition. She wonders why John gave her the information on a plate, but she will think about that later. Right now, she is in a kind of hole in which, except for the church and her hotel, there is almost nothing. She does not even have her measuring equipment with her.

While mechanically flicking through the pages of the hotel magazine she comes across an article on the Viking invasions, which took place around the time of the construction of the towers. She is attracted by the word 'polarization'. Taken aback, she re-reads the paragraph that says that the Vikings used a 'sun stone' that polarized daylight and told them where the sun was behind the clouds in order to navigate the seas. So, the polarization of light was a known phenomenon in northern Europe at the time!

Susan had picked up a piece of rock at the foot of the tower and decides to examine it in the lab on her return.

She puts the magazine down and lies on the bed, looking at the ceiling.

"There can only be two reasons for raising the height of the door, either to match another height – like the monastery – or the level needed to get a precise value related to a phenomenon that was still unknown. Since the floor was always in direct contact with the ground because of the rubble, the second option seems more likely. So, if the ground had an effect, there must be some kind of geomagnetic phenomenon or something to do with the ionization of the air. We know that ionization electrifies the air in a particular way, and that the level of electrification changes depending on the height. They must have looked for a certain level of ionization so that that process that took place around the tower would work as best as possible. If the tower could reflect the waves from Venus onto the monks the benefit of maximum elongation would be missing, which would make the polarization negative. So, if they had found a device to do it, the monks could enjoy the benefits of Venus all year round, a little like in the hibernation chest in the Serapeum. If the towers vibrated at the frequency of granite, maybe they could also amplify the waves, and the rock they were made of could reverse their polarity?"

What about the monks, then? Susan now understands why all monasteries were built of wood while the towers were always made of stone. The towers had a function, and the monastery was made as permeable as possible to the waves produced by the towers. The monks, then, saw their ability to read the future improved. At the time, the Church ran the country. Saint Patrick brought Christianity to Ireland in the 5th century, insisting unusually strongly on the role of the Holy Trinity, and by extension, that of the Holy Spirit. The monastery of Glendalough was built around that time. In those days Ireland had around one hundred kings who shared the governance of the island among them; there are about one hundred towers. The Vikings started to attack around 800 AD, but only carried out minor expeditions for many years and only took away the treasures that their ships could carry. They really concentrated on the monasteries, because they contained more precious objects than any other places. We can easily imagine that these towers were built for the sole purpose of shelter against attacks. Would they have been built to improve the capacity of precognition of the monks, and therefore their ability to predict Viking incursions? No, that does not seem to fit; towers were already there centuries before the first invasions.

In ancient times there were oracles, prophets, soothsayers and astrologers to help emperors govern their empires, not forgetting their ability to train new soothsayers and other specialists in precognition. However, we have very little information on how this knowledge subsisted in the 6th century, when the first towers were built. All this knowledge has been recovered for Christianity. One can guess that the recluses in the Serapeum of Memphis gave way to other recluses and hermits controlled by the Church, but what remained of the divine aspect behind it all? Everything was transformed into acquiring the Holy Spirit, but with the historical blur that surrounds this notion, typical of the Trinity since the creation of the Bible.

We should also remember that Ireland was still largely governed by Celtic rituals in the 5th century. Basically, the Celts built strong citadels and forts to defend themselves from invaders, all of them large structures in stone. Glendalough is just a simple tower with minimal interior dimensions. Instead of having a 'reactive' attitude, i.e., wait until the invader approaches to start fighting, why not have a 'proactive' attitude, by doing everything possible to predict the arrival of the invader and take the necessary measures to prevent him arriving?

For the Celts, a soothsayer was called a 'vate', which is really a Gallic term; the Irish word is 'faitsine'. All the Druid priests became Christian priests after they were converted to the faith, although they still retained certain features of their ancient practices. Some people even speak of 'Celtic Christianity'. Ireland is the last European bastion to remain Celtic for so long, and there are very few descriptions of its pre-Christian era.

So, are these towers linked to some kind of ancient knowledge held by the faitsines, those Celtic soothsayers who were converted to Christianity? This could explain why they were only found in Ireland, but they would also have been built at the start of the Christian era. Christian Guyonvarc's well-documented book titled 'Magie, médecine et divination chez les Celtes' does not even mention these towers. Susan decides that no conclusions can be reached unless one of the towers can be reactivated, checking the effect of it on people living nearby. Disappointed, she gets up from the bed with the idea of taking a final stroll to the tower.

She passes it and walks towards the lake beneath the tower. The lake is only three hundred yards or so long. She walks a little farther and sees the tower reflected in the water. She sits down on a rock and continues to think, all the while looking at the still water.

Why has Man built such mysterious monuments, sometimes enormous, for their function to be lost over the centuries? The same thing seems to have happened to pagan festivals; all that is left is a kind of simulation.

How many thousands of years did Man need to observe, understand, interpret and implement the phenomena related to Venus and precognition?

What did the Mysteries of Antiquity have to do with these monuments? Freemasonry might have picked up the rituals and symbolism, but the real reason still escapes us. Susan wonders if she is going to carry on with her research for long, and if she will ever find the key to it all.

Will she abandon this difficult assignment and rejoin Alex? The team is making progress on the design of the machine and there will surely be a place for her in the new structure that will be set up in the near future.

She has heard that Jacques Vallée has been criticized by some people in SAIC who do not want to admit that all apparitions of UFOs come from these disembodied beings. Jacques has successfully demonstrated that these beings existed and were able to 'materialize' a series of molecules collected from the surrounding environment, but this does not really prove that all the observations are linked to these beings.

Susan starts to walk back to the hotel. The time has passed quickly and the light is fading.

Suddenly something happens above the lake, to her right. Susan turns round a sees a mist forming above the water. Little flashes of light streak through the dark cloud, like discharges of static electricity. The cloud grows in size until it covers the lake. Suddenly, in total silence, the cloud gives way to an enormous object – dark, triangular, almost as big as the lake. It is only a few hundred yards away from Susan at this point.

She can see the details of the inner face of the enormous thing, as if it was crossed by pipes and grooves. The object hovers about one hundred feet above the water.

After a few seconds of immobility, three enormous lights appear at the three angles of the triangle. It makes a quarter turn, but Susan cannot make out the geometry of the object. It seems to transform itself as it turns on itself, and although it resembles a large triangle with a thickness of around seventy feet, she is still not sure of what she is looking at. The object rises gently towards the sky, and stops when it reaches a height of around 200 yards.

Susan is not carrying a camera. Just her luck! She grabs her smartphone, but realizes that it is too dark for her to photograph anything worthwhile.

Suddenly, a red light appears in the center of the device. Like the others, it is enormous, and several feet wide. The lake is lit up and seems to turn red.

While she is taking as many photos as she can the object suddenly disappears, right there, but on the circumference Susan can see around a hundred small light spheres like the ones she saw in Arizona.

The spheres move towards the center of the figure and blend into one, slightly larger, sphere. Once the maneuver has finished the sphere moves towards the tower, to the right of Susan. She cannot believe her eyes; this is not happening by chance, she is receiving a message. Something enormous passes in front of her and Susan understands it all now.

She is effectively receiving an answer to the questions she asked herself a few minutes before. She follows the sphere as it approaches the tower. She sees it go inside the tower, as if it had been absorbed by the blocks of rock. Then, nothing else. She only hears a few blackbirds, singing as they hunt earthworms, and frogs croaking at the edge of the lake.

It all happened so fast, in probably less than ten minutes. Her first idea is to call Jacques and tell him what she has seen. Her heart beats fast in her chest as she reaches the base of the tower. The ladder is no longer there and she cannot go in again, but however hard she tries to look inside, nothing is happening inside. She stays for another thirty minutes, just in case something else happens.

What beauty, what joy at witnessing that!

She has a vision that links the spheres, flying saucers and mysterious monuments. So, the Ankh was not something in isolation, there was certainly something that tied it all together.

Excited but happy, Susan opens the door of the hotel. She looks at the person behind the reception desk but does not pay him much attention apart from a simple and courteous nod of the head. Apparently nobody else saw anything. It was dark and the lake was separated from the village by a wood and some fields.

She goes into the bar as asks for a caipirinha.

ALAIN HUBRECHT

Chapter 35

June 14th 2011, San Diego, California

Susan shuts her laptop and puts it back in her bag. Almost six months have gone by since her trip to Ireland. She has not been able to control events after that; in any case, what she observed there was too important to keep quiet. After putting Jacques in the picture, she returned to San Diego immediately. Her encounter – not of the third kind, but a new type that still had not been catalogued – had to be followed up. Jacques organized meetings with several people, who remained anonymous, and she had to be present each time. They were lucky to have a private SAIC jet to take them to the places where these people worked. She saw people from Congress, the CIA, NSA, the Pentagon, and others whose logos or passes she did not recognize, often because they were dressed in civilian clothes. Poor Alex had to stay behind in San Diego each time.

A team was sent to Glendalough to take the measurements that Susan was unable to record. They observed, with a fair degree of precision, that the tower door is located at a height at which the ionized layer of air changes quickly. This has to do with the composition of the soil and the relief of the surrounding area. Provided that nothing changes in these two parameters, the level remains constant. By using filters they were able to measure and check that the light reflected by the tower was indeed negatively polarized, which confirms Susan's hypothesis that the tower increases the beneficial effect of Venus throughout the year for people located within a radius of around one hundred yards. This also happens even if they are behind wooden or stone walls. Alex confirms the capture of axions during the experiments in the Great Pyramid and on opening the Ark. These particles with incredible properties are capable of penetrating matter as if it were butter.

The most interesting meeting was the one with the fewest people present. She travelled to Washington with Jacques and they went to a small building on the heights of the city, where they met a certain William Skinner, a giant in civilian clothes but with a military air. They went to the Pentagon together, where William showed his pass, but the guards did not ask them to show anything else as they went through three consecutive checkpoints, while everyone else had to show their white pass each time. They then went up one of the enormous ramps that connects the different levels of the building and entered a windowless office, where William asked the person who was working there to take a stroll outside for about an hour. After closing the door, William approached a cabinet and put his hand in the space between the cabinet and the wall to activate a releasing mechanism. He then pushed the cabinet to the right as if it slid on rails. This led to a bay in the wall where there was a staircase, which they then took, sliding the cabinet back into place behind them before going up. William turned back to them to tell them that the architects of the Pentagon had great fun and games while they were designing it, but this was nothing compared to what they would never see.

Once at the top of the stairs, William pressed a button that set off a signal. After a few moments another cabinet slid on rails and they entered another office, just as nondescript as the one they had just left.

Two people were waiting for them in this office. They both seemed well into their seventies, and both were wearing civilian clothes, which after all is normal at their age.

They were asked to take a seat and if they wanted anything to drink. After a few words aimed at breaking the ice, introductions were made, which Susan certainly did not expect after all the precautions taken for them to arrive there. William introduced Henry Kissinger and Étienne Davignon to them. Susan only knew the former by name, but it was pointed out that Henry was a member of the Council on Foreign Relations ('CFR' since 1955) and that Étienne was the President of the Bilderberg Group. She wondered why these big shots might be interested in UFOs.

Susan recalls that the CFR was a think-thank set up in 1921 and had been followed that same year by a number of international or national think tanks that brought the most influential thinkers together. In England it was called Chatham House (or RIIA), chaired by no less than the Queen of England, and in Belgium, the home country of Étienne Davignon, the Egmont Institute, chaired by Davignon himself. It is too difficult to say what spurred the creation of these groups of the most powerful people in the world. The Bilderberg Group was set up later, after the Second World War. Susan wonders what hat Étienne is wearing in this meeting: Bilderberg or Egmont?

Even so, she is told things that she swears never to repeat outside, information that clarifies the world situation regarding the observations of flying saucers.

Clearly, these groups know what UFOs are, but have never wanted to tell the truth, preferring to let people believe that their secret prototypes are flying saucers, or that flying saucers come from some other world and could attack us.

They are told that no debris from a real flying saucer, with real aliens, had ever been found anywhere. They are also told that no approach of a spaceship from outer space had ever been observed on Earth. They had never understood what was happening, but thanks to the means deployed to observe airspace and the cosmos they soon learned that these objects did not come from somewhere else. They decided, however, to let the idea of the threat of attacks by aliens hang in the air, to maintain a kind of strategy of tension, which is always useful to keep control over people. The CIA paid Disney a lot of money over many years to produce films showing flying saucers and aliens attacking Earth, and Hollywood continues to do this without even being asked. The subject of long and hard reflections, this strategy of tension, if well used (depending on your point of view, of course) means that people will accept almost anything. As for the famous UFOs, very few people know what is going on, i.e., the clear lack of risk, or at least absence of a direct link between the thousands of sightings every year and potential visitors from outer space.

Now, ninety years later, however, the situation has suddenly become very different thanks to Susan's latest observation.

Everything Jacques Vallée has told them about for the last year, corroborated by Susan's observations, proves that there would be quite a few alien civilizations in the Universe, and that at least one of them would have crossed Earth's pass thousands of years ago.

It is more than likely that they would have applied construction techniques to Earth that would have helped to make tools and machines that no longer exist, and they would have taught sciences such as mathematics and astronomy and explained how astrology could influence not only character, but also – and above all – the capacity of precognition, later renamed by the Christians as the Holy Spirit. This last concept came later, however, after the Age of Enlightenment, floating in the well of spiritualism and other paranormal practices that were discredited in the new way of thinking.

Nowadays people are taught how to draw up strategic plans in business and politics schools, to have a vision, but without realizing that these terms had real meaning in the past. They now seem to have more to do with lotteries and chance than anything else. These courses based on case studies do not pay any attention to the ability to predict what will happen or help people to make the right decisions as a result. Our society is in trouble now, whichever way you look at it. Nobody seems to know what to do on any scale – macroscopic, international, or microscopic. The media and communication technologies have shortened the cycles of influence considerably. Twenty years ago a strategic plan was made for five years, but now nobody knows how tomorrow will work out. Icons of our economic history tremble and collapse in the space of a few months: Kodak, Polaroid, Chrysler, General Motors ... Other companies in the world of finance make bad – or corrupt – decisions and go bankrupt in just a few years. Why, oh why do they make these choices knowing full well that they will be found out sooner or later? Not long ago, the banks themselves dug themselves into a hole after creating, and then betting on, toxic products. The repercussions of that catastrophe have not ended yet, and we should pray that Western society does not collapse completely, if there is still time to rescue it. Prayer ... the word is closely linked to the notion of precognition, so why does it not seem to work anymore? The Church has replaced ancient gods with the Holy Trinity, plus the list of saints it has created over the centuries. Anything in the Christians' Heaven, or linked to it, is worth a prayer, because it comes back to universal consciousness. Praying to something virtual is a way of addressing the Whole, that form of intelligence that governs universal consciousness and provides good answers when it is questioned about a particular thing or about the past or the future. What is not taught is the art of listening. Hermits and recluses dedicated time to learning how to listen, but nowadays who knows how to decipher messages from the beyond? Nobody teaches us the difference between our intellect, which is like a wired machine in our brain that deals with ideas sequentially, one after the other, depending on what our brain has recorded as a fact (from our five senses, our conversation, of what we see) and the latest information that we access in our memory. This intellect only strings pearls, always choosing the closest one; we act and speak like robots, with no real free will. No school teaches us how to tell the difference between the ideas and information that comes from this intellect and those from our consciousness, which, as can be seen, is part of universal consciousness, therefore it speaks to us in the same way. Courageous people know how to listen to their consciousness; those who speak to animals listen to the consciousness of those animals; mediums, spiritualists and fortune tellers also know how to read the consciousness of their clients, but no school tells us how to distinguish between these two categories of information. Not even mediums and other similar people talk about it, thinking that they have a gift for hearing voices. Nobody talks of developing this gift or improving it, and even less of using astrology or light machines to make getting access to this incredible source of information a more efficient process.

Susan looks at the streets as she is driven back to her hotel. Once there, she says goodbye to Jacques, who is staying somewhere else, and is entering her room when the phone rings.

The caller is a Frenchman who introduces himself as François Favre (P-4). He had heard of her during a meeting of his Study and Research Group into Parapsychology, which he set up in the early 1970s. He would like to meet her, saying that it is important but he cannot go into details over the phone. Susan suggests that they meet on her next trip to the East Coast, which is planned for soon.

François gives her his details and promises to get on the next plane to Washington.

Susan hangs up and falls back on the bed. It is 7 p.m. already, the lunch was not that great, and she has the impression of being in the back of beyond, out there north of Washington. It is raining. Lifting her head, she only sees boulevards, street lamps, grassy strips and cars with their headlights on that come and go in a kind of silent ballet, the roads reflecting the light from the headlights. What a sad view!

She is fed up of these meetings, these open secrets and unsaid things. She wonders where Jacques wants to get to with all this. Nothing interests her here, and now she has committed to wait for François Favre. Now what could he want?

She switches the TV on and starts to undress for a shower before going down to the hotel restaurant. She will order some salmon and go to bed early. She is tired, and even a little annoyed by the way things are going. Something is not quite right.

ALAIN HUBRECHT

Chapter 36

June 16th 2011, Washington, Virginia

Susan wakes up to a fine clear morning, which helps her mood. The previous day she visited Washington and its different monuments; a good way to relax. At the White House she saw how the squirrels no longer fear the tourists and come up close to try and get some food. Then she went for a real Italian pizza served on Kraft paper and a wooden board; she had never eaten one that good. She must remember to thank the person who recommended the restaurant. She takes her time over breakfast this morning, has already packed her suitcase to check out, and now waits for this Frenchman who is crossing the Atlantic to see her.

Phew, these guys are complicated, but then so is the subject, and its implications could have unforeseeable consequences. She had already seen, with the Chinese, what a nation could try to do to get hold of knowledge, even going so far as killing one of its nationals.

She hopes that Favre will not pull her into one of these endless stories. However, his voice on the phone gave her confidence, his English was not great but Susan's French was not exactly state-of-the-art either, but they could communicate, which is the most important thing.

She waits in the hotel lobby, flicking through the pages of (always thick) magazines. She is thinking about the waste they represent when the door opens and an absent-minded professor kind of figure enters the lobby rather awkwardly. The hotel is not very big, nor is the hall, so she sees him immediately. He comes up to her and puts his hand out, even before she has time to get up to welcome him.

His clothes are crumpled after the long flight. The lower part of his face is unshaven, giving him an eccentric and rather untidy appearance, but nevertheless quite pleasant overall.

"Madame Gomez, I presume?"

"Yes, that's right, and you must be Monsieur Favre?"

"Yes, I'm pleased to see you. I've just come from the airport and am quite hungry. Do you mind if we go into the bar so I can order a sandwich?"

They walk towards the bar, which is completely deserted at this time of day.

"Thank you for waiting for me. I know you live on the west coast but it's much easier for me to come here. You know, I am just a simple independent researcher and I have no grants or budget to cover my expenses, but the important thing is that I am here. I trained as a psychiatrist and have dedicated my life to the study of parapsychology. I have concentrated on the phenomenon of precognition and flying saucers and have created a study center on these phenomena."

"Ah, but why did you want to see me here rather than the specialists in those areas, or Jacques Vallée, who was with me here two days ago?"

"Well, I've known all those people for years, and have often fought hard with them in debates or conferences, but you are the person I wanted to speak to. They don't understand me … or rather don't want to understand me."

"Well, how can I understand you better? I'm not a psychiatrist, and even less of a specialist in flying saucers."

"True, but you have witnessed one of the most amazing things in history, and very recently, and you are also at the heart of one of the greatest advances in these areas, whatever you might say."

"How come you know all this? What are you referring to when you talk about this marvelous event?"

"Don't get upset. You know, rumors travel fast in our little world. There are only around twenty specialists in UFOs, and even fewer who link them to psychic phenomena. I know about it thanks to your experiment in Ireland. I admire you for it, but what I wanted to say to you will help you see things in a completely different light, believe me!"

"OK, we'll see. Order your sandwich and tell me all about it."

Favre takes a few minutes to read the menu in English with the different varieties of sandwich and hamburger, and finally decides. The two are comfortably seated on leather sofas in the subdued atmosphere of the bar.

"I should be honest with you and warn you that a lot of people don't like me. Some ignore me, others criticize, but very few praise me. There's a reason for that. After publishing the results of my research on parapsychology nobody endorsed my findings. No doubt I was too far off the trends of the time, and I am even more so now! My ideas and my theory are not convenient, either for scientists or enthusiasts of unexplained phenomena. I think I demolish their convictions a bit too much. I bring the whole concept back to the individual, not to the outside world. I explain that it all happens in our head, and the only factor that is difficult to understand is time. It is time that triggers and explains these events, these unexplained visions."

"I'm not following you. I admit that our ideas about flying saucers have evolved enormously this year, but how can you explain these appearances through the notion of time? And precognition … is that explained by the fact that people access universal consciousness?"

"Be careful there. Time is the key to it all, and there's no need to look for a solution outside our heads. Nothing goes out and nothing comes in, not yesterday, tomorrow, or today."

"Surely that's not possible. In the last few months we've demonstrated more than once that we can access information that was not known to us before, information that we would never have known under normal conditions."

"Exactly, that's what you don't understand. Precognition is simply memory that comes from the future. What's more, all memories are precognition. Making the effort to remember something means waiting for the information to reach you from the future. When you try to remember an event, you prepare the information in the future, let's say two seconds later, and once that period has passed you discover the information. Precognition just uses a longer period, which could be days, months and even years."

"I'm finding it hard to believe you. For example, the case of that Russian plane that crashed in a remote part of Africa. The Americans wanted to get their hands on it before the Russians and used the skills of the Stargate team. Nobody in the world knew where the plane was, but the team located it to a precision of less than one mile and clearly saw that it had landed in a river bed. They even made a drawing which was later successfully compared with a photograph taken on the site. How can you explain that?"

"All right, imagine that the plane hadn't been found by that team. Let's say that it was discovered later, by the Russians or explorers, or by the local people. Photos would have appeared in the press, and the members of the Stargate team would have learned of it, even a few years later. Well, that information, created in a possible future, is accessible in the present. Do you see what I mean?"

"Not, not really. I understand the principle behind what you say, that I can have access today to all the information that I might acquire in all the possible futures throughout my life. However, I don't understand how I could know about things located in places I would never go, like the Moon, for example. Ingo Swann did some exercises on the Moon."

"Once again, the reported information comes from the future, or from photos or films that he saw years later."

"No, that's not possible. Nobody has yet seen what he saw."

"OK, then it's still to come, or he saw it badly."

"Yes, the way you see it, it's easy to explain everything. Let's take what happened in San Diego the other day when the Chinese kidnapped us. Jacques Vallée saw the route to the place where we were being held in his mind. He did not know the place, had never been there before and probably will never go there in the future, and he didn't come and save us himself but sent specialists to do the job."

"Well, normally in one way or another he will be able to see something he saw in precognition some time later in his life. We can imagine a future in which he would have gone there after you had been found, dead or alive."

"But he saw us, he saw the people in the rooms, it was as if he was watching us at that very moment."

"He could have reconstructed it all unconsciously, after learning all the pieces of the puzzle. I'll give you an example. Nowadays, when research departments set up very complex projects, for planes, factories or buildings, for example, they deploy a whole range of simulation software that will recreate a virtual model of the construction under all possible conditions, to see what happens. When a breakage or problem is identified, they go back, modify the project and start the simulation over again. Do you follow me? Let's take a Formula 1 race car. Dozens of engineers simulate its performance on all the circuits it races on, and in all weather conditions. They will carry out dozens of repeats, each time changing the car's design to get to the first race of the season with a car that has already raced, in virtual terms, on all the circuits. As for premonitions, that's just repeating a simulation, nothing more! Many people are still surprised that I always restrict premonitions to information that has to do with problems, danger, or accidents, but simulation is also like that. You only look for possible problems, and it's only on the real circuit that people will enjoy the car's performance."

"I'm not with you all the way on that. True, spontaneous premonitions or premonitory dreams are related to potential problems, but when mediums or clairvoyants such as the people in the Stargate program start work they can see everything."

"Yes, I grant you that, the difference is related, as they say in computer science, to the technique applied to transport the information, for example e-mails. Premonitions are part of 'push' and precognition part of 'pull'. I agree, however, that I have not covered this aspect of things in sufficient detail.

"OK, one point to me, then! And since you seem to be in the picture about our activities, what do you think of UFO apparitions? We can contact them by telepathy, and we believe that they are the 'souls' of the fallen angels of ancient times. These souls would still be on Earth, and since they'd be sad at not having been able to help the human race with their knowledge, they'd try and suggest ways for us to develop our science, simply by showing us that it could be done with technology we don't have yet."

"Yes, I know about that too, about your experiments in the desert, and, as I told you, about your trip to Ireland. These beings don't exist, any more than flying saucers do. It all comes from ectoplasm. They are created by our race, and it stops there. There is no telepathy, only precognition with oneself in the future. Remember that it is only a temporary loop with oneself."

"What about the Ankh we received from those spheres that paid us a visit in the desert, and the same spheres I saw in the dark triangle in Ireland?"

"Unfortunately, it is only ectoplasm formed by your spirit or that of another person. Even the Ankh is an ectoplasm. Its meaning or use is perhaps the one you worked out, and that information might come from the future, but the being that materialized it is certainly a human being who was most likely right next to you, if not you yourself."

"But if it was me, surely I would remember?"

"No, no more than if you remember to ask something of the future or make an object appear. Think of what Méheust wrote in his books. He explains that in the years after a writer or a cartoonist describes a scene with UFOs the craft appears in reality, almost to the smallest detail. You have determined, or rather your colleagues have, that these UFOs are materializations of thought forms, wished by dead aliens who helped us thousands of years ago. I say that we materialize these objects, which is why they evolve with our technology, sometimes slightly ahead of its time. So, a writer who describes a scene of science fiction sees, in his spirit, what will happen in the future, but in fact what happens several years later are the thoughts of another human being, of which he will be informed by the press."

"Oh, all this seems to be a bit farfetched!"

"I admit that what Méheust demonstrated is a great example of a temporary loop. Everything I am explaining has been clearly demonstrated, and the example proves it."

"So, you mean that these beings that visited us and the spheres only exist in our heads, or that we effectively created them?"

"Yes, exactly, but it doesn't take anything away from the interest of the phenomenon. If they were visitors from space, what they could teach us would be limited to their knowledge at the time of their arrival, whereas my theory sustains that we would have access to all future knowledge."

"Hey, wait, I'm going to stop you there. You said it was limited to our lives, and that we can't access something that will happen after we die."

"Yes, sorry, but endless possible futures and discoveries can be made, and you can benefit from them. When Nicolas Tesla said that he could connect to a zone containing all these discoveries, he might have seen inventions that were, during his lifetime, made in the possible futures that never happened."

"Yes, that's possible, but it still sounds far-fetched, what you say about each individual having access to an incredible potential knowledge. Unlimited!"

"No, the only limitation is linked to physical limits, to the realizable aspect of an invention on the basis of the time that a new technology takes to be developed, or its material impossibility."

"I'm trying to follow you. Take the case of those big black triangles that come to a standstill and defy our technological knowledge. They must have some incredible source of energy to be able to levitate like that. If it were 'feasible', an inventor would perhaps have 'perceived' it in his dreams. However, if it is not realistic, that doesn't stop people dreaming about it and materializing it in the way they want to see it evolve. However, we cannot discover how to make a thing fly like that. We could say that any invention can be made ahead of its time because the inventor is able to see things in another way in a probable future through precognition, and, therefore has the technological ability to make it happen. The material and physical feasibility of an invention is an important thing. You can see flying ships or saucers, little green men and big black triangles without any of them being feasible. They are simply dreams in material form, like your spheres and your Irish triangle; they have no technological coherence. However, an inventor can perceive an invention that will be made in the future. I must admit that we cannot explain today what decides to give us access to a particular piece of information, because we only see the problems or inventions that work, and not inventions that don't work. When he saw a new apparatus Tesla knew that it would work right from the start. He was always staggered by his visions, and did not know how to explain them."

"So, does this mean that there is a selective system, a kind of filter, which only allows us to perceive useful things, either to avoid unhappiness or discover new inventions?

"The system could be in our heads. As for inventions, imagine that you can read the newspapers of the future in which different inventors' results appear. They would indicate if each invention worked or not. Admit it, it would be a pity to remember inventions that don't work; you see, the logic explains the phenomenon."

"Yes, but once again there is a 'push' system here, never the opposite, regarding inventions. I don't know of any inventors who claim that they can 'look for' inventions on demand. They all seem to have different types of doubts, like others have premonitory dreams."

"Yes, I acknowledge that I have limited my reflections to mechanisms that 'push' information from the future into our heads, and not to those that will look for it in the future."

"Well, I don't know if we've really nailed the question. To be honest, I doubt it. While you were talking I was thinking about the theory of

Rupert Sheldrake (P-10) about waves with shapes. I think your theory explains what could happen better than his, and I must admit that this all seems to stand up very well. What would you like from me now?"

"I would ask you to try and get people to understand me and take my theory into account. OK, it might not be the right one, but at least it will be considered by the people who work with you. Your work is not fully affected by my theory, because it is quite possible that our ancestors knew how to improve our ability to see into the future. The hypotheses linked to flying saucers and the so-called possibilities of precognition and mediums are the ones that should be reviewed. The ability of the human body to create thought shapes, ectoplasms as the mediums call them, should also be studied in more detail. The fact that they have a physical existence like your Ankh also calls for a study. Almost all ectoplasms disappear after a certain time, whether they are apparitions of UFOs, the Virgin Mary or 'angel hair', but others survive, such as the remains of molten metal and the Ankh.

"As for theories on visitors from outer space in ancient times, i.e., those contained in the Book of Henoch, I think we should put them aside, at least for the areas that we are interested in. Indeed, I don't know anything about this. Maybe they did really exist, and perhaps they built mechanisms in Egypt to improve their capacity for precognition, and maybe they taught astrology to help men improve it. Clearly, we will never know, because, as they say, it was already known."

Susan watches Favre in silence and wonders what to make of it all. She realizes that he came to see her as soon as he could, and that what he says seems to be credible, well thought out, and she cannot find fault with his line of thought. But should she tell Jacques and the others? How can she tell them that he came to see her? Being a woman, maybe she is leaving herself open?

"Listen, what you tell me is not easy to digest, but I understand and accept your process. Could we imagine a demonstration of what you are saying? Could it be demonstrated that the cross and the Ankh, the spheres and triangle are actually produced by us? I think it would be much more difficult to demonstrate the fact that premonitions and other forms of precognition or visions of inventions are only linked to one brain and to innumerable futures, through which we can project ourselves before coming back with the findings."

"Yes, I admit that ... while you were talking, coming back to the Ankh again, I was wondering if the fact of touching an object that has belonged to someone else could stop us from making a selection – among the innumerable futures – and from taking those that contain the presence of that person or information related to him or her. As for demonstrating the basis of my theory through some kind of demonstration, I fear I cannot help you much there. Your group is in a better position to do that than I am. You have people who have the gift of precognition, and you should do tests that will allow you to define the limits of the phenomenon."

"That's precisely what they are doing."

"Yes and no. I fear that they are only doing tests that subconsciously confirm their ideas. That's the danger of getting too enthusiastic."

"Just like you!"

"Well, if we put our ideas together I think we would arrive at a better result!"

"Would you like a drink? I'm starting to get thirsty."

"Yes, thanks, sure, the same again for me, but please put it on my bill. You are my guest today."

Susan walks towards the bar and uses the time to organize her thoughts. Either she agrees to the researcher's request, or she refuses. He seems to be walking on hot coals and does not even give her a few minutes to reflect. She tells the waiter to take his time preparing the drinks, and looks at her watch. They have been talking non-stop for two hours; it's no surprise that she's thirsty.

She returns carrying two drinks, a beer for Favre and a Campari Orange for herself.

"Listen, I suggest that we stop discussing this for now. I'm going to make a few calls and we can meet for dinner this evening if you like. I take it you're not returning to France tonight?"

"No, not knowing when you would be free I booked a flight for tomorrow. My hotel is very close by. Please let me invite you to dinner this evening."

"OK. Let's meet in the lobby at 7 p.m. That gives you time to go back to your hotel, freshen up and maybe even rest for a while. And think about what I just suggested to you."

Favre says goodbye and leaves the hotel. She watches him as he walks away. He walks in a funny way, looking for a sidewalk to get back to his hotel; naturally, there isn't one. He does not seem to come over to the States very often!

Susan goes back up to her room. She takes a shower, puts on a bathrobe and lies on the bed. She thinks about who she is going to call first. After a good five minutes she picks up the phone and dials a number.

Chapter 37

June 16th 2011, the rooftop terrace at the W Hotel, Washington

Susan enters the felted atmosphere of the rooftop restaurant in the W Hotel, located very close to the White House with a view of the Washington Monument. She had heard of this place before and wanted to see it at least once. The reason for her meeting with Favre made the place well worth a visit. She would suggest sharing the bill with him, after giving her name and explaining that she had already reserved a table. The waiter accompanies her and she realizes that François is already there. She sits down on a large and comfortable red seat. To her left, the window looks out over the Monument; the view really is magnificent. You can see all the lights of Washington from here. The discreet atmosphere and the distance between tables mean that they can talk without worrying about eavesdroppers. She almost decided on the 1789 restaurant, where Obama regularly dines, but she was not sure they would find the peace and discretion of this restaurant. Anyway, the view is wonderful. François stands up to greet her and offers his hand.

"Good evening, I hope you like the place."

"I have seen very few places as beautiful as this, and I thank you for letting me experience it. So, have you thought about my request?"

"Wow, you don't hang around, do you? First of all, let's order an aperitif, then we'll look at the menu, and later we can get down to more serious things."

"OK, that's fine by me. Sorry to be so impatient."

"Don't worry, I understand."

Susan asks for a caipirinha, called a 'Mixed Berry Caipirinha' here, while François decides on a glass of white Chardonnay from Magnolia Grove in Napa Valley. Susan has a bit of fun watching the Frenchman trying to decipher the menu. He confesses his surprise at seeing sandwiches as a starter in such a classy restaurant, but Susan points out that they are only served at midday. He then sets off in search of a good steak with French fries, but there is no sign of that typically European dish. He continues, in vain, to look for something substantial before asking Susan for help, and she suggests a giant scampi cocktail as a starter and spicy chicken as a main course.

"Thanks, I must confess that these names bamboozle me, and they don't give me any idea of how many things I am going to find on my plate. I do have a small favor to ask you, however."

"Go ahead."

"Every time I come to the United States I ask for cheesecake for dessert. I love it and it just isn't so good in France."

"Don't worry, I found it on the menu. You will have your favorite dessert."

They place their order, and while she sips her drink Susan starts to explain what she decided to say to the professor.

"I called Jacques Vallée and told him about your work and request. He was very surprised that I had accepted to meet you without telling him first, but I told him what you said to me. He calmed down and listened carefully to my summary of our discussion. He already knew about your theory, and had stated his objections, but seeing the progress that's been made in the project he's now more open to listening to alternative explanations, and yours is compatible with what we saw and observed. Before, with no arguments clearly indicating one direction or another, it was quite normal for each scientist to stick doggedly to his or her position. If you're right, it means that we can never expect any technological contribution from another civilization, like the expectations created by the 'fallen angels' theory or who knows what other alien visitors to Earth a few thousand years ago. But our theory admits that they're capable of accumulating molecules through thought, while yours says that it is us who are capable of it. When we see that the phenomenon of premonition or precognition affects 99% of the human race, it's possible to believe that any psychic phenomenon might only be related to humans. By the same rule of thumb, so are UFOs."

"Well, I'm happy to hear that. What did he decide, then?"

"Nothing for now; he wants to think about it. He feels that your theory stops halfway. On the one hand, it doesn't deal satisfactorily with 'proactive' precognition, and on the other it doesn't try to understand what activates a 'reactive' premonition. The terms 'proactive' and 'reactive' refer to the 'push' and 'pull' technologies. Nor does it deal with the case in which a possible future could lead us to know where the sought after information was, and that inevitably requires the intervention of a third party ... animal, vegetable or mineral. You say that everything goes on in our brain and never leaves it, except over time. He'd like to produce a unified theory and not leave gaps in the reasoning. We've already spent a lot of money on this project, and with the results obtained so far it'd be a pity to give out incomplete or wrong information."

"Do you think I could join the team to improve the theory?"

"I don't know. We're very grateful to you for your contribution, really, but we don't think it would be a good idea to bring you into the team. The risk is that you would push it towards what you believe. It's the classical case of people who are passionate about what they are doing."

"Yes, that's true. It would be hard for me to make people think I'm not passionate!"

"I hope you're not disappointed. We are pleased that you contacted us, and we will keep you up to date with the progress of our work as far as we are allowed to reveal things."

Chapter 38

September 10th 2011, Huntsville, Alabama

Following Susan's meeting with François Favre the team radically changed its action plan and spent two months checking out if the researcher's theory had a good foundation.

It was considered plausible, and a real battle emerged as a result to study the phenomenon of temporary changes to the brain, its ability to interconnect with the information from a universal consciousness, and the way in which the phenomenon of premonition works and the materialization   of   thought   take   form. At SAIC's request Susan had moved to Huntsville with Alex to work for the Missile and Space Intelligence Center (MSIC). The base is still active, and shares the site with the American Army, specifically the base at Redstone where the MSIC is located. The MSIC works on espionage in space, but also on wave-directed weapons and, reading between the lines, anything to do with thought control. Since the Cold War this work was hidden behind the code name MKULTRA. The center also seems to be the place where all the information collected by Nikola Tesla was sent after his death. There is still a company called Intergraph on the site; it developed revolutionary computer components in the 1980s that were restricted to a very small number of selected companies. The company designed a superscalar and super vectorial 64-bit computer that is still unrivalled today. The person behind its design also designed Windows-based software with an incredible performance, but when they saw how powerful it was they decided not to present it in public for fear of harming the computing industry as a whole. At the time, the Intergraph office where the team worked was guarded by the military police. None of their inventions remain today. Susan found this information in the internal database of SAIC, and reached the conclusion that strange things had been happening in Huntsville for around fifty years.

The unit where she is working with Paul is charged with studying ways of controlling the brain remotely, either through reading or writing, basically to see what people are thinking or to give orders. At first sight, the results are not so great. On the other side of the corridor is the service that works with satellites, and farther to the right the people working with the HAARP team (T-7), which runs the network of giant antennae that send waves into the ionosphere.

Susan is not too happy to be here. She does not like the environment; it is too military and too oriented towards psychological warfare. She has already had a few rows with Alex, who does not seem to bother too much about other people's moods. Nevertheless, she accepted to come here, because the resources available are even more impressive than at SAIC in San Diego. Well, she would see what happens. She has put her archeological activities on hold as a result of events, her meeting with François Favre and her meetings in high places with Jacques Vallée. Four research themes have been identified: what leads to the 'push' effect; how to gain access to the information stored in universal consciousness; how to influence the performance of the human brain, and how materializations take place. A fifth theme – how universal consciousness is fed – is left aside for the time being, because it is the one with the closest links to the basic principles of matter. It is rather 'static' as a result. Each atom has its life, and stores its history inside itself. That is more or less what Jean-Emile Charon (P-2), a CNRS researcher, said in the early 1980s. He explained that matter is made of eons, easily assimilated as a counterpart to electrons, and that these eons need to increase their power along four axes: reflection, knowledge, love, and action. Each eon possesses its own knowledge and has existed since the beginning of the universe. His theory has aged a little, but its basis, which says that it is possible to gain access to universal consciousness from the smallest particle, is still valid until proven to the contrary, and it is the one they have decided to adopt for the time being.

Even though the basic mechanism is not understood, they decided to look at everything related to it that leads to measureable effects, even though it might not be possible to reproduce them.

Jacques Vallée has taken over the leadership of the group working on the materialization of aerial phenomena, and Paul Smith heads the group studying the precognition effect. François Favre, after long reflections and discussions, agreed to lead the group studying the 'push' effect, which is really his pet subject. Susan is in charge of the improvement of human skills. She has the best knowledge of what has already been done, and Alex contributes his work on the light machine.

This Sunday, Alex and Susan, recently arrived, visit the space museum as a way to relax after their move from San Diego. They are in front of the main entrance, admiring the enormous mass and sleek lines of the SR-71, the famous 'Blackbird' that revolutionized the history of supersonic flight and espionage techniques. They are still amazed that this aircraft, which entered service in 1968, could fly at over Mach 3. No airplane has equaled it to this day, at least no known aircraft!

"Can you imagine flying in that thing at top speed, seeing the curve of Earth under you from such a height?"

"No, it'd scare me to death. You're a guy, and I know you, you love thrills and spills, but I prefer old stones and I want to stay alive. Did you see the size of those engines? I could park my car inside one!"

"Yeah, you must really feel you're dominating the world from up there, it must be great. Look, there are two seats, we could go together!"

"Are you kidding? You'll never get me in that! Come on, let's go inside the museum."

The collect their tickets and start to stroll around the rooms with reproductions of original objects that took part in the conquest of space. Outside, they could admire natural-sized rockets like the ones that took men to the Moon, but it is too hot out there and they prefer to stay in the air-conditioned area.

In one of the rooms they notice an unexpected object. Next to the LEM is the spacesuit and helmet of the hero of Stanley Kubrick's film '2001, Space Odyssey'. The helmet is easily recognizable; seen from above it looks like an ant's head with two big eyes painted on top. It is red and draws your attention. Susan thinks of the film, in which Arthur C. Clarke, the science-fiction author who wrote the screenplay based on his novel of the same name, had amazing ideas about the universe, the appearance of intelligence, aliens and time travel. Kubrick wanted to make a science-fiction film that would be as credible and realistic as possible, with unnoticed special effects. Susan tries to recreate the film in her head, seeing it from the perspective of her new knowledge. Could it possibly contain some interesting information?

"Do you remember the movie?"

"Of course, I've seen it over and over again. It's great. The special effects make it incredibly realistic. The modern super-productions certainly have nothing on it."

"But what stays with you from the film?"

"Well, let's see, yeah, a monolith that floated over Earth at the time of prehistoric man. If he touched it, Man acquired intelligence."

"Exactly, and can you remember what happened at the end?"

"I remember that the last survivor disconnected the computer, which had become too independent, and the craft was sucked into the gravitational pull of Jupiter."

"Nothing else?"

"Well, I remember seeing a baby floating in space, but I didn't understand the symbolism."

"The astronaut sees himself back on Earth, older. Then he dies, and is reborn in the form of an astral baby that announces the Superman, all under the benevolent eye of the monolith. Did you know that Clarke based himself on the Book of Henoch for the screenplay?"

"Why are you telling me this? You know that theory has been put on ice since your meeting with François?"

"Yes, but why am I looking at this helmet right now? It refers to aliens and the improvement of our intelligence."

"That has nothing to do with it …"

"No, just think of Méheust's theory, which says that science-fiction writers seek their inspiration in the future, and that the future shows them thought forms imagined by other human beings. Maybe you're right; I should stop trying to see relationships where there are none. Come on, let's go outside and take a look at the rockets."

ALAIN HUBRECHT

Chapter 39

September 11th 2011, Huntsville, Alabama

Susan arrives at her office early. From there, she can see the enormous grey buildings lined up in parallel rows, devoid of any frills and scattered across the enormous site. They are very tall and can either house offices, hangars or manufacturing units. On the corners, a big number indicates each block. Those occupied by her unit are not different in any way from those of NASA or Intergraph. Fortunately, there are still a lot of plants and trees to look at, and she is also lucky to have a window in her office. Alex has not arrived yet; he has some paperwork to do in town related to their house move.

After the visit to the museum she took time out to think, and started to elaborate an idea. She would like to check if it is feasible before telling Alex about it. She leaves her office, crosses the corridor and talks through an interphone to request access to the offices of HAARP. An employee opens the door after checking her out on a camera located in the corridor. She then puts her pass in a slot and waits for the door to open, which happens after the employee asks her some questions about the reason for her visit.

She asks to speak to the manager and is taken to a windowless room. In the corner on the right she notices a sideboard with a telephone on top marked with the word "SECRET" in red letters. Even the connecting cable is red! She had seen one of these in the Pentagon in her meetings with Jacques Vallée, and knows that the people who have this kind of telephone are pretty important. The man who now stands before her is imposing, gray-haired with a crew cut, but has a kindly face. That's good, she thinks, because the atmosphere here is not exactly light-hearted.

"Hi, my name is Susan Gomez, and I've just arrived in the Brain Control unit on the other side of the corridor. I have some technical questions that I'm sure you could help me with."

"Go ahead, I'll answer when I can, otherwise I'll tell you what you have to do to come back and see me another time."

"Thanks. I've read several articles on the HAARP project. I don't want to know what's it's for, but I would like to know if it can help me in my work."

"The HAARP project is at the service of the scientists, outside military working hours, so I think that my first answer could be positive. What is it you want to do exactly?"

"I'd like to know if it's possible to polarize the particles that cross the waves emitted by HAARP's antennae."

"That depends on what particles you're talking about. We can act on certain wavelengths and in a certain electromagnetic spectrum."

"I am thinking of acting on axions, the particles from photons that have been passed through a strong magnetic field. I can give you the wavelengths and the time slots."

"What area would you like us to act on?"

"The whole of the United States, but at different moments."

"Wow, that's quite something! We would need to do a lot of paperwork before getting authorization, but it is technically possible. Do you have a date for this experiment?"

"No, it's a purely theoretical thing at the moment. Could your technicians look at the feasibility of the exercise? I can send you the wavelengths by e-mail, plus the polarization characteristics and the trip schema for the exposure window."

"OK, I'd be happy to do that for you. You know, we're always open to new applications of HAARP, because nothing valuable has come out of it so far."

"Really? I read that the project had achieved a new feat of technology."

"Well, in that case you're better informed than me!"

"No, I'm joking, I read in an engineering magazine that the thirty-five generators that power the 20-kilowatt antennae were designed to be undetectable by infrared rays. No calorie can escape, either through the exhaust pipes or through the ground."

"It seems that you know a lot of things that the public shouldn't, but seeing the pass you're wearing I'm not going to worry about it. Give my team a few days to give a technical answer to your question, and in the meantime I'll deal with the administrative end. As soon as I know anything I'll let you know."

"That's great, thanks very much. I'm looking forward to hearing from you."

"Oh, by the way, my name is Harry Meessen."

A few days later, Harry paid Susan a visit in her office. His smile suggested some good news.

"Good morning, Susan. I hope I'm not disturbing you."

"No, not at all. I was going to make a phone call, but it can wait."

"I have the information, and except for a few details I think you're going to like what you hear. You made my guys' life a little difficult with your negative polarization idea. You know that it can only be created by reflection on a plane. In your case, as you explained, it's the cloudy surface of Venus when struck by the sun's rays at a certain angle. You want to re-create this effect for all the other moments in which this angle is not suitable. HAARP's first objective is, effectively, to create a reflecting plane, but for waves that will bounce at the same angle as they arrived, like a ball on a pool table. My boys thought about uncoupling the antennae. Some of them will create a lower reflecting plane, with neutral characteristics, while the others will create an upper plane capable of negatively polarizing your particles. We can ensure that they don't bounce back onto the first plane again but pass through it to reach Earth's surface. We checked out your data and it seems possible to sweep the country in the way you suggested."

"That's great, and thank you so much for having worked so fast!"

"Nah, that's nothing, it was just the technical part and that's my job. I don't think it'll be so easy on the administrative side. Have you spoken about this project outside your unit?"

"No, not yet. As soon as I get your reply, if it's positive, I'll organize a conference."

"Are you authorized to tell me what it's about?"

"Yes, I think so. In any case, it's up to me to decide. The result of the sweep should improve people's precognition skills."

"Are you serious?"

"Completely. We've been doing research on this in SAIC for over a year, and recently in your offices on the other side of the corridor. We've have obtained very convincing results and my job is to see how we can achieve a strategic advantage for our country."

"But surely, however well the thing works, you're not going to give the entire population of the United States the benefits of state-of-the-art technological discoveries?"

"Why not? From homeless people to top-line executives, I aim to boost everyone's decision-making capacities, which should lead to an incredibly competitive population. Where do you see a snag?"

"Well, this kind of discovery is usually reserved for the elites."

"No, that's a mistake. I would even say that, ideally, the world's population should benefit, but my patriotism ends there."

"Mm … so your plan would greatly improve the competitiveness of all our companies without any distinctions or favoritism?"

"Exactly. A gift for every American citizen. But wait, it still has to work! In any case, we're not just swimming around in science fiction. It's a major strategic project that has no precedent."

"Well, hell, and on top of it, it's a woman telling me this. What a kisser for our strategists in the Pentagon!"

"To be honest, I'm quite proud of it."

"But what real effect will the project have on the population? What will they feel? Will they be aware that something is happening?"

"No, not directly. First of all, as I say, the thing has to work. Then we'll see how much time it takes to expose the population so that an effect can be felt. If everything goes well, each individual will be better placed to see what will not work for him or her in the future, and take decisions to avoid situations that lead to things going wrong. They can also gain access to inventions tens of years before they would have been discovered normally. Those will be the most useful benefits if the project is successful."

"Yeah, but what you're saying sounds incredible. If it works, it should be restricted to the Army or a particular elite, but you want to give the whole population of the United States access to it? That's crazy; it's like giving gold to pigs! Are your superiors in the picture?"

"No, not yet, I wanted to hear your opinion, but it's clear to me that all the people in the country should benefit. I'm sure that the end result will be much better than if it is reserved to a select few, and I don't know what would be done with HAARP. Anyway, there's already a solution for that, and I'm not involved there. Listen, the situation of the economy is serious. World wars are well behind us, but what is shaping up on the horizon is just as serious as wars: blind economic superiority without scruples, the removal of social conquests, bankrupt countries because of the banking crisis and independent groups of speculators as powerful as nations. Nobody has a magic formula to get out of it, people try to hide the reality of the situation, and the poor suffer more and more. Tomorrow we might be governed by China or Qatar, who knows? Our debts, and those of countries friendly to us, just go on rising.

"Believe me, there needs to be a radical change in our ability to produce, to innovate, and only my idea can get us out of the quagmire."

"I admit that your arguments sound convincing, and I must say I tend to agree with you."

After swapping a bit more information about the study, Harry leaves and goes back to his office.

Susan prepares to send an e-mail to Jacques Vallée.

She is sure he will follow her line.

Her gaze wanders out the window to the distant forest as she thinks about the best way to announce her project.

Epilogue

June 2028, Paris, at the foot of the Eiffel Tower

Susan has been waiting for François Favre for a few minutes. There are lots of people milling around the base of the Eiffel Tower. Maybe it was not the best place to meet, she thinks, but fortunately the weather is on their side and it is a beautiful day.

François is 86 years old now. Susan has a son by Alex who will turn 16 this year. They are living happily in California.

Susan has returned to her great passion, archeology, and Alex works in a division of SAIC.

"Hello!"

"Oh, hello François! Excuse me, I was lost in thought. What a lovely day! Do you know where you want to go for a drink?"

"Listen, despite the crowds, I would really like to take you up the tower. It would give me great pleasure to invite you to the Jules Verne, as a souvenir of our first meeting in Washington, in the POV lounge. Do you remember that?"

"Of course I remember, and I like your idea. Hey, you look great for your age, but are you sure you really want to be up there more than 400 feet off the ground?"

"Yes, of course, and anyway my age has nothing to do with what we talked about the first time we met, and largely thanks to you. Come on, follow me!"

The two friends join the queue for the elevators and the time passes quickly because they are pleased to see each other again. After ten minutes or so they finally stand at the entrance to the highest restaurant in Paris.

"I reserved a table, because I knew you would say yes. There's our table, at the end on the right."

"The view from here is incredible. We're used to skyscrapers at home, but here we're really isolated in the middle of the sky. What a great idea you had!"

"The pleasure is all mine. Did you have a good flight?"

"Of course. Just one hour from California. I took me longer to get here from the airport than from California to France. Isn't it amazing that we still can't get local transport right!"

"What would you like to eat?"

Susan and François study the menu for a few minutes and carry on with their discussion after ordering.

"So, tell me, how are things going?"

"Oh, great. Alex is now head of the production unit for light apparatuses. They're selling like hotcakes. Their efficiency is proven and the patent has allowed SAIC to create a division dedicated to them, and it now accounts for a large part of their revenue. He's happy. When business goes well, everyone is always happy. Our son Michael is finishing college this year, and he's been running his own company for the last two years."

"College? Isn't he a bit young?"

"No, back home kids can go to college starting at twelve now. You know that education has undergone an authentic revolution after our discovery and the implementation of my plan, sixteen years ago. It's amazing that the project with HAARP was able to change the world."

"You said it, and for once, for the better! Look at world peace, which we've had for ten years, the revival of the economy, good healthcare and a decent income for people all over the world. It's almost paradise on Earth, and all thanks to you."

"Come on, don't exaggerate! Thousands of people worked on it. What we had to do was to make the decision, on a national level, to give up our strategic lead for the benefit of the human race as a whole."

"I believe that the key was the invention of controlled fusion. At last, the only inexhaustible energy source that does not harm the climate or our resources! Every attempt to create new, free energy has been opposed worldwide, and each time people had to face the fact that if all the world's energy had to be created by one method or another it would lead to a global imbalance that would inevitably destroy Earth in the end. Gravity is only used to keep objects in the air that should be there, like aircraft or cars, and not to supply energy. Luckily, our researchers' intelligence has multiplied perhaps a hundred times, or at least their inventiveness has. Just think, there are no patents any more. No invention can be patented, and the notion of benefit to the human race has become universal."

"It hasn't been any easy ride, though. Look what happened in 2018 with religion, when the United States succeeded in eliminating the notion of religion as a financial movement. Fortunately, the Pope agreed, and it was his gesture that pushed the other religions to take the same line. There are no places of worship now. They've all been replaced by areas of well-being and contemplation. The one who came out of it best was Buddha. If he knew 2,500 years ago that he would ultimately triumph …"

"It's not really Buddha, but his doctrine of spirituality and wisdom that has won the day."

"Yes, of course, I was joking. So, what's up with you here in France?"

"Oh, you know that the notion of 'State' will be abolished next year, and the word 'France' will just be a reference to a geographical area, a mark of history. Even the world government will disappear, as it has no reason for existing. There are no public bodies anymore; everything is run by the private sector. Now that there's no more corruption, criminality or economic problems, simple private entities can start managing all the infrastructures. The notion of money still exists, but for how long?"

"All the same, things have been really simplified with this idea of a working hour that is the same for everyone. One Mondo is equivalent to one hour of work all over the world, whatever the status of the person who does it. The collapse of the birth rate has led to a re-examination of all the plans for demographic growth and has revalued property. Every human being has the right to a house at sixteen years of age. The removal of roads and highways has allowed us to completely rethink the distribution of the land.

Distance is no longer seen as an obstacle. Total telepresence has led to the disappearance of offices. Organic teletransporters have led to the elimination of all warehouses. Our cities are now just museums; Paris still exists in the form that we can see now. The only new spaces are dedicated to recreation and physical fitness, theme parks and nature parks. All monuments and buildings of a certain interest have been classified and will never be destroyed. All the rest will be demolished to the benefit of the new 'group housing units'."

"You worked as a psychiatrist. Aren't you worried that there might be a drift back, that we're all becoming too passive?"

"First of all, I should tell you that I am still working! Age is not an obstacle any more. Our dear researchers have found so many miraculous ways to stay in shape that I will soon be joining the lower levels of the elderly! Drift back? No, I don't see it happening. Our world government got to a stage in which everything seemed to work on its own. No problems have been detected for over five years. The stock exchanges and speculation have been eliminated, thank heavens, and there are no more traces of mafias or drugs. Most illnesses have been eradicated and the rest are likely to disappear within the next two years. Average life expectancy is estimated at 200, with excellent health right up to the last few years. The Spectra program wants to extend that figure to 1,000 years, but they still have some concerns. The number of discoveries and inventions made has been incredible, Susan. I'm not surprised they gave you the Nobel Peace Prize. You fought hard with the President of the United States for him to open up the frontiers to your technologies. In less than six years your country has become the world leader in all areas, it has paid off its debt, developed defense technologies that allow you to do without an army, and you have sold these technologies to other countries that wanted them. That was a clear demonstration of the efficiency of your HAARP project. Then you convinced your country to offer all its knowledge to the rest of the world. That was the really big challenge and you achieved it. Here in France we watched the situation evolve, wondering which American solution would end up devouring us. Your only condition was to stop supporting religions. You asked each country that inherited your discoveries to break all links with religion and stop financing it as well. That was really brave."

"Not really. Don't forget that other countries had been watching us and the progress we were making for years. The fact that we called our HAARP project 'Operation Holy Spirit' was not by chance. That allowed us to set our watches in terms of the materiality of the phenomenon and take all mystical elements out of it. You know, we communicated a lot on that. Naturally, it was a question of challenging people head on. We didn't want to attack or upset anyone, and what's more we had to come up with solutions to replace notions. You can't lead a people dying of hunger without some kind of religion; we had to provide a solution to that hunger. The hungrier a person is, the more he or she needs to believe something. Economic prosperity is no longer a Holy Grail. Controlled fusion provided the solution, as did material teletransport. Everyone, everywhere, has access to food and clean drinking water. We have no need to build roads, canals, or lay cables any more. Our fusion machine is enough, you just throw microscopic quantities of garbage or whatever into it and you have energy for years."

"Yes, I know. That discovery moved everything forward. Anyway, tell me more about your son Michael. Did he benefit from your discovery when he was born?"

"Yes, he did. He was the first baby in the modern world to be exposed at the moment of his birth, and I must confess that I am happy with the result. He's capable of materializing matter at will, and his inventive spirit is really quite extraordinary. Fortunately, he kept his human emotions, and he loves us just like children have always loved their parents."

"What will it be like when all children born like him start to produce things? We can already see the results of your exposure of the population."

"Hah, don't make me laugh! You've reminded me of the side effects that we didn't think about. Animals that changed their behavior and new species that appeared all over the place. We didn't reveal that at the beginning, because we didn't know what effect it would have on fauna and flora. Their reproductive cycles are shorter than those of humans, and we soon observed that the species improved considerably in just a few generations. We decided to stop that early on. The period of exposure had been long enough anyway for our population. The patents office saw an incredible rise in the number of applications, and a 100% increase in the creation of new companies, but some of them took advantage to improve their criminal methods. We hadn't foreseen that either, but luckily the negative side soon came to an end thanks to our prosperity, making criminality a waste of time. The HAARP system was stopped after three years, and replaced by exposure sessions in movie theaters with informative films and people were invited free of charge. In any case, we realized that each individual has a limit, and more exposure above that limit is no use at all. What we wanted to do above all was avoid segregation, so that everyone could have access to the same beneficial effects."

"Looking back, what do you think of it all now?"

"Complete success, wouldn't you say? Seventeen years ago nothing was going well on Earth … religious wars, terrorism, banking crises, sky-high food prices, unemployment, and almost-bankrupt states. In the US we had bankrupt cities and states and an astronomic financial debt, rampant climate change and the exhaustion of fossil fuel resources. That's all behind us now, thank goodness. At last we can focus on our wellbeing, protecting Earth against a potential Near Earth Object, improving our climate, recovering endangered species and or wildlife that were suffering the most. There is work for those who want it, and leisure for those who prefer that. Nobody is forced to work. Everyone has guaranteed earnings, and those who want to work a bit more can, but they can't earn more than the hours they have in their lives."

"What about the fallen angels and the UFOs?"

"Oh, that's well in the past now. We might think we've reached their level of civilization, but we've decided not to attempt the exploration of space outside our solar system. We understood that this would be like arming a time bomb. The result of an encounter with an alien species is totally unpredictable, so we'd rather not induce it. That's why we've stopped the SETI program and sending waves outside the solar system. The farthest we'll go is the asteroid belt, with the Souillier project. We'll soon be in a position to go up there and look for minerals and water. There are resources for thousands of years there."

"Wow, you move fast! I can see that you're already thinking about the long-term future, but what about yourself? What are you doing now, and what would you like to do?"

"Well, our son is finishing college soon, so I can go back to archeology full-time. You have no idea of what the new soil scanning techniques can reveal. We can even identify the different stages of construction, destruction and reconstruction of ancient sites layer by layer, and digitalize the information differently. Virtual reality allows us to bring these places to life again in theme parks where people can travel back in time and believe that they're surrounded by real buildings. We now understand that our ancestors achieved a very high level of spirituality and technology, because they understood that there was no point in replacing men with machines. They also understood, very early on, that speculation through interest rates had to stop. The only difference is that we chose to grant spiritual wisdom and the gift of precognition to everyone, rather than preserving an elite and using the knowledge to conquer empires."

"Yes, that's true, but at the time the lack of modern communication resources prevented the spread of knowledge, and it was normal for people to keep knowledge secret. What was needed was a way of distributing information immediately across the entire planet, so that everyone could have access to it at the same time. What you did is magnificent, you managed to avoid any attempt to leave the straight and narrow, and you held back the government of the most powerful country on Earth almost by yourself. Without that, we would have embarked on a spiral of conflicts and wars for the control of power."

"Oh, come on! Stop exaggerating!"

"No, really, you are the exceptional one!"

ALAIN HUBRECHT

ABOUT THE AUTHOR

Alain Hubrecht has worldwide experience in multiple areas such as energy, industry, safety and defense, having worked with the major players in the world such as NATO, Pentagon, SAIC, NASA and several other defense agencies. He is passionate about new technologies and challenges. He was trained by former STARGATE members, worked for the Blue Brain project, was member of the scientific study group of UFOCOM and co-founded the Belgian Transpersonal Association with Carlos Castaneda.